Traitors
Sneer

Books by Pat Anderson

NOVELS
The McGlinchy Code
The Crimes of Miss Jane Goldie
Torrent
A Toast to Charlie Hanrahan
Catalyst

THE NEO-GERS SAGA
Clash of the Agnivores
Never Mind the Zombies
Rattus Agnivoricus
Damned Agnivores
Another Agnivore in a Different Kitchen
A Trip to Agnivoreville
Hell of the Voidoids
X-Ray Agnivores

FACTUAL
Fear and Smear
Up to Our Knees
Get Over It
The Boattum Line (by Billy 'Burger' King)
The People
Jesus Was A Protestant

FOR CHILDREN
The Skyscraper Rocket Ship
The Ceremony at Goreb Ridge
The Brain Thing
The Football Star
Mighty Pete and the School Bully School

Traitors Sneer

WORKING-CLASS TORIES

Pat Anderson

Snowy Publications MMXXI

'No attempt at ethical or social seduction can eradicate from my heart a deep burning hatred for the Tory Party. So far as I am concerned they are lower than vermin.'

Aneurin Bevan

Contents

<u>Preface</u>

Regular readers of my books might notice that the endnotes look a lot tidier than usual. I took advice and started using Webpage Archive (Thanks DouglasFM!), meaning that the links are a lot shorter than usual. There were some pages that I could not put on Webpage Archive since they contained videos or comments. For these I used tinyurl.com. unfortunately, tinyurl.com does not archive the pages, so fingers crossed that none of the pages disappear.

I don't think I need to go into any detail on what the book is about; the title is self-explanatory. I know not everyone will agree with some of what I have to say but, hopefully you find it both informative and entertaining. Thanks for buying.

Pat Anderson
December 2021

Follow me on Twitter: @PatAndrsptr

Read my blog: https://paddyontherailway.wordpress.com

Introduction

The Representation of the People Act of 1884, also known as the Third Reform Act, tidied up the British electorate so that there was equality between the boroughs and the counties.[1] It hardly turned Britain into a democracy; 40% of men still could not vote and neither could any woman. The Tories, however, did not see it that way; in fact, it frightened the life out of many of them. Conservative power was based in the counties, and they feared that working-class voters in the countryside would destroy that power. Some of them believed that it was simply political opportunism on the part of the Liberal Party. As one Tory MP put it when the Bill was introduced to the Commons,

> The men who demand it are not the working classes... It is the men who hope to use the masses who urge that the suffrage should be conferred upon a numerous and ignorant class.[2]

Even some Liberals were concerned about the future of politics. William Harcourt, Home Secretary at the time, said,

> The Bill is a frightfully democratic measure which I confess appals me. Its effect will not be felt at once but in a few years it will come with a rush. I don't see any hope for the Tories anywhere or anyhow.[3]

As it turned out, all the fears were misplaced. Certainly, in the 1885 election, the Liberals made great strides in the counties, but many boroughs returned Conservative MPs.[4] Ever since that time, whether the Tories have been returned to government or not, many working-class people, in the boroughs and the counties, have voted Conservative. Even when all men were given the vote in 1918 and all women ten years later, the Tories maintained a solid vote among the working classes. The question is, why?

Although there are some altruistic souls out there that vote for the general good rather than their own, most people go into the polling booth determined to look out for their own interests. Any neutral observer would consider that the best interests of working-class people are decidedly *not* served by the Tories. So why do many working-class folk insist on voting for them?

There are always, of course, the Hyacinth Buckets of this world, folk that have done a little better for themselves and feel that voting Tory, or even joining the local Conservative Club, is commensurate with their new position in life. Even those that have bought their council house think that they are better than everyone else in the street. The whole idea of his neighbours being better paid or receiving more in the way of benefits fills him with dread. His best bet is to vote Tory, which party will ensure that he can still strut about like the big 'I am'.

In fact, misanthropy plays a major part in why working-class people vote Tory. Whether it is a hatred of people 'sponging' off the taxpayer, a hatred of black people, brown people or foreigners in general or a hatred of LGBT people, the reasons for voting Tory among the working classes are wholly negative. What they are voting for is to stop society changing and, hopefully, take it back to a previous, so-called simpler time.

That simpler time might have been an era of low wages, poor housing, hunger and disease, but that is not what matters. What is important is that there was nobody moaning about the words one used to describe people. Words like 'darkie', 'Paki', 'poof', 'spazzy' etc. were commonly accepted, everyday expressions. In those halcyon days, there were very few 'darkies' and 'Pakis' around to claim they were being offended. Those few that were around kept their mouths shut if they knew what was good for them. Meanwhile, 'poofs' and 'spazzies' were safely locked up out of everybody's way.

As we shall see, nostalgia plays a great part in many working-class, British people's lives as they pine for the good, old days of 'free speech' and no 'woke' characters around to pull them up for being racist or homophobic. And those 'woke' characters nowadays tend to be middle-class liberals and Labour supporters, whom only the Tories are able to counter.

But wait, are the middle classes not the ones that are the Tories' main supporters? In fact, are they not the ones that make up the Conservative Party? Well, yes and no. If one were to look closely, one would find that there are just as many of the middle classes that are members of the Labour Party than there are of the Tories. The Tories' great success in recent years has been to make many of the working classes believe that Labour is the party of the middle classes.

Of course, the Tory Party could not do this on its own; The UK media play their part. The press especially are mostly right-wing organs that use propaganda and downright lies to convince working-class people to vote Tory. This is nothing new. The right-wing press has been doing this kind of thing since the Victorian age, so they are well practised in how to do it right. As we shall see, everyone in the UK has been bombarded with right-wing propaganda since the last quarter of the 19th Century.

It is a long story, so we had better get started. And where better a place to start than at the beginning, when working-class men first had the vote. We need to look at how such men were persuaded to use their vote in the right way – the Conservative way.

Traitors Sneer

1
The Road to Mandalay

If you have studied the history of the Nineteenth Century at any level, you will have come across the term Free Trade. This was the great desire of the manufacturing classes in Britain in the Nineteenth Century, and, in the middle of the century, they got their wish. Free Trade became the economic model for Britain's commerce with the world. All ports should be open, including those of Britain, and there should be no tariffs whatsoever to hinder trade.

Free Trade had a double advantage for the factory owners. On the one hand, they could produce goods at much lower prices than anyone else in the world, so stood to make a fortune. Another benefit was the opening up of home ports to imports of cheap foodstuffs. The abolition of the Corn Laws meant that they did not need to increase wages, and in some cases could even cut them.[1] The middle classes had finally flexed their political muscles.

Of course, Free Trade was only beneficial so long as Britain could produce manufactured goods cheaper than everyone else. In the last quarter of the Nineteenth Century, however, Britain began to see competitors coming to catch up with it, and maybe even overtake it. Other European nations, the USA, and even Japan had become industrialised and were looking for markets. And that was the least of Britain's worries.

In what became known as the New Imperialism, industrialised nations began to snap up colonies to supply them with raw materials and as markets for surplus products. The USA concentrated not only on Spain's old territories in the Americas and Caribbean, but, along with Japan, in the far east as well. This could potentially bring them into conflict with Britain, who already traded extensively in the area.

European nations, meanwhile, concentrated on the relatively virgin continent of Africa. There were already European ports dotted about the African coast, but the interior, especially in the tropics, had always been guarded by disease-carrying mosquitoes and tsetse flies. Improvement in drugs that could combat malaria and sleeping sickness, however, meant that the interior was now open for conquest.

The so-called 'Scramble for Africa' was a rather unsavoury business where European nations, keen to avoid war, divided up the map of the continent with no thought to the indigenous populations. A straight line might serve to demarcate one nation's colony from another, but it could also run through a tribal kingdom, leaving said tribe split in two. Not that anybody in Europe was particularly concerned about that!

In a sense, Britain's empire was forced upon it. As other nations snapped up colonies, it was pretty obvious that they would be following protectionist policies. Britain had to step in to safeguard its trading partners in the name of Free Trade. It was the last thing Britain wanted.

Empires cost money to run, which was the main reason that the British Government had tried to avoid having one. Colonies like Canada, Australia, New Zealand and the ones that became the USA were different. The indigenous populations had, quite considerately, contracted European diseases and died out. Those that had not were systematically wiped out or forced off their lands. This left white, settler populations that could contribute taxes to Westminster's coffers. The other countries that were to be subsumed into the British Empire were a different matter entirely.

Making a virtue out of a necessity, Britain claimed to be taking on the 'White Man's Burden'.[2] This was all about those of white, European stock taking charge of the savage, heathen native for his own good. The stated aim was to guide indigenous populations toward running their own affairs in a western European way. Quite how this was to be achieved when the white man retained all the power in his own hands was not clear. What was clear, though, was that the British would do a much better job of things than Johnny Foreigner. This distinction hardly figured in the natives' thinking; it did not matter to them who was trying to 'civilise' them with a Maxim gun!

At any rate, Britain now had a formal empire, which was going to cost the taxpayer dear. Getting the manufacturing classes onside was easy; it was the trade in their products that was being protected. The upper classes, meanwhile, would be involved in governing the colonies as well as being in charge of the armies that would 'pacify' them. The middle classes would be providing the civil servants and minor officials. But what of the working classes? Many of them had been given the vote in 1867 and even more in 1884, so their opinions mattered as well. In fact, since working men now made up the majority of the electorate, their opinions were of paramount importance. So, how were they brought on board?

The answer to that is straightforward; propaganda was exercised to an enormous extent. The late Victorian and Edwardian period was when most literature, as well as songs, devoted to the cause of empire were written. Books like those of H. Rider Haggard[3] and Rudyard Kipling[4] were extremely popular, as were the *Boy's Own Paper* adventures (Fig.1). Music halls resounded to the strains *of Land of Hope and Glory*, *Soldiers of the Queen/King* and *On the Road to Mandalay*. Newspapers too were full of news about the Empire and wars against savage tribes. The big question is, though, did it work?

Historians are divided over how much working-class people were invested in, or even cared about, the Empire. Some argue that the Empire had only a marginal influence on Britain, while others see it as the root cause of racist attitudes.[5] The ones that do not believe that the working classes were affected point to the lack of any mention of the Empire in correspondence. But, as the historian Daniel Jonah Goldhagen points out,

> Notions fundamental to the dominant worldview and operation of a society, precisely because they are taken for granted, often are not expressed in a manner commensurate with their prominence and

3

significance or, when uttered, seen as worthy by others to be noted and recorded.[6]

In other words, just because people do not mention things in their letters, that does not mean that they are unaware of them or do not care about them. People, of whatever station in life, tend to speak of things that are important to themselves and the ones they are corresponding with. The Empire might only be mentioned if it affects them directly; for example, if a member of the family is in the army and is posted to some far-flung corner.

Working-class people might not have been directly involved in the running of the Empire, but that does not mean to say that they were not interested. They certainly showed an interest when it came to imperial wars. Gladstone and his government discovered this to their cost in 1884, when the Mahdist War in Sudan was in full swing.

In 1882 Britain invaded Egypt to put down a rebellion and put the Khedive back in charge. They stayed, making Egypt part of the British Empire in all but name. The Egyptian army came under the control of British officers, who were, nominally at least, under the command of the Khedive. In reality, it was Britain that ruled the roost.

At that time, Sudan was part of the Khedive's extensive possessions and had an Egyptian army of occupation, led by British officers, of course, imposed on it. Understandably, the Sudanese were keen to throw off the shackles of Egyptian and British rule, but they were hopelessly disunited. That was until a leader called the Mahdi arose to bring them all together. The Mahdi claimed to be God's latest prophet on Earth, a new Mohammed. Whether or not the Mahdi believed this about himself was immaterial; everybody else in Sudan did.

The Mahdi's army defeated all that stood against it and looked set to drive the foreigners off their soil. The Liberal Government at Westminster considered that Sudan was not worth fighting over and looked to evacuate everyone, Egyptian, British and European. Someone would have to be sent over to take charge of this exodus. But who?

4

W.T. Stead, editor of the *Pall Mall Gazette*, had the answer. A bona-fide hero of the Empire was in London, kicking his heels until he went to the Congo to work for King Leopold of Belgium: General 'Chinese' Gordon. Stead interviewed the great man, who had been in Sudan before and who felt that the Mahdi needed to be stopped in his tracks.[7] In the same edition of his paper, Stead called for Gordon to be sent to Khartoum, where most of the foreigners were trapped.[8] Soon, every newspaper, and the British public, were demanding that Gordon be sent to Sudan.

Like the Mahdi, Gordon was a religious fanatic and, also like the Mahdi, he was convinced he was always right. Stories about his sexuality can be discounted;[9] some folk simply cannot accept that a man can remain celibate into middle age. Accusations of pederasty against such men stem from a deep-rooted anti-Catholicism, which goes all-out to insist that celibacy in a man automatically leads to deviant sexual practices. Equally, the pop psychology used to somehow prove that he was a repressed homosexual[10] is a load of rubbish.

Gordon was sent to Khartoum to evacuate the place but decided that he knew best. He disobeyed his orders and started to fortify Khartoum, making ready to defend it against the Mahdi's army. The British public and the press,[11] of course, were right behind him and pressurised the Government to send reinforcements. Gladstone and his ministers dithered; they did not want to get embroiled in a war just for the hell of it.

Apparently, it was Queen Victoria that ordered Gladstone to send reinforcements to Khartoum.[12] Unfortunately, it came too late and the British and Egyptian forces did not arrive in Khartoum until two days after it had fallen, and Gordon had been killed. The British press and public were outraged and Gladstone, who was known as the G.O.M. (Grand Old Man) became the M.O.G. (Murderer of Gordon).[13]

People of all classes went into a 'frenzy of public mourning' and stones were thrown through the windows of 10 Downing Street.[14] It is not too presumptuous to suggest that those stones were thrown by working-class people. It is hard to imagine anyone of the Victorian middle classes being involved in such a demonstration, while upper-class elements would have confined themselves to attacking Gladstone in the Houses of Parliament.

It could be claimed, of course, that, aside from wars and other crises, working-class people were apathetic about the British Empire. The fact was, however, that many working-class jobs were dependent upon it. Stevedores and shipbuilders are the ones that immediately spring to mind but there were many others. Cotton mills were dependent more and more on raw cotton from the colonies (instead of America), while Jute production needed raw material from the subcontinent. Coal mines, meanwhile, depended on factories for much of their sales and the railways did a lot of their business taking raw materials to the factories and manufactured goods from them. Those factories, of course, depended on the Empire for much of their sales. Many other jobs depended on the factories, railways and coal mines for their existence, which ultimately meant that they relied on the Empire.

Foodstuffs too came from the colonies, the most important of which for working-class people was tea. And what was a cup of tea without a couple of spoonsful of sugar? The smooth running of the Empire was essential to keep these commodities coming and to ensure that the prices stayed down.

The most direct involvement of working-class men in the Empire, though, was in the army. While the upper classes ran the colonies and commanded the armies and the middle classes were responsible for administration, it was the ordinary soldier that was the one on the ground, shooting at any restless natives. That was his only interaction with the indigenous population, except when he was on leave.

We are probably all familiar with the scene in the film *The Man Who Would Be King* where the Indian man is thrown off the train. That, unfortunately, was no exaggeration. My father served in Egypt in the early 1950s and regaled us with stories of how they would throw 'wogs' off the buses if they smelled of garlic. No doubt other soldiers had similar tales to tell their families about how they lorded it up over the 'wogs'.

That gentleman that was thrown off the train by Sean Connery and Michael Caine, moreover, looked rather well-to-do. Ordinary, working-class soldiers were free to treat the natives however they wanted, no matter to which station those natives belonged. Obviously, they would never come into contact with upper-class natives, who would not be seen travelling on public transport. There were plenty of middle-class natives, though, especially in India and it must have been a heady experience for private soldiers to be treated with deference by such men; the kind of men that, back in Britain, those soldiers would have to treat with respect.

Those soldiers would bring their racist attitudes back home with them and pass them onto friends and relatives. They would have had a willing audience; most people like to think that there are others they are better than. Folk that are near the bottom of the heap, living in a slum and barely keeping the family fed, could find some comfort in knowing that they were still better off than others in the world.

It was not just ex-servicemen telling working-class people that black and Asian folk were lesser beings than them; there were plenty of reminders all around. There were gollywogs in toyshops and in adverts for Robertson's marmalade. Posters advertising soap showed it as so powerful at removing dirt that it would turn a black child white (Fig.2). Camp Coffee showed a soldier from a Highland regiment being served by a Sikh (Fig.3). Other adverts portrayed British heroes standing firm against a pack of bloodthirsty, black savages (Fig.4).

Produce tended to be advertised according to whichever colony or country it came from, which seems fair enough. Africans, Indians (real ones, from India) and Chinamen were common characters in adverts. The problem was, though, that they tended to be portrayed as caricatures.

At any rate, there were plenty of racist images around to influence the thinking of both children and adults. As Professor Richard Evans pointed out in his lecture entitled, 'The Victorians: Empire and Race',[15] racism and Empire were intimately entwined. Glorification of the British Empire necessitated a chauvinistic doctrine of the British being a superior race.

To reinforce these feelings throughout the British population, a new day of celebration was instituted at the beginning of the 20th Century: Empire Day. Jim English wrote an excellent article for *The Historical Journal*, which goes into some detail about Empire Day and how much working-class people were involved. In it he argues that the notion of empire changed in the inter-war period. It was no longer about jingoism but emphasised its moral purpose of civilising the world.[16] The accounts he gives of inter-war Empire Day celebrations, however, contain much that is jingoistic and about British superiority.

Films of the period invariably reinforced imperial attitudes that were supposed to be old-fashioned by that time. 1939's *The Four Feathers* is a prime example, with the hero facing hordes of screaming 'Dervishes'. The same year saw the release of *Beau Geste*, in which English heroes, members of the Foreign Legion, bravely face hordes of screaming Arabs. In fact, most of the films set abroad at that time have stiff-upper-lipped, white heroes seeing off hordes of screaming natives of all different hues.

Sometimes, though, films portrayed *good* natives. What was seen as good in a British gentleman, however, was not what made a good native. To reach that hallowed state a native had to be faithful, loyal and obedient; what Bernard Porter, in his book *The Lion's Share*, called 'doggy virtues'. Intelligence, outspokenness or self-reliance in a native were sure signs of a troublemaker. Examples of both these kinds of native were provided in the 1935 film, *Sanders of the River*.

The same film betrayed another aspect of racism and white supremacy; one, yet again, that continued into the late 1970s and even into the 1980s. This concerned not the behaviour of the natives, but the way they dressed. Many of the women in the film were topless. Well, it could be argued, that was how they were in real life. If those women had been white, however, they would have been covered up, whether that was true to life or not. The implication was that white audiences would find nothing titillating about the breasts of young, black women. It

8

was as if those women were simply animals and there would have to be something wrong with a white man that found black breasts sexually exciting. TV programmes in the 1970s were guilty of the same assumptions and black tribes often appeared on 'nature' programmes.

Of course, to a certain extent, Jim English was right in his assessment of the British Empire, in later years, being about bringing civilisation to the world. But then, an element of that moral crusade had always been present. It eased the consciences of imperialists to think that one day, in the far-off future, they could hand over the reins of power to natives that were ready for the task.

This way of looking at empire was just as racist as that which portrayed natives as mindless savages. In this mindset, natives were like children, who had to be trained and educated and sometimes punished for transgressions. This simile, however, could only be taken so far. Children know that they will reach adulthood at a certain time and be ready to take on the responsibilities of that role. The Empire's indigenous populations, on the other hand, were given no such certainties. They would only be ready to govern themselves when the white man said they were.

Working-class people, however, had no time for such highfalutin, paternalistic notions. They were influenced by the films they saw and the books they read. Black people were either screaming savages, intent on murdering everyone in their path, or incredibly stupid. Brown people were of the same ilk or treacherous and unscrupulous. The Chinese and Japanese, meanwhile, were sly, underhand individuals, addicted to opium and determined to take over the world. These stereotypes were constantly reinforced in films, books, radio plays and, later, on television.

Films with screaming natives continued long after their need as propaganda was gone. *The Naked Prey*, released in 1965, was full of bloodthirsty savages with some novel ways of killing white men. There was even a remake of *The Four Feathers* as late as 1978, complete with a *good* native. The real shocker, though, appeared twelve years earlier, in 1966. This film did not only portray stereotypically savage (and screaming) natives but was about a hero of the British Empire.

Khartoum was pretty much a hagiography of General Gordon. Gone were any references to him disobeying orders and, effectively, failing in his duty. History was distorted to make it look as if Gladstone and his government had abandoned Gordon. The 'Dervishes' were the usual screaming bloodthirsty savages, and the film offered no explanation as to why there was an uprising in Sudan in the first place. To add insult to injury, the Mahdi was played by a blacked-up Lawrence Olivier.

Also continuing long after the Empire were adverts depicting racial stereotypes. Everybody of a certain age in Glasgow remembers the huge, lit sign of Ba-Bru outside Central Station (Fig.5). It was not removed until the late 1970s. Also continuing into the late 1970s was the Lees Macaroon Bars TV advert, with cartoon black people and the lyrics, 'For piccaninnies and grandpapas…' (Fig.6). Even in the 1980s, racial caricatures galore appeared in an advert for Kia-Ora.[17]

As well as adverts, caricatures were the norm in children's comics too. In the 1940s and 1950s, there was a regular feature in various comics, notably the *Wizard*, called *Spadger Isle* (Fig.7). The eponymous hero, along with his friend, lived on an island populated by black natives. Each story had a couple of small frames by way of introduction and then a larger frame showing the natives doing stupid things. None of the natives had names and were referred to by Spadger and his friend as 'the nigs'.[18] (*Sparky* readers of the 1960s might remember this comic strip when it was resurrected as *The Moonsters*.[19])

Speaking of the *Sparky*, the comic had a character of the same name who was another racial stereotype. (Strangely enough, I thought Sparky was an alien when I was a child!) Any representations of black people in comics were of the 'big rubber lips and grass skirt' variety, like Sparky (Fig.8). There was even the appearance of the odd bone through the nose. Chinamen, meanwhile, had Fu Manchu moustaches, pigtails and wore coolie hats and long, loose robes with wide sleeves, into which they usually tucked their hands.

The exception to all this racism, apparently, was Charlie Williams, the Yorkshire comedian, who had his own comic strip in *Shiver and Shake*. An online database of British comics says, 'Little or no reference was made to Wlliams' (sic) colour'.[20] Actually, that is not strictly true. There were at least a couple of times when white people got covered in soot or black paint and Charlie mistook them for his cousins (Fig.9)!

It was hardly surprising that working-class people were racist when even their children were bombarded with such propaganda. The beneficiaries of such attitudes were the Tories, who had long associated themselves with the Empire and, by extension, racism. That became clear in 1964 in Smethwick, in the English Midlands, where the Tory candidate, Peter Griffiths, won the seat with the slogan, 'If you want a n_____ for a neighbour, vote Liberal or Labour.'[21] (Fig.10)

The comments from some of the ordinary people of Smethwick in 1966 show how ingrained the propaganda expounded in the interwar films had become. 'They're a nuisance when you've got to walk past them in the street, they won't move,'[22] said one man. They obviously did not come from *good* native stock, then! Other comments betrayed similar racist notions.

> 'They should live in a district by themselves. They're not clean.'[23]

> 'They're content with Kitekat [cat food] and dog food, instead of ordinary meat.'[24]

Almost as soon as immigrants got off the boat from the Caribbean, they faced discrimination. Many shops refused to serve them, they were housed in slums and the only jobs they could get were those that white people did not want, with long hours and low pay. This discrimination was considered justified since black people were lesser beings than those that were white. As one Tory MP, Beresford Craddock, said in the House of Commons in 1953,

> Let us remember that 95% of them are primitive people. One of the reasons why they are not generally accepted into hotels is because their sanitary habits are not all that could be desired... It is well known that a large number of Africans in East and Central Africa are riddled with a disease of a very unfortunate kind... I will not dwell on that very delicate subject but I think that Honourable Members who have experience will agree that the attitude of the African towards women and sexual matters is entirely different from the attitude of the general run of Europeans... it is a common practice among Africans to put children to sleep by excitation of their urogenital organs... The effect of alcohol upon an African is remarkable. I admit that sometimes alcohol has a remarkable effect on Europeans. But speaking generally, alcohol seems to bring out all the evil instincts in the African in the most astonishing way... these views and practices are due to the psychological makeup of those primitive people from time immemorial.[25]

Ironically, these were the kinds of sentiment the British claimed to have been fighting the war against less than a decade before. But it was not just discrimination that black immigrants had to put up with. Gangs of working-class youths roamed black neighbourhoods at night, armed with chains, cutthroat razors and flick knives, attacking anyone they found there. These attacks were egged on by the likes of Oswald Mosley and the right-wing press.[26]

The racist reaction to these immigrants could easily have been predicted. All one had to do was look back to another group of immigrants that came to Britain in the 19th Century. England's oldest colony, Ireland, was part of the UK in the 19th Century so, technically, those immigrants were not immigrants at all. They were treated as such, though, and unwelcome ones at that.

During the Famine, the British public was generous in giving to charity to help feed the starving in Ireland. And there was a huge public outcry about the practice of *Souperism*.[27] Obviously, there was great sympathy with the Irish but, when they began to move to England and Scotland, attitudes changed. Then again, they probably did not change at all. The normal image of the Irishman was as a dirty, lazy, feckless, drunken individual that was always looking for a fight. It was hardly what you wanted living next door to you!

One could feel sorry for the Irish when they were at a distance; not so much when they were living in one's town. The Church of Scotland's infamous *On the Menace of the Irish Race to our Scottish Nationality* merely summed up what a lot of people in Britain thought.[28] If that was the way they reacted against other white people coming to their country, it was hardly surprising that they went crazy about black and Asian folk turning up on their doorstep.

In the same way as they had done with the starving Irish, British people were generous in giving to charities to build schools and churches in Africa, or to clothe poor natives around the world. Also, in the same way as they had done with the starving Irish, the British public were only sympathetic as long as the natives stayed 'over there' instead of 'coming over here'.

In the midst of all this racial discrimination, along came Enoch Powell with his *Rivers of Blood* speech. What Powell was arguing against was not immigration *per se*, but the Labour Party's impending Race Relations Bill, which would make racial discrimination a crime. Powell quoted one of his constituents, who said, 'In this country in fifteen or twenty years' time, the black man will have the whip hand over the white man.'[29] Essentially, what Powell wanted was a continuation of racial bigotry by whites against blacks.

Incredibly, or perhaps not so, thousands of dock workers and meat packers marched in support of Powell when he was sacked from Edward Heath's Shadow Cabinet.[30] Meanwhile, Powell received thousands of letters of support and a Gallup poll showed that 74% of the population supported his speech.[31] Despite the fact that he was sacked, Powell's speech showed that racial bigots could still count on Tories to rally to the cause.

As late as the 1990s, Norman Tebbit, the Tory politician, questioned the loyalty of Asians living in Britain. (There were those 'doggy virtues' again.) He said that many of them failed to pass the 'cricket test', meaning that they supported the cricket teams of India, Pakistan or whichever other country they had come from.[32] Quite what he intended to do with those that failed his 'test' he neglected to say. His words, though, were certainly inflammatory and came at a time when conspicuous racism had become a problem yet again.

By the 1980s, the effects of being crammed into poor housing began to show among immigrant communities. Like all poor communities, the young people did not do at all well academically. This, coupled with racist attitudes, led to high unemployment among Afro-Caribbean and Asian youngsters. They ended up doing what disaffected youths have always done in Britain's cities; they formed gangs and indulged in criminal activity. This rise of criminal activity among black people was exaggerated in the media and it was often portrayed as if gangs and certain crimes never existed in Britain before black immigrants arrived.

In January 1978, Margaret Thatcher, then Leader of the Opposition, was interviewed on Granada TV. Much of the interview was concerned with immigration, still a major issue among Tories. Thatcher spoke of how a committee had projected that, by the end of the 20th Century, there would be four million Pakistanis in Britain. She said,

> Now, that is an awful lot and I think it means that people are really rather afraid that this country might be rather swamped by people with a different culture and, you know, the British character has done so much for democracy, for law and done so much throughout the world that if there is any fear that it might be swamped

people are going to react and be rather hostile to those coming in.[33]

She went on about tackling immigration policy and bringing back voters from the National Front. To this end, it looked as if she was prepared to steal some of the National Front's rhetoric, if not policies.

> We are a British nation with British characteristics. Every country can take some small minorities and in many ways they add to the richness and variety of this country. The moment the minority threatens to become a big one, people get frightened.[34]

Once Thatcher was elected as Prime Minister, she was as good as her word and, as well as clamping down on immigration, it was open season on black people already living in Britain. What were known as 'SUS' laws (short for 'suspicion') were used to disproportionately harass black people. 44% of those arrested in London under SUS were Afro-Caribbean, even though they only accounted for 6% of the population.[35] Then there was the infamous Special Patrol Group, whose remit often appeared to be to go around beating up black people. A raid on lockers at SPG headquarters uncovered a stash of illegal weapons and even Nazi regalia.[36]

Things eventually erupted into what were termed *Race Riots* in the 1980s.[37] Although investigations revealed tensions in poor, immigrant communities and institutional racism among the police, right-wing papers, like the Mail, blamed everything squarely on the immigrants themselves. In fact, forty years after the Brixton riots of 1981, they still insist that the violence was caused by criminal elements.[38]

Tory politicians behaved likewise, claiming that immigrants had refused to integrate and did not behave in a 'British' way. Tebbit's 'Cricket Test' was just the latest in a long line of fingers of blame being pointed at immigrants. And as recently as 2011, when riots broke out again, David Cameron said, 'It is criminality pure and simple. And there is absolutely no excuse for it.'[39]

Tebbit's 'test' went to the heart of the integration argument; these people did not see themselves as British. It was difficult, however, to see how they could possibly have integrated when they had been barred from jobs, shops and even churches.[40] Besides, British people rarely integrated with the local population when they went to live abroad. But then, they were not *immigrants* but *ex-pats*.

All these racial tensions, along with runaway unemployment and an inflation rate that stubbornly refused to come down, meant that the Prime Minister, Margaret Thatcher, was extremely unpopular. In fact, by the end of 1981 and into 1982, polls showed her to be the most unpopular prime minister since the Second World War.[41] There was still a while to go until the next election, but it looked as if Thatcher would not be leading the Tories into it.

And then, redemption appeared in the shape of Argentina invading the Falkland Islands. Apparently, the military junta in Argentina planned the invasion as a diversion from all the social problems going on in the country. Fortunately for Margaret Thatcher, it served the exact same purpose in Britain. If the Argentinian generals had been bribed by the Tories to provide a sideshow, they could not have planned things better. The British public was outraged, even though 99.9% of them had never heard of the Falklands and had no idea where they were.

All the old, imperialist feelings came to the fore once again as if they had never gone. Of course, a bit of racism was thrown in for good measure. Who could forget the troops on the SS Canberra singing their pleasant, little ditty to the tune of Cliff Richard's *Summer Holiday*?

> *We're all going to the Ma-alvinas*. (The Argentinian name
> for the Falklands.)
> *We're all going to kill a spic or two*.[42]

Tory ministers seemed to revel in the conflict as they appeared on various news and current affairs programmes. Thatcher herself came out of 10 Downing Street to tell reporters to 'Rejoice!' when news reached her that the island of South Georgia had been taken.[43] The Sun newspaper, meanwhile, was in the forefront of all the jingoism, accusing other papers of treason if they questioned what was going on.[44] When the Argentinian battleship, the *General Belgrano* was controversially sunk with the loss of hundreds of lives, all the Sun had to say was, 'Gotcha!'[45]

In June 1983, the Tories, still under Thatcher, rode on a wave of jingoism to a huge majority in the House of Commons.[46] Just as they had done in the interwar years, the Tories had commandeered the Union Flag; the party conferences were like the *Last Night of the Proms* with all the flag waving and imperialist songs. Thatcher was to remain Prime Minister for another seven years, while the Tories governed Britain for another seven after that.

Even now, there is something there in the Tory Party for the racist. Boris Johnson is on record talking about 'piccaninnies' and black people with 'watermelon smiles'. Attempts have been made to play down what Johnson said, claiming that the phrases have been taken out of context and that he was attacking Tony Blair and the Queen.[47] The truth is, though, that reading the context only makes things worse. Here are some examples of what he wrote:

> It is said that the Queen has come to love the Commonwealth, partly because it supplies her with regular cheering crowds of flag-waving piccaninnies.[48]

> They say he (Tony Blair) is shortly off to the Congo. No doubt the AK47s will fall silent, and the pangas will stop their hacking of human flesh, and the tribal warriors will all break out in watermelon smiles to see the big white chief touch down in his big white British taxpayer-funded bird.[49]

> The continent (Africa) may be a blot, but it is not a blot upon our conscience. The problem is not that

we were once in charge, but that we are not in charge anymore.[50]

Although such utterances are condemned in the media, the sad fact is, as many have pointed out, they actually increase Johnson's popularity. There is nothing your regular Sun reader likes more than 'plain speaking' from a politician. And as is evident from Johnson's last comment above, the glorification of the British Empire has not gone away.

2
But Emily Loved Him

As everybody knows, if one goes back in history, the upper classes provided all Britain's prime ministers. It was the same as Britain moved into the modern age of the 19th Century. Even those from a middle-class background, like Gladstone and Disraeli, bought large country estates and became part of the local gentry. Gladstone had an easier time of it than his great rival since he had mixed with the ruling elite as a child at Eton. Disraeli's education had not been so illustrious, so he felt the need to invent an aristocratic background for himself.[1]

Obviously, with the electorate composed of upper- and middle-class men, one would expect an element of deference to be involved in politics. With the extension of the franchise in 1867 and 1884, however, one would expect that such deference would eventually, if not immediately, disappear. The facts, though, say otherwise.[2]

Since 1884 there have been twenty-six separate prime ministers. Of those nine went to Eton, two went to Harrow and one to Rugby. Others went to less prestigious fee-paying schools and, indeed, only eleven out of those twenty-six prime ministers did not attend a fee-paying school at all. Two of those eleven, however, went to the High School of Glasgow, which, although not a fee-paying school at the time, is the oldest school in Scotland and was a rather elitist establishment.

It is interesting to note that another two of those eleven, Gordon Brown and Theresa May, were never elected prime minister. That leaves only seven prime ministers elected by the British public that went to ordinary schools. Actually, Britain did not become a full democracy until 1928, when working-class women were granted the vote. Looking at elections since that date, there were seventeen separate prime ministers. Of those, only eight, including Brown and May, attended ordinary schools. That means that nine elected prime ministers went to fee-paying schools, while six did not. It is a rather skewed picture, which shows that the elites of the 18th and 19th Centuries are still pretty much in charge.

Only two of those prime ministers, Clement Attlee and Tony Blair, were not Tories; the rest most decidedly were. Two of the last three of our prime ministers went to Eton, while, as mentioned above, Theresa May, who was sandwiched by David Cameron and Boris Johnson, was not voted into the job in a general election. So, what makes an overwhelmingly working-class electorate choose such upper-class characters to be prime minister? The answer is rather obvious: propaganda.

We saw in the last chapter how adventure novels and magazines like *Boy's Own Paper* helped to instil the importance of empire into the population at large. They also served another purpose. The heroes of practically everything put in print were upper-class. There were even stories set in fee-paying schools, with the understanding that the pupils would grow up (if they ever did) to be the protagonists of those stories of 'derring-do' that existed elsewhere in the magazines.

George Orwell published a piece about these magazines in 1940, looking closely at the *Gem* (Fig.11) and the *Magnet* (Fig.12), both of which started in 1908 and were still in existence when Orwell was writing (sometime in 1939). Orwell recognised the propaganda inherent in these periodicals, saying,

> *All* fiction from the novels in the mushroom libraries downwards is censored in the interests of the ruling class. And boys' fiction above all, the blood-and-thunder stuff which nearly every boy devours at some time or other, is sodden in the worst illusions of 1910.[3]

The *Gem* stopped publishing at the end of 1939,[4] while the *Magnet* ended in May 1940.[5] By that time, though, their job was done, and they had been superseded by another medium entirely. The *Boy's Own Paper* continued until 1967,[6] but that was the exception. From the 1930s onward, films took over as the propaganda medium of choice. (By the way, if anyone finds out what a 'mushroom library' is, could they let me know!)

It was the arrival of talking pictures that heralded films' possibilities as propaganda. Silent movies were quite useless in this respect since nobody knew what accent the actors had. Even foreigners with little English could pretend to be a British aristocrat, given proper direction. The Talkies, of course, changed all that.

While Hollywood made films with a social conscience, like *I Am A Fugitive From A Chain Gang*, *Mr. Deeds Goes to Town*, *Angels with Dirty Faces*, *Of Mice and Men* etc. British cinema regurgitated old, time-worn tales of upper-class heroes. Films like *Sanders of the River*, *The 39 Steps*, *The Drum*, *The Four Feathers* and *Goodbye, Mr. Chips* were straight out of *Gem* and *Magnet*, with upper-class heroes keeping the world safe and secure.

British films made in the 1930s were full of upper-class characters, with clipped tones, who resided in huge houses that ordinary folk could only dream about. Well-loved films from the period, like those mentioned above, portrayed the upper classes as the norm, as the way people *should* be. Working-class, and even middle-class, folk were usually just there as comic relief, or to demonstrate what a good person the hero was: 'Thankee kindly, guv'nor, yer a real gent an' no mistike!'

Quite often, the actors were from middle-class backgrounds, but had to affect upper-class accents to succeed in their profession. Robert Donat, for example, owed his clipped tones to elocution lessons.[7] The hero and heroine always spoke in upper-class accents, even if they were performing in a comedy. Aside from the God-awful *Aldwych Farces*, comedy protagonists with upper-class accents were still of the heroic mould. They might be a bit dull-witted, but they were mostly played straight. You would not see Rex Harrison behaving the way Cary Grant did in *Arsenic and Old Lace*!

Of course, there were working-class film stars, but they were of the harmless, and even gormless, type, like the Crazy Gang, Will Hay, George Formby or Gracie Fields. Ordinary people might enjoy them, laugh at their antics and jokes, or even be inspired by them to sing or play the ukulele but they did not want to *be* them or be *with* them. They were not the ones that women fell in love with or copied their clothes and hairstyles. They were not the ones that men wanted to sleep with or, like their womenfolk, copied their clothes, hairstyles and even mannerisms. Most of these fantasy figures were provided by Hollywood but those that were British were decidedly upper-class; at least, the *characters* were.

Strangely, when Hollywood made movies that were based in Britain, it adhered to the British format. *Cavalcade* might have won the best picture Oscar in 1933 but it is a pretty boring film, concerned with an upper-class family's travails in the first three decades of the 20th Century. The family faces everything that life throws at it with stiff-upper-lipped, stolid fortitude. The working-class characters, meanwhile, are stereotypes, who lose their way when they stop being servants to the upper-class family and leave its benign influence.

Other movies set in Britain stuck to the *Boy's Own* formula of upper-class heroes fighting off hordes of screaming savages. *Beau Geste* was a prime example. Even when Hollywood tried to transpose its social conscience onto Britain, it made a complete mess of it. Like *Cavalcade*, *How Green Was My Valley* won the best picture Oscar, but it was total fantasy. Although set in Wales, it was filmed in California with mostly American actors. The book on which the film was based, with its union activism and political anger, was tossed aside in favour of a sentimental tale of salt-of-the-earth miners that knew their place. Happy workers went to the mine every morning singing, as they left their clean, spacious cottages for the day. It was a sanitised view of the working classes of which the British Establishment would have approved.[8]

The British leading men in Hollywood films were all of the upper-class type, even if, like Robert Donat, they did not belong to that class at all. David Niven, Ronald Colman, Stewart Granger, Rex Harrison and George Sanders were all matinee idols, who spoke in those clipped tones so familiar to British cinema-goers. Perhaps unconsciously and inadvertently, American film makers helped to perpetuate the myth that the British upper classes were all cast in the heroic mould and were the best people to run the country.

One of those matinee idols, Leslie Howard, returned to Britain to do his bit for the war effort. Too old for military service, he worked at making propaganda films and radio broadcasts and writing articles.[9] Of course, everyone realised that propaganda was ineffective if it was boring. Propaganda films were made in the form of feature films for maximum effect. Howard was no different in this respect.

Inspired by Churchill's speech that referred to the pilots that fought in the Battle of Britain, Howard directed and starred in *The First of The Few*, a biography of Reginald Joseph Mitchell, who had designed the Spitfire aircraft that played such a significant role in the conflict over British skies. Also in the film was David Niven, who played a character that was a composite of the different test pilots that Mitchell had worked with before his death in 1937.

Wikipedia describes Mitchell as being 'working class,'[10] although, as the son of a headmaster, he is probably more accurately described as lower middle-class. Whatever class one places him into, though, the fact is that he would have spoken with a 'Stokie' accent. Leslie Howard, however, played the man with his usual, clipped, upper-class accent. This was the start of a major rewriting of history; that the British upper classes won the Second World War for us.

If one were to make a list of all the heroes of WWII, there would be very few, if any, from an ordinary, working-class background. All the heroes promoted by the British media are posh and public-school educated. Attendance at Oxbridge does not go amiss either. Essentially, the Establishment has put forward members of its own class as the ones that won the war. The ordinary rank and file have been mostly forgotten and even deleted.

War films that feature prisoners of war in German camps are always full of officers, sitting around making plans to escape while playing games and putting on concerts. There is a reason for this. The Geneva Convention specified that captured officers could not be put to work. The other ranks were not so lucky. It was permitted to use ordinary soldiers for any type of work except for armaments factories and the like. Germany pretty much kept to the Geneva Convention, especially the bit about the special treatment of officers.

Ordinary soldiers had no time for planning escapes; they were far too busy working all day in factories and in fields. At night, they would be exhausted and ready for sleep, not sitting around a candle discussing how they were going to get back to Blighty. It is an aspect of the war that has been hushed up. Nobody wants to know about these forgotten prisoners; or, rather, their story is kept buried by the media. Much better to concentrate on the 'heroes' that were constantly trying to escape and were a thorn in the Nazis' side. Ordinary soldiers taken prisoner by the Germans were used in another way; a way that has been expertly hidden.

> A limited number of non-commissioned soldiers working as orderlies were allowed in Oflags (camps for officers) to carry out the work needed to care for the officers so don't be too surprised to find a Corporal in Colditz!
> A few of these orderlies had been assigned as 'batmen' to senior officers and were incarcerated along with them, however, most were assigned by the Germans once captured and many disliked their new role intensely and suffered because of it.[11]

No wonder those British officers could sit around making escape plans; they had skivvies to look after them, no doubt doing their laundry, repairing their uniforms and even making their tea. A disgusting example of this practice concerns another WWII hero, one Douglas Bader. His batman was captured along with him and was assigned to still look after him while in captivity. The batman, Alex Ross, was a medical orderly and, as a non-combatant, was required to be repatriated according to the Geneva Convention. The Germans were all set to send him home, but Bader would hear none of it, demanding that his batman remain with him in Colditz.[12]

You will not find any of this in any mainstream accounts of Bader. Instead, he is put forward as one of the great heroes of WWII; a man who lost his legs but still fought the Nazis. It is the same with all the other posh, pampered officers that took part in the war. Compared to all the ordinary soldiers, sailors and RAF men, they had a relatively easy war. And yet, they are the ones that people are supposed to look up to; and many, in fact, do.

Films and TV series set during WWII always have posh officers as the heroes and memorable scenes always involve them. Who can forget Kenneth More, as Naval Captain Colin Maud, in *The Longest Day*, strolling about Juno beach with his bulldog on a leash as if he were out for a Sunday picnic? Then there is Lee Remick, as Eisenhower's personal secretary and driver Kay Summersby, in *Ike: The War Years*, shaking her fist at the English Channel, threatening what she is going to do to Hitler.

And then, there are 'The Few', whom we have already met. Not only have foreign pilots been erased from the Battle of Britain, but working-class pilots have been overlooked as well. Many pilots from a working-class background took part,[13] but movies and TV programmes have conditioned us to accept that they were all upper-class, stiff-upper-lip types, who, for some unfathomable reason, all seemed to be called Ginger.

Those pilots, moreover, relied on ground crew to keep them in the air and those characters had to work around the clock. Then there were the ack-ack, anti-aircraft artillery, crews and spotters, not to mention the ARP wardens making sure there were no lights to guide the bombers in. Not just pilots were involved in the Battle of Britain, although Churchill and subsequent media have told us otherwise.

Since it has been accepted that the upper classes and the upper middle classes won the Second World War, it stands to reason that the First World War would be seen in the same light. It is not easy to do since the Great War did not give as many opportunities for grandstanding as WWII but, still, the media try.

In the early months of the war, it must have been confusing for soldiers on both sides when they were ordered to dig trenches. The Germans had been all set to overrun France and now, suddenly, they were digging in to defend what they had won so far. At least the Germans could still feel that they were winning; they were in enemy territory, after all. For the British, it was a different matter entirely. They had come to drive the Germans out of France and Belgium, but now were going to defend a position against an enemy that did not look as if they were going to attack any time soon. They had been told that the war would be over by Christmas; that hardly seemed likely now.

Once they were dug in, it became difficult to get the soldiers to fire on the enemy. A 'live and let live system' predominated in several areas on the Western Front.[14] There are stories of soldiers on both sides letting the enemy know when an artillery attack was going to happen, so they could take cover. One story tells of a high-ranking British officer touring the front line, asking a soldier why he does not shoot a German sniper. The reply was, 'He's never done me any harm!' There are even tales of fraternisation taking place in No Man's Land.[15]

Of course, the top brass on both sides were unhappy, to say the least, at this state of affairs. The officers on the ground tried everything they could to stir up their men to fire on the enemy, including threats of courts-martial and even of being shot there and then. Often, officers would throw grenades into the opposite trench to get the enemy to fire so that their own men would have to fire back. Still, though, the policy of 'live and let live' continued.

The climax of these 'truces' came at Christmas 1914. The 'Christmas Truce' relies wholly on anecdotal evidence, but it has been generally accepted that it did actually happen. It did not just occur in one place, but apparently at several. Soldiers on either side of No Man's Land started to sing Christmas carols and then climbed out of the trenches to meet each other. It seems that football matches took place as well.[16]

There are some folk prepared to deny that any such thing took place, and it is difficult to argue with their logic.

> The officers on both sides would have lined up their machine guns and artillery and conducted massive summary courts-martial. That's just the way they did it back then.[17]

> A lot of insubordinate soldiers would of (sic) been shot, or at the very least locked up.[18]

Officers would have been dead against their men fraternising, but they would have been averse to mass court-martials and even more so to slaughtering their own men. Such an officer might find it difficult in the future to get men to obey his orders. Worse, there are plenty of stories around about officers being shot in the back by their own men during WWI.[19] It would have been easier, if not safer, to just turn a blind eye and not mention the incident in official reports.

The story of the Christmas Truce might be heartwarming, but it does not fit the usual representations of war: ordinary soldiers were involved, rather than officers. And then, in 2014, came Sainsbury's Christmas advert.

Remarkably clean soldiers sat in remarkably clean trenches, dreaming of home at Christmas. Singing began from the German side and the British joined in, singing the English-language version. Then, a brave British soldier sticks his head above the parapet, causing consternation in the trench opposite until a German soldier climbs out too. Eventually, both sides meet in the middle, in No Man's Land, shaking hands, wishing each other a Merry Christmas and, finally, organising a football match.[20]

It was an extremely popular advert, probably more so than the programmes around it, but not everyone was impressed. Many viewed it as disrespectful and in very poor taste. Others did not like the way it was all sanitised, especially No Man's Land, where the filthy water-filled craters, dead bodies half-eaten by rats and the ubiquitous mud were all removed so as not to offend people's sensitivities at Christmas.[21] Those, however, were not the only changes.

The young British soldier that is the first to climb out of his cosy trench looks remarkably like an officer. There are no pips on his shoulder, but that requires a close look and when he opens his mouth, he certainly sounds rather posh. Another close look is required to notice that, as the young British soldier walks toward the Germans, behind him, his comrades are all following him, led by their officers.[22] All was right with the world again; the officer class were leaders in the Christmas Truce.

After WWII was over, there was immediately another war; a Cold one. In an uncertain world, we had to be sure that the upper classes were still there to protect us. The movies had to give us another hero to look up to and, as usual, they rose to the task. Fighting against the Commies, thinly disguised as an international terrorist organisation or even individual megalomaniacs, James Bond has become the archetypal British hero. The definitive portrayal might have been by a Scotsman from a working-class background, but the character was decidedly upper-class.

Of course, there was always Harry Palmer, the handsome, working-class spy, who, albeit reluctantly, did his bit to protect the West from those nasty Commies. Although not on the scale of James Bond, he managed to get beautiful women falling into bed with him, which was something relatively new for a working-class character in a British film. He was also unusual in that Michael Caine was a bit of a heartthrob, with whom women might well want to sleep and men would want to be. That was not quite the whole story, though.

In the same year as the second Harry Palmer film, *Funeral in Berlin*, was released, Caine also starred in *Alfie*, a cautionary tale of what could happen when a man goes about having casual sex with lots of women. Or, rather, what could happen when a *working-class* man goes about having casual sex with lots of women. One could easily imagine Harry Palmer having to procure a backstreet abortion. Meanwhile, James Bond shagged his way through the world's female population with no worries of an unwanted pregnancy or, God forbid, an STD!

The character of Harry Palmer, moreover, could well fit into the category of an Angry Young Man. The term 'Angry Young Men' usually referred to the writers of the books and plays that the films were based on but could equally apply to the protagonists. It must have seemed like a breath of fresh air at the time, with working-class lives presented as dramatic, rather than comical. Looking back at the films, decades later, however, they seem rather bland and steeped in bourgeois moral values.

The typical protagonist of these films was a vicious, selfish, arrogant brute, who cared nothing about his fellow man. They were not concerned with tearing the system down and starting again with a more egalitarian society. All such a protagonist cared about was his own place within that system and the obstacles that stood in *his* way. His own ambitions were all that mattered and to hell with everybody else.

Jimmy Porter, in *Look Back in Anger*, lashed out at everyone around him, often literally, as he ranted and railed about his own situation, not that of people like him.[23] Joe Lampton equally was concerned mainly with himself in *Room at the Top*.[24] Joe, if you remember, ended up marrying the boss's daughter. Both these characters, and others, used people, especially women, without a second thought for their feelings. In fact, female characters in these films rarely escaped without being slapped viciously.

Conceited to the point of narcissism and self-centred to the point of solipsism, these characters were not heroes by any stretch of the imagination. The fact that they all ended up as miserable failures or hopeless, bitter drunks made the films a bit like Greek tragedies, with the main characters paying for their hubris in the final act. None of the characters evoke sympathy in the audience. Instead, one cannot help but feel that they deserve all they get.

Back to James Bond and it is notable that practically all subsequent British spies and secret agents were from upper-class or even aristocratic stock. John Steed in *The Avengers*, Lord Brett Sinclair in *The Persuaders* and the eponymous heroes of *Adam Adamant Lives* and *Hannay*. Even George Smiley was a rather posh individual, with an aristocratic wife. And then there are the more modern heroes, like Lorraine Broughton in *Atomic Blonde* and Eggsy in the *Kingsman* movies.

But wait a minute, I hear you cry. Eggsy's from a working-class background! That is certainly true, but it is clear from the films that he is going to become a member of the Establishment. Besides, as Stuart Jeffries pointed out in the Guardian, Eggsy is not your typical working-class 'oik'.

> There is a parallel genius in the casting. Taron Egerton is lantern-jawed, with Men's Health

muscle definition and fetchingly symmetrical features that distinguish him from his frankly troll-like, convincingly English underclass coevals.[25]

Rather worryingly, there is a whiff of the Nazis about *Kingsman*. Eggsy's difference from those around him and his being selected to be a Kingsman is redolent of Nazi scientists measuring people's heads etc. and deciding that they were 'Aryan', even though their friends, neighbours and even family were not. It even reminds one of old fairy stories, where a commoner is recognised as having 'noble blood' and becomes a knight or even a king. At any rate, you know that Eggsy will no longer speak with that common accent once he is a fully-fledged adult. In fact, he will become, for all intents and purposes, James Bond!

If anyone questions the propaganda effect of James Bond, they might like to consider a short scene in the film *Goldfinger*. Ian Fleming included many pieces of absolute nonsense in his books that purported to be true; for example, that homosexuals cannot whistle.[26] The only one that made its way onto the screen, however, was that painting the skin was a dangerous business. According to Fleming, a piece of skin had to be left uncovered so that it could breathe.

One of Goldfinger's henchmen painted Shirley Eaton's character's entire body with gold or gold paint, causing her to die of 'skin suffocation'. This is absolute rubbish and would not happen at all since there is no such thing.[27] That has not stopped people believing that this is true and acting accordingly. In fact, most people would think twice before covering all their skin in body paint.

If the film *Goldfinger* has had that effect, what else have people swallowed whole from it and other movies? As we have seen, whenever a film or a TV series is made about a spy, he (or she) has to be an upper-class, fee-paying-school type. Folk have fallen for this myth, even though the truth is somewhat different. The infamous Soviet double agents Kim Philby, Guy Burgess and Donald Maclean, were all upper-class types that attended top, fee-paying schools and studied at Cambridge. This, however, tends to be ignored and James

Bond and the rest are most people's idea of the archetypal British spy.

Books, comics and films were not the only media pushing the propaganda myth that the upper classes were the saviours of Britain and the best ones to run the country. Other media pumped the same propaganda directly into people's homes. In the 1930s and during the war years, the BBC, through its radio programmes, reinforced the message. As in the cinema, the only working-class voices to be heard were in comedy shows like *It's That Man Again*. The serious business of announcements or reading the news was all done in the clipped tones of the upper classes. Those accents were the ones you could trust; there was nothing jokey about them.

The BBC carried this practice over into its television service. News and current affairs programmes were presented by the likes of Robert Dougall, Kenneth Kendal, Richard Baker and Richard Dimbleby, well into the 1960s and beyond, in accents that would not have been out of place on the radio in the 1930s. Children's programmes were presented or voiced by the same types; *Muffin the Mule*, *Andy Pandy*, *The Woodentops* and *Bill and Ben* were repeated, often ad nauseum, from the 1950s to the 1970s. Richard Baker narrated *Mary, Mungo and Midge* and *Teddy Edward* and then there was Oliver Postgate, with *Pogle's Wood*, *Noggin the Nog* and *Bagpuss*.

Some of these children's programmes were well-loved and many people have happy memories of them, but that was purely serendipitous. The BBC was like an Old Boys' club, with friends and acquaintances brought on board to provide programmes. Of course, given the upper-class, fee-paying-school background of those in charge, it was obvious that the same types ended up in charge of making programmes. It was no wonder that children's programmes were essentially posh. Everybody might love *Bagpuss* as much as Emily did, but there is no denying that the programme had a very old-fashioned, upper-class village feel to it.

Presenters, no matter what their background, had to have 'BBC' voices to fit in. It was a continuation of the agenda of the 1930s and 1940s; only über-posh voices could be the voices of authority and trustworthiness. So ingrained has this become with us all that it can be quite a shock when other voices are used. Channel 4 currently (2021) has a couple of continuity announcers that are anything but posh. One speaks in a broad Brummie accent, while the other has a Caribbean accent. These voices sound strange and even a bit grating. They are not the voices we are used to when hearing announcements on national television.

As well as a plethora of snooty voices, the BBC used to have their family-friendly serials on a Sunday afternoon. These were usually set in Victorian times and invariably had some aristocrat or member of the local gentry arriving, *deus ex machina*, to sort everything out. *A Little Princess* was one such popular drama. Another was *The Railway Children*, which you would swear had been written with the BBC in mind. Its plot was about an upper-class family forced to move to the country, where they helped everyone from the station master to local schoolboys. They, in turn, were helped by an upper-class gentleman on a train. It was so suited to the BBC's agenda that three versions were made in 1951, 1957 and 1968. The 1970 film version has since become a holiday staple on the BBC.

The *noblesse oblige* inherent in *The Railway Children* makes it sound as if it were written by Conservative Central Office. In fact, it was written by one Edith Nesbit, who was a founder member of the Fabian Society.[28] So, why would an avowed Socialist write such a book? Well, although nominally Socialist, the Fabian Society was every bit as paternalist as any Tory group. They wanted to help the working classes, but on their terms; they knew best. Their adherence to the doctrine of eugenics proved that.[29] It was hardly surprising that some of its members and ex-members, including Bernard Shaw[30] and HG Wells,[31] became fascinated with fascism.

Anyway, all this propaganda has had the desired effect that many working-class people look up to and revere the upper classes; they are manifestly the best type of people, are they not? This has translated into votes for the likes of Boris Johnson, as well as a hatred of anything even remotely liberal or left-wing. They are also prepared to believe in upper-class individuals no matter what. This brings us to yet another element of propaganda in the media.

In 2009, the BBC broadcast a special, Easter edition of *Doctor Who* called *Planet of the Dead*. One of the characters, played by Michelle Ryan of *Eastenders* fame, was a thief. This, however, was no ordinary thief. Her name was Lady Christina Da Souza, a member of the aristocracy. She was a sympathetic character, whom we all wanted to escape the clutches of the police. It was a familiar character from books, films and other TV shows: the Gentleman (or Lady, as in this case) Thief.

The Saint was one such character, as was *Raffles*. Usually, this kind of character only robbed people that deserved to be robbed, often returning the loot to somebody it had been stolen from earlier. At other times, the Gentleman Thief gave the proceeds of his crimes to charity, a bit like Robin Hood (another aristocratic Gentleman Thief). Even though the police might be after the character, we all root for him because he is on the side of all that is good.

Working-class thieves, on the other hand, are always vicious gangsters, who usually get their comeuppance, like Bob Hoskin's character in *The Long Good Friday*. Then there was *The Cook, The Thief, His Wife & Her Lover*. One got the impression from the film that Michael Gambon's character was hateful, not for being vicious or for taking revenge on the man having sex with his wife, but for his pretensions of being a gourmet and connoisseur. He should have been eating at the local Greasy Spoon with others of his ilk.

In the stark, black and white world of fiction, upper-class thieves are all good, while working-class thieves are all bad. This might help to explain why it is that many people are ready to condemn somebody that swindles a couple of thousand from the DWP but say nothing about a toff swindling millions from the tax man. It also explains why a lot of folk were prepared to turn a blind eye to posh people in government handing contracts to their friends and family in the middle of a pandemic.

THE BOY'S OWN PAPER

No. 684.—Vol. XIV.   SATURDAY, FEBRUARY 20, 1892.   Price One Penny.
[ALL RIGHTS RESERVED.]

THE ORCHID SEEKERS:

A STORY OF ADVENTURE AND PERIL IN BORNEO.

BY ASHMORE RUSSAN AND FREDERICK BOYLE.

"'How dare you attack a British ship!'"

Fig.1 Boy's Own Paper 1892
Note the chauvinistic cry of the man with the sword.

Fig.2 Advert for Pears' soap showing a black child being turned white.

Fig.3 Camp Coffee advert.

Fig.4 Advert for tobacco showing a brave officer holding off natives in South Africa.

Fig.5 Irn Bru advert featuring Ba-Bru outside Glasgow's Central Station.

Fig.6 Lees' Macaroon Bars.

Fig.7 Spadger Isle.

Fig.8 Sparky.

Fig.9 Charlie Williams cartoon.

FACE THE FACTS

IF YOU DESIRE A **COLOURED**
FOR YOUR NEIGHBOUR

VOTE LABOUR

IF YOU ARE ALREADY BURDONED
WITH ONE

VOTE **TORY**

The Conservatives once in Office, will bring
up to date the **Ministry of Repatriation**, to
Speed up the return of home-going and
expelled immigrants.

Fig.10 Cleaned-up version of 1964 election poster.

Fig.11 The Gem comic.

Fig.12 The Magnet comic.

3
One World Cup and Two World Wars

Visitors to the Lincoln Memorial and the Washington Monument, in the area known as the National Mall in Washington DC, will find plenty of other things to see between the two buildings. Points of interest include the Vietnam Veterans Memorial Wall, the spooky Korean War Veterans Memorial and the National World War II Memorial. You can always pick out British people among the crowds of tourists as they all say the same thing when they notice the dates on the latter memorial. It says that WWII lasted from 1941 until 1945. 'But it started in 1939!' you will hear the British tourists exclaim.

If you were to follow some of those British tourists for a while longer, you would be bound to hear somebody say, 'Bloody Americans! They think they won the war and it only started when they arrived!' Actually, the British are just as parochial as the Americans when it comes to WWII. It could well be argued, and has been, that WWII began in 1935, when the Italians invaded Abyssinia, or even earlier, when Japan invaded Manchuria in 1931. To the British, however, the war only started when *they* got involved. And they have the nerve to go on about the Americans!

The similarities between the Americans and the British, or, rather, the *English*, do not end there. If Hollywood films all imply that America won the war, British films are just as chauvinistic. Very rarely do other nationalities feature in British war films, even though, as its name proves, practically the whole world was involved. The common theme of most British war films is that Britain stood alone. This is most evident when it comes to the Battle of Britain.

Pilots of many nationalities took part in the air defence of Britain in 1940, including Poles, Americans, Canadians,

Frenchmen and Irishmen.[1] These pilots are, however, totally ignored in accounts of the conflict. Even the Encyclopaedia Britannica omits their contribution.[2] It is hardly surprising that people have swallowed whole the myth that Britain alone conquered the Nazis.

And it is not just World War II this myth has been applied to. The Napoleonic Wars have received the same treatment. You rarely hear of the involvement of Austria, Russia and Prussia, even though they were major players in the wars. Prussian forces were even present at Waterloo, along with the armies of the Netherlands, Hanover, Brunswick and Nassau.[3] Nobody, in Britain at any rate, knows that; all they have learned is that the Duke of Wellington led British troops into victory over Napoleon.

It can come as a shock to those studying History to discover that Britain did not dominate the ensuing peace. The Congress of Vienna,[4] where Austria's Count Metternich was the major guiding force, seems like an almost impudent affair. Britain had defeated Napoleon, had it not; so why were all these foreigners involved in discussing the future of Europe? It takes a major reboot of one's mindset to undo all the preconceptions one has about the Napoleonic Wars.

The same preconceptions, or misconceptions, are also rife when it comes to the First World War. Apparently, the French, the Russians, Australians, Italians, Indians etc. were not really involved. And those 'Johnny-Come-Latelies' the Americans, only arrived to help mop up at the end of things. Again, Britain stood alone and stopped the Germans from taking over the whole of Europe. The ingrates in Europe, however, seem to have 'forgotten' this.

There are plenty of books, television programmes and even websites that can easily disprove all these notions, but they tend to be ignored. Politicians, newspaper columnists and talking heads on television and radio are fond of pointing out that History, as a subject, should be patriotic. To be fair, Britain is not the only place where this happens. Fritz Fischer's huge 1961 tome, *Germany's War Aims in the First World War*, which showed that the whole idea of *lebensraum* and conquests in the East did not start with the Nazis, caused a political uproar in

West Germany at the time.[5] Instead of just blundering into the war, Fischer showed that Germany had actively sought the conflict.

Needless to say, nobody has examined Britain's leaders in the run-up to WWI in the detail that Fischer did with Germany's. This has resulted in two, distinct, narratives existing together in Britain. What we learn in school is that Britain blundered into WWI, as did other nations, tangled up in alliances and ententes. The other narrative, the more popular one, is that Britain responded to German and Austrian aggression and were fighting to maintain freedom and democracy. The truth, however, was somewhat different.

Going into the First World War, many of the British soldiers did not have the vote and neither did women. One of Britain's allies, Russia, moreover, was still an absolute monarchy;[6] even Germany was more democratic. As for the British Empire, it was hardly what you would call a democratic institution, which makes the claims about defending democracy appear rather hollow.

The Treaty of Brest-Litovsk showed how keen the Germans were to make conquests in the East.[7] Germany never showed any interest in establishing hegemony over Europe and certainly none in taking over Britain. The immediate German attack to the West in 1914 was intended to knock France out of the war before the Russians got themselves organised. As Fritz Fischer's research confirmed, the Germans' main area of interest was in the East, as it always had been.[8] The stories of us all speaking German if we had lost WWI are just that: stories.

In the decades leading up to the First World War, it was unclear who Britain's enemy in an expected war was going to be. The Fashoda Incident pitted Britain and France against each other as imperial rivals,[9] while Britain and Russia were almost continually at each other's throats throughout the Nineteenth Century and even into the Twentieth.[10] Talk of an 'inevitable' war was rife from the late Nineteenth Century onwards. That 'inevitability' came from the fact that, for the first time in a hundred years, Britain was facing competition in world trade. Economics were the principal reason for Britain

44

being willing to enter the First World War. There was, possibly, another reason.

If the Treaty of Brest-Litovsk and Fritz Fischer's research showed that Germany had reasons for wanting to go to war, the Sykes-Picot Agreement[11] showed that, perhaps, the same was true of Britain and her allies. It was an agreement among Britain, France, Russia and Italy to divide up the Ottoman Empire between them after the war. For Russia it was going to mean the long sought-after access to the Mediterranean. For the others, especially Britain, it meant taking over the Levant – Palestine, Syria, Persia etc. But why would Britain want to expand its empire into this region that had been nothing but trouble for at least 2,000 years? The answer was simple.

In the years leading up to the war, oil was rapidly replacing coal as the fuel of choice for ships. There was also the new-fangled motorcar that looked to be the transport of the future, as well as aeroplanes, which were obviously going to be important too. The biggest producer of oil in the world was the USA, although Britain bought most of its fuel from Royal Dutch Shell.[12] Although Royal Dutch Shell was a partly British company, it would obviously be better if wholly British companies could control oil supplies.

In 1908, oil was discovered in Persia (modern-day Iran) by a British company. The Anglo-Persian Oil Company was set up, in which the British Government became a majority shareholder during the war.[13] Oil exploration took off in the whole Middle East in the years after WWI, with Britain playing a major part.[14] This helped keep Britain an important player on the world stage; a role that, otherwise, would have passed her by completely. The truth was that Britain was already in economic decline.

We saw in Chapter 1 how Britain, during the 19th Century, became the world's largest producer of manufactured goods. We also saw how, by the end of the century, other nations had begun to catch up. Britain stuck to its policy of Free Trade, which had served it well when it was the only industrialised country in the world. Other countries, however, could ill afford to allow cheap British goods to flood their markets and destroy their own, nascent manufacturing industries.

Countries that were part of the British Empire had no choice in the matter, but the likes of Germany and the USA were outside that hallowed sphere. To safeguard their own industries and economies, they followed protectionist policies. By the start of the war, 'Britain was merely first among equals, as opposed the unrivaled (sic) superpower she had been a half-century earlier.'[15] Having control of the expected oil fields in the Middle East might bring Britain back to global dominance again.

If the First World War was not fought for the altruistic reasons that are claimed, the Second World War appears, in retrospect, to be a different matter entirely. 'Retrospect' is the operative word here as we all know now how evil Hitler and his Nazis were. At the time, though, nobody, among the general public at any rate, was aware of millions of Jews being systematically killed. And Hitler showed, both in *Mein Kampf* and in his actions, that he intended to seek conquests in the East, just like his predecessors in Germany. Unlike his predecessors, Hitler was quite prepared to take over Europe to get what he wanted. As such, he posed a threat to Britain and her empire. That was why Britain went to war.[16]

AJP Taylor said of the Nuremberg Trials that they had hanged a few Nazis and assumed that the rest of Germany had been somewhere else at the time.[17] Taylor hated Germany with a passion that deserved a better cause but, in this instance, he was right. There was supposedly a process of de-Nazification in Germany after the war, the famous 'Persil' Certificates[18] that cleared individuals of being *too* Nazi. In practice, however, de-Nazification was just a case of pretending that Nazi Germany did not happen.[19] This was the theme of Adam Curtis's documentary, part of his *The Living Dead* series, called *On the Desperate Edge of Now*.[20] As the programme points out, there was a lot of denial going on among the Allies as well.

Curtis focuses on individual experiences among allied soldiers, but the denial went much further than that, especially in Britain. With the benefit of hindsight, everyone looks with disgust and dismay at the pictures of Neville Chamberlain, waving his piece of paper and declaring 'Peace for our time.' At the time, however, Chamberlain was hailed as a hero, with crowds lining the streets to cheer him lustily.[21] He has been damned for this ever since, with one observer saying what a lot of people think, '...in pursuit of this heroic image, Chamberlain placed personal publicity success ahead of good diplomacy.'[22]

Despite all those cheering crowds greeting Chamberlain, it did not stop many people, during the war and after, convincing themselves that they had never agreed with the policy of appeasement. Nobody was more convinced of this than Winston Churchill, who took over as Prime Minister in May 1940. He was determined to prove his prescience to everybody and, to this end, published, in collaboration with his son, Randolph, the book, *Arms and the Covenant* in 1938.[23] This was a collection of his speeches from 1928 to 1938, warning of the dangers of fascism and Nazism and calling for Britain to be ready for the coming conflict. His pose as a prophet, however, was not the entire truth.

The International Churchill Society exists, as it boasts, to preserve 'the historic legacy of Sir Winston Churchill.'[24] The Society's website seems to present that legacy both good and bad and gives a remarkably 'warts and all' portrayal of Churchill. There is a piece about Churchill's position in the 1930s, which shows that Churchill and his son were pretty selective over what was included in *Arms and the Covenant*.[25] In fact, Churchill was not very anti-fascist at all before the war. If anything, he was pro-fascist.

Churchill saw fascism as a great movement to stop the spread of communism, which he abhorred. He supported both Franco in Spain and Mussolini in Italy, and even as late as 1940 tried to recruit them as allies in the fight against German aggression in Europe.[26] In 1935, he had described Hitler's

> long, weary battle for the German heart. The story of that struggle ...cannot be read without admiration for the courage, the perseverance, and the vital force which enabled him to...overcome all the...resistances which barred his path.[27]

As part of his reinvention, Churchill even changed his public opinion of Oliver Cromwell from one of hero worship[28] to one of painting him as an authoritarian villain.[29] His strategies certainly worked as it is difficult to find anyone that believes otherwise than that Churchill was foremost in Britain in warning about the dangers of fascism and Nazism. 'If only we'd listened to Churchill, we could have strangled Nazi Germany at birth!' is the prevailing view. This way of thinking explains why folk were so ready to accept the invasions of Iran, Afghanistan and Libya. Things had to be nipped in the bud before it was too late.

As we move into the third decade of the 21st Century, the World Wars are more and more part of the distant past. The combatants of WWI are all dead and buried, while those of WWII are well into their nineties, if they are still around. It will not be long before both wars are beyond living memory, and this has prompted some to start revising history already. Of course, they have not touched upon WWII yet; there are still folk alive that took part, after all. There is plenty to be going on with, though, concerning WWI.

Poet Ian McMillan has argued that our perception of the First World War has been 'skewed' by reading Wilfred Owen and other war poets in school. He says,

> In the 1960s a literary elite decided this was the most authentic view of the conflict because it chimed with their own anti-war feelings.[30]

This seems to be a developing agenda that seeks to show that the 1960s and early 1970s were an anomaly; the anti-war feelings extant then did not exist at other times. Quite what the purpose is of this agenda is unclear but there definitely appears to be a revisionist programme looking to make out that the two world wars, and WWI in particular, were not as bad as has been previously thought.

Amanda Phipps, for example, uses reactions to three major runs of R.C. Sheriff's play, *Journey's End*, to gauge popular feelings about the Great War.[31] Those runs were in 1928-30, 1972 and 2011. This allows her to follow the same agenda as Ian McMillan in singling out the 1960s and early 1970s as a time of pacifism and acute class consciousness,

48

unlike, she argues, the interwar years. But were 1920s and 1930s attitudes so very different?

Phipps points out that

> ...it was Rupert Brooke's patriotic poetry, not Wilfred Owen's sombre verses, which the nation still bought. Thus, whilst some did begin to question certain aspects of the conflict in the late 1920s, there was no overriding resentment to the First World War. Many still wanted to feel that loved ones had been sacrificed for a worthwhile cause and were too personally connected to the conflict to accept its failings.[32]

The 19th Century, often called the Long Century, is usually considered to have come to an end in 1914, with the Great War destroying all the old Victorian certainties and values. The study of history, however, is about continuity as much as change and one can easily discern many elements of concern to Victorians that were still important in the 1920s and 1930s and beyond. Respectability was still the overriding concern of most of the British population in the interwar years and that included attitudes to death and bereavement.

In Victorian times, the rules for mourning were hard and fast and the stiff upper lip was not confined to the upper and middle classes. Even the Queen herself was castigated for wearing her widow's weeds for far too long. In an age when death was an everyday occurrence, it made sense to regulate how mourning should be conducted. It was cathartic in the way a children's game might be, removing the need to dwell on one's loss. Rending one's clothes, weeping and wailing and tearing one's hair out like a character in a Greek tragedy was simply not the way the British behaved.

The interwar years were just as death-filled as Victorian times. Not only had many young men lost their lives in the war, but there was the flu pandemic and, especially, if one lived in a closely packed, working-class area, deaths from tuberculosis (consumption) affected practically every family. It was hardly surprising that spiritualism, seances and the like, became even more popular during this period than it had been in Victorian times.[33] In public, however, everyone still felt compelled to put on a brave face.

Part of that stolid façade was having a copy of Rupert Brooke's poems in the house. It would be placed where everyone could see it, next to the family's copy of the Bible. Just like the Bible, it would rarely, if ever, be opened; being read was not its purpose. It was for show, proving one's conformity to what one was *meant* to believe. Like all the old rules about mourning, it was a pretence and Brooke's poems were well-suited to that pretence.

Brooke wrote his poems at the beginning of the war and they are full of patriotic lines about glory and dying for king and country.[34] The irony was that he never saw a gun fired in anger and died of an infected mosquito bite in April 1915.[35] He had no idea at all what war was like and yet was celebrated as a great war poet. It summed up the unreality of the way that grief was dealt with in public after the war. What people's private feelings were was a different matter entirely and much more difficult to gauge. It is possible, though, to get some idea.

Although the zeitgeist in Britain seemed to be one of seeing the war as a worthwhile endeavour and the deaths of all those young men being for a legitimate purpose, that did not tell the whole story. It was customary at the time to call the Great War 'The war to end all wars'[36] and certainly nobody wanted to have to go through it ever again. As we saw earlier, cheering crowds greeted Neville Chamberlain when he arrived back from Munich and, despite later suggestions to the contrary, appeasement was an extremely popular position in Britain at the time.

Amanda Phipps's examination of reactions to the play *Journey's End* gives rather a distorted view of the 1920s and 1930s. The problem is that ordinary, working-class people were not great theatre goers; not when it came to plays at any rate. *Journey's End*'s first run, from 1928-1930, was in London's West End.[37] It is doubtful that many working-class people would venture into such a posh area, and even less likely that they would have been welcome. The attendance figures given

50

by Phipps[38] would have been entirely made up of middle- and upper-class patrons.

Working-class entertainment was provided by variety theatre, gramophone records and, increasingly during the interwar years, radio. The most important source of entertainment, however, was the cinema, which British people attended at least once a week. More people probably saw the film of *Journey's End*, which was released in 1930 (Fig.13), than ever saw the play. Fortunately for Amanda Phipps's thesis, it proved extremely popular.

Another film released in 1930, however, was probably far more popular than *Journey's End*. That film was *All Quiet on the Western Front* (Fig.14). Facts and figures are difficult to come by, but All Quiet on the Western Front won the Best Picture Oscar for that year and was the third-highest grossing film in the USA in 1930.[39] To suggest that the film was popular in America but not in Britain is ludicrous. Besides, an even more explicitly anti-war film was doing the rounds in 1930 and was well received by British audiences and critics.

Peace on the Western Front[40] (Fig.15) was a short 'B' film, intended to be shown along with a main feature film. With an obvious nod to *All Quiet on the Western Front*, the film was sanctioned and supported by the Imperial War Museum, who provided archived film for the movie.[41] And just in case anyone missed the point of the film, an extended press release rammed it home forcefully.

> As is stated in the accompanying press brochure, the purpose of the film was to impress upon younger generations, for whom the Great War was ancient history, that war 'is not a childish game, a glorious adventure', but 'a hideous ugly thing.'[42]

These short films were usually made to have a short run, but *Peace on the Western Front* was still being shown in cinemas two years later.[43] That fact is a serious slap in the face to the arguments of Phipps and others that the Great War was still seen as something glorious by people desperate to find meaning in the deaths of their loved ones. The truth was that pacifism appeared to be the overriding concern of practically everyone in Britain.

Surveys showed that the British people were against war,[44] while most people thought that Germany had been treated too harshly at Versailles and was only taking back what was hers in the first place.[45] Although there were voices opposed, in the main the Labour Party supported the policy of appeasement right up until the end of the 1930s.[46]

There was a broad consensus, then, in the interwar years, in politics, media and popular opinion, that there should never be another war. This was reflected in another of those Victorian-style regulations concerning mourning: Armistice Day. The very name of this occasion suggested that it was not just about remembering the fallen. It highlighted the peace at the end of the war; a peace that should be maintained at all costs. The film *Peace on the Western Front* was actually released to coincide with Armistice Day,[47] which shows how much the day was dedicated to peace.

Armistice Day, or Remembrance Day, as it was renamed after WWII, gives us an insight into the agenda behind the efforts to rewrite the history of WWI and the interwar years. To uncover this agenda, it is worthwhile looking at how the Royal British Legion nowadays describes the relevance of Remembrance Day.

Remembrance Sunday, which falls on 14 November in 2021, is a national opportunity to remember the service and sacrifice of all those that have defended our freedoms and protected our way of life.[48]

Poppies are worn as a show of support for the Armed Forces community.[49]

As you can see, the whole emphasis of the occasion has changed. There is still mention of peace, but only in passing and as if it is somehow incidental to the occasion.[50] The main focus is now on 'service,' 'sacrifice' and 'support for the armed forces.' Obviously, things have changed since the interwar years, but what? That can be answered in one word: Churchill.

Between the years 1956-1958 Churchill published his four-volume *The History of the English-Speaking Peoples*.[51] His history was an old-fashioned, Whiggish view, which saw history as a march of progress towards a perfect society. It would pain Churchill to have accepted it, but, in many ways, it was similar to Marx's theories, both influenced by Hegel's dialectic theory of history. Churchill held racial views that went along the same lines with different races at different stages of development, the British and Americans being the most advanced.

Many condemn Churchill for his racism, which inspired a lot of his actions, such as his advocating using poison gas against insurgents in Iraq.[52] Others, though, are prepared to overlook these faults, saying that he was 'of his time' and a product of his Nineteenth-Century upbringing. (Of course, the exact same could be said of Adolf Hitler, but nobody makes excuses for *him!*) Whatever one's thoughts about Churchill, though, one has to admit that he was the right leader for WWII.

Churchill had started writing his history in the 1930s, but the war got in the way, and he could not finish it until the 1950s. His views on British history, however, were already formed and informed and inspired his speeches during WWII. Such was the power of his speeches that the adjective 'Churchillian' has been coined to describe them and others like them. He imagined that it was his destiny to lead his country in time of war[53] and he managed to sweep the British population along with him; it was *their* destiny too.

Churchill was acutely aware that he was standing at an important point in history and his speeches reflected this. His genius was to imbue the British public with the same sense that they were all doing something vital to the very existence of Britain. They were making history as well as living it. It was what made Churchill the ideal war leader. Unfortunately for him, the end of the war meant that a war leader was no longer needed.

Despite the huge Labour majority in 1945, there were still plenty of people that swallowed whole Churchill's vision and refused to let it go at the end of the war. Not all of them totally understood it, however, and never bothered to read Churchill's books. This led to some rather skewed ideas about history and Britain's place in it.

Adam Curtis's third episode in his short series, *The Living Dead*, was called *The Attic* and was about this legacy of Churchill and his historical views. Among those giving their opinions was a London police officer, who had this to say about Britain:

> Our history is special inasmuch that everyone has tried to give us a good hiding since the year dot. The Romans failed, I think, really miserably. They didn't really succeed in conquering the *whole* of England.[54]

Actually, it was *Scotland* that the Romans failed to conquer the whole of. The whole of England and Wales was a Roman province for nearly four hundred years! And the Romans were not the only invaders. After the Romans left, there were Angles and Saxons, Vikings and then the Vikings' descendants from France, the Normans. The Picts mounted several invasions of England and were invaded themselves by Scots and Vikings. The upshot is that there is no such thing as an indigenous Briton; everyone in England, Scotland and Wales is of mixed pedigree. You try telling that to your average Brexiteer, though!

This mistaken idea of Britain standing up to all and sundry has engendered a strange notion regarding Britain's historical relationship with Europe. It has become one that sees European nations as constantly squabbling and fighting and Britain needing to come in, *deus ex machina*, to sort it all out. If Britain had not been there, Europe would have been a smoking ruin a long time ago. Folk that believe this tripe are also guilty, necessarily, of believing in some pretty offensive national stereotypes.

Germans, to these people, are all humourless boneheads. The comics of the 60s and 70s, like *Commando*, reinforced this attitude with dolts on sentry duty regaling each other with gems like, 'Ach, zis is a waste of time!' Meanwhile, their fanatical, monocle-wearing, Junker commanding officer berates his own men and is even prepared to shoot them if they show any hesitation in obeying his orders. British soldiers, like Captain Hurricane (Fig.16) in the *Valiant*, called the Germans 'squareheads' and 'sausage-noshers'.

As well as being stupid, Germans are incredibly arrogant and have been looking to take over Europe, and even the world, since time immemorial. Most of them seem to be content to do it one poolside lounger at a time; others, however, view the European Union as their big chance to rule the roost without having to lose another war.

The French, according to this mindset, are cowards and are prepared to surrender at the drop of a hat. This viewpoint stems from events in World War II but ignores the fact that the British ran off and left their allies under Nazi occupation for four years. Dunkirk is always spoken of as if it were a victory, rather than the ignominious defeat it actually was.[55] With their allies having deserted them, the French had no option but to surrender. And yet, British chauvinists are prepared to blame France for the defeat.

The 'live to fight another day' myth has helped excuse Britain's behaviour in deserting her allies, but the truth is that, without the Americans, Britain was in no position to fight any other day. In reality, it was the Americans that liberated Europe, with British help, not the other way around. It is, perhaps, surprising that the French welcomed the British troops, rather than spit in their eyes!

Anyway, there are plenty among the British working classes that believe that the whole of Europe, apart from Germany, owes Britain a massive debt of gratitude. The Germans, meanwhile, should be constantly apologetic and grateful that their country is even allowed to exist. English football supporters like to remind the Germans of their inferior status with their song, *One World Cup and Two World Wars*.

As for the Empire, it has become the norm again to argue that it was a good thing. This is what Churchill believed; that it brought civilisation where there was none. In

Chapter 1, we saw Boris Johnson's view of the Empire in Africa. It is worth repeating.

> The continent (Africa) may be a blot, but it is not a blot upon our conscience. The problem is not that we were once in charge, but that we are not in charge anymore.[56]

There are many in Britain that would wholeheartedly agree with those sentiments. Meanwhile, there appears to be an agenda, whose narrative is that the British Empire was nowhere near as bad as is made out.[57] One character even argues that the Empire was beneficial to the conquered natives.[58] The comments section has some agreeing with him, while others call him naïve. This is true since he obviously does not think things through. Another of his blogs rails against Britain and America trying to force their political and cultural systems on foreign countries.[59] It totally undermines what he says about the benefits of the British Empire, but, then, he probably does not care about that.

This glorification of the British Empire is part-and-parcel of the general revisionism about Britain's past, including WWI. As we have seen, all of this comes from the mind of Winston Churchill and from those that refused to abandon Churchill's vision when WWII ended. These attempts to rewrite history, however, are not propaganda; they are preaching to the converted. They are a reaction to public opinion, rather than an attempt to influence it.

The big question, though, is why all this rewriting of history is going on now. The answer lies in this tweet by a Brexiteer:

> When will remainers get it through their thick skulls that we want brexit at any cost? Even if it means tanking the economy. Even if it means mass unemployment. Even if it means a crashing pound. Even if it means starving. We say loud and proud…YES to brexit, NO to foreigners![60]

Now, that level of xenophobia and racism did not start with the Brexit referendum; it pre-dated it by many years. In fact, this existing zeitgeist was exploited by those looking to leave the European Union. This zeitgeist expresses itself in a love of the military, a mawkish preoccupation with Remembrance Day, an unhealthy obsession with Britain's past glories, especially the Empire and a desperate and unrealistic longing for Britain to go back to those days. Again, this is all part of Churchill's vision, but why did it take so long to assert itself?

These beliefs and feelings existed during the 1960s and 1970s too, but certainly not to the extent that they do now, in the 21st Century. What happened to throw out all the idealism and liberalism of the 60s and 70s and go back to beliefs and opinions that belonged to the period of the Second World War?

If we go back to Churchill's vision of Britain during WWII, among those that were influenced by it and carried that belief beyond the war years was a teenage student at Oxford University. That student was to have a bigger influence on Britain and British opinions than Churchill ever did. That student's name was Margaret Thatcher.

Airey Neave was one of those upper-class heroes of WWII that we encountered earlier. He was educated at Eton and Oxford and eased his way into being an officer when the war started. Unfortunately for him, he was captured in 1940 and sent straight to a POW camp. As you will remember, officers in the POW camps had not much else to do but plan to escape and Neave was no exception.

After a few escape attempts, Neave was sent to Colditz, which was supposedly escape-proof. After a failed attempt in 1941, he managed to escape in 1942, no doubt leaving his batman to the tender mercies of the Gestapo! As the first to escape Colditz, his reputation as a hero was assured. With the level of fame and respect earned by Neave during the war, a career in politics was inevitable: as a Conservative, of course.

Post-war Britain was a shock for Neave and others of his class. They thought they had been fighting to keep Britain and its empire as it had been in the 1930s. they remembered how things had been before the war, a stable, structured, hierarchical society. Unfortunately, ordinary people remembered it as well and had no great desire to go back to it. The Beveridge Report[61] promised a fairer society and was the main feature of the

Labour Party's election manifesto. To the disgust of Neave and his ilk, Labour was elected with a huge majority.

As time went on, Neave grew more and more concerned. By the 1970s, he was convinced that something had to be done. That something could only be achieved by the Tories, but not in its current manifestation. It needed somebody as leader that was in tune with Neave's own ideas. He chose Margaret Thatcher, who was a firm believer in Churchill's vision of Britain, as his protégée. With Neave's help, Thatcher won the leadership contest against Edward Heath and the road was clear for a return to the old days.[62]

With her head full of Churchill's view of Britain and its history, it was obvious that Thatcher desperately wanted to be a war leader, like her hero had been. As we have seen, she got her wish in 1982 with the Falklands Conflict, but that was not enough. After the conflict, everything had to be a 'war'. There was the war against the unions, the war against Communist infiltration, the war against Irish terrorists and, most importantly, the war against the European Economic Community. Her fights against these different organisations were named as 'wars' by Thatcher and her associates and were reported as such by the media.

So why did working-class people vote for Margaret Thatcher and support her, even though her policies were all against their best interests? Well, it was partly due to her Churchillian rhetoric about 'making Britain *great* again'. It was also due to the myths that were put about concerning the unions in the 1970s; myths that many people still believe.

4
Everybody Out

If you were to watch any pre-war British films, you could be forgiven for thinking that trade unions simply did not exist. The simple fact is that the British Establishment did not want unions and the film industry, as part of that Establishment, felt the same. The last thing they wanted was for ordinary people to think that unions were a good thing. At the same time, producing anti-union films seemed like a dangerous thing to do politically. The best thing all round was just to leave well alone.

In the post-war period, trade union officials merited a mention in films and in the new medium, television, but it was usually as comedy characters. Miriam Karlin's shop steward in *The Rag Trade*, with her cry of 'Everybody out!' (Fig.17) was a case in point. Every TV comedy that involved some kind of workplace, like *On the Buses* and *Are You Being Served*, had its shop steward or union rep that nobody, least of all the workers, could be bothered with.

Films did the same, with even the *Carry On…* series having its share of union rule-book-checking bores, most notably in *Carry On Cabby* and *Carry On at Your Convenience*. The union official got in the way of folk doing their jobs properly and was a thorn in the side of the bosses and the workers. Such pests were ridiculed mercilessly in the film *I'm Alright Jack*.

While British films portrayed unions and shop stewards as figures of fun, Hollywood went into all-out attack mode. Movies like *F.I.S.T.*, *Hoffa*, *Once Upon a Time in America* and the more recent *The Irishman* have shown us how corrupt unions were and possibly are. One thing most of these films never explained, however, was why American unions got mixed up with gangsters in the first place. In the Nineteenth Century and well into the Twentieth, the bosses controlled the local police and often had their own, private police forces.[1] There was also the Pinkerton Detective Agency, which, although credited with solving crimes, mainly provided armed thugs, spies and agents provocateurs to break strikes.[2] Bosses in Pennsylvania even invented the myth of the Molly Maguires to justify the murders of union men and to keep down Irish Catholic immigrants.[3] Without the financial resources of their bosses, it was hardly surprising that unions welcomed the protection of the Mob with open arms.

On a side note, one ostensibly anti-union film actually had a different agenda entirely. *On the Waterfront* was directed by Elia Kazan, who had appeared before the House Committee on Un-American Activities a couple of years before and grassed up everyone he knew that had flirted with Communism in the 1930s. The screenwriter of the film, Budd Schulberg, did the same. It puts a totally different slant on the movie to view it in the context of these two men justifying their actions.[4]

Anyway, British people were bombarded with the idea that unions were worthy of nothing but, at best, ridicule and, at worst, fear. It was a simple matter, then, for the Tories to convince the working-class electorate that the unions were to blame for the economic mess the UK found itself in at the end of the 1970s. It was not just the relentless propaganda of the media, however, that provided an environment where ordinary people could be so easily gulled. The truth is that the British working classes have never been united.

Actually, it is debatable rather than being the absolute truth; the fact that I use the term 'working classes' shows which side of the debate I am on. While at university, I had quite a few friendly arguments with tutors and other students that thought that working-class solidarity was a real thing. My opinion was, and is, that such solidarity has never existed at all.

Take the Chartists, for instance. As probably everyone knows from their schooldays, the six-point Charter was written by William Lovett and the London Working Men's Association.[5] The nationwide movement, however, was led by Fergus O'Connor and the LWMA was left behind. Lovett and his associates were all artisans and looked to get the middle classes to work with them. To this end, they were desperate to appear 'respectable'. O'Connor had no time for these namby-pamby ideas; he was going to show the power of the working classes, who would force the Government to give in to their demands.[6] The Chartist movement, then, ended up hopelessly riven.

As the Nineteenth Century progressed, the differences between artisans, men who had a trade, and the ordinary working classes became more marked. When unions were made legal in the last third of the century, these unions were almost overwhelmingly comprised of tradesmen. In fact, one aspect of these unions was to keep unskilled and semi-skilled workmen out of jobs that were deemed to be only for artisans.[7]

After 1867, most tradesmen had the vote, which set them apart from the mass of working-class people. Many of them also owned their own homes, thanks to the building societies that had been established to provide them with mortgages.[8] Tradesmen and their families lived next to small shopkeepers and the like, bringing them closer to being middle-class. The fact that they lived apart from other members of the working classes reinforced this difference.

Some tradesmen banded together to build their own houses, the famous Edinburgh Colonies being an example of this.[9] These were built well away from the slums of Edinburgh's Old Town. Even pastimes became different, with tradesmen more likely to be seen on the golf course of a weekend, rather than down the pub. No wonder historians speak of these people as being an 'aristocracy of labour'.[10]

Even into the 1950s and 1960s, tradesmen were desperate to hold onto their superior status. In the Glasgow shipyards, not only did their unions insist on strict pay differentials but unskilled and semi-skilled workers, when assisting at a job, had to walk behind the tradesmen at all times.

And it was not just these distinctions that stopped there from being a united working class. Most union members saw the need for going on strike, but often did not extend the same courtesy to other unions. If bus or train drivers came out on strike, for example, other workers complained that it made it difficult to get to their places of work. A binmen's strike would be cursed by all, union members or not. And most griping was saved for when teachers went on strike, forcing parents into the unwelcome situation of looking after their own children!

The 1970s, according to many people, was a time of never-ending strikes, with the whole of Britain suffering because of them. Read these summations of the decade:

Three-day weeks, candles at night, cold dinners, and power cuts and all because of what? A union who used that (sic) decided to hold the country to ransom! Strikes seem (sic) to be the only thing on the news back then. As a child growing up, I believed this was how adults always behaved.[11]

> I remember the three-day week; going to school in groups, all wearing luminous yellow bands on our coat sleeves so that we could be seen in the dark. Then coming home and huddling round the gas cooker for heat.[12]

> The nice thing about electricity shortages was that they were announced on the wireless, by area, beforehand. Candles could not be found in hardware stores, but were plentiful in Harrods. We used Artic (sic) candles and camping lanterns. One could be somewhat prepared. No bread? They flew in bread from France until that was stopped and, if there was flour in the house, one had to bake (or not). The worst strike for many was on throwaway nappies. I am sure that hurt many people. I seem to remember contests of how to get along with tiny amounts of water - winners combined boiling food, washing dishes, bathing, washing clothes and finally, using the remains to water the garden, in about the same order with the same water. Hosepipes were banned in London.[13]

Reading those comments, one might well believe that the 1970s was a time of constant hardship, with fuel shortages, food shortages, children having to walk to school in the dark and even water shortages. Like all such memories, they are flawed, believing that everything happened at the same time. The truth was that all these 'hardships' occurred in different years and, more importantly, the unions were not always to blame.

Those children walking to school in the dark, for example, was caused by a Government experiment whereby the clocks where not put back in October. This made for lighter evenings, but darker mornings. The experiment took place from 1968, with the clocks not going back again until October 1971.[14] It was hardly what you would call something that happened throughout the 1970s and it was certainly nothing to do with the unions.

Interestingly, there is debate over whether keeping the clocks at British Summer Time all year round or sticking with the present system would be better. Some are even calling for an alternative method entirely. This debate shows again the divisions between working-class people, since everyone wants what would be best for his own job or life.[15]

The Three-Day Week only lasted two months, as did the blackouts. The miners accepted a deal from the new Labour Government and returned to work in February 1974.[16] People talk about it, though, as if it lasted for years. As for the bread shortages, they were caused by the shortage of petrol for delivery vans engendered by the Oil Crisis.[17] This was over by March 1974. There was another bread shortage when bakers went on strike in 1977, but that was three years after the Three-Day Week and lasted just over a week.[18]

The most ridiculous suggestion from those comments above, however, is the implication that the unions were somehow to blame for hosepipe bans. This happened only once in the 1970s, during the summer of 1976 when the whole of Britain baked in a heatwave.[19] Many folk in the 1970s, and afterwards, believed that union leaders thought the sun shone out of their arses; to blame them for a heatwave, though, is taking that belief to extremes!

Union official and author, John Medhurst,[20] wrote an article for *Red Pepper* a few years back, in which he dispels many of the myths of the 1970s.[21] It is certainly worth a read, if only to counter all the anti-union propaganda found elsewhere. One myth that he was more than happy to lay to rest is that Margaret Thatcher 'saved Britain'. In fact, she did more harm than any amount of unions ever had.

In 1979, when Margaret Thatcher became Prime Minister, she quoted St. Francis of Assisi on the steps of 10 Downing Street,

> Where there is discord, may we bring harmony. Where there is error, may we bring truth. Where there is doubt, may we bring faith. And where there is despair, may we bring hope.[22]

It was not clear if she said 'we', meaning the whole Tory Party or if she was employing the royal 'we', probably the latter. It was a strange speech to give since it soon became obvious that she and her government intended to do the *exact opposite* of everything she had detailed. She revealed herself to be every inch a dogmatist and, like fanatics everywhere, she was determined to do what she thought was right no matter who got hurt in the process.

How the hell Milton Friedman won a Nobel Prize for his rehashed ideas is one of the great mysteries of modern times. *Monetarism*, his economic theory was called, though, as Michael Foot never tired of telling everyone at the time, it was simply plain, old-fashioned *Deflation*. Deflation had been the norm in economic theory and practice in the pre-war years, when bringing down inflation was seen as the best thing a government could do to salvage the economy. Doing this, however, resulted in high unemployment, which was viewed as not necessarily a bad thing. Wages could be kept low since there were plenty of unemployed people out there that would be happy to take the job of any troublemaker that asked for higher pay.

After the war, the theories of Maynard Keynes held sway, with both Labour and Conservative governments making sure that unemployment was kept low while inflation would take care of itself. Keynesian theory also advised that government spending was an important way of keeping the economy on track. Now, here was Margaret Thatcher, ready to resurrect the old economic shibboleths of the 1920s and 1930s.

Unemployment stood at 3m in 1982,[23] while the Employment Secretary, Norman Tebbit, intimated that the unemployed should get on their bikes and go and look for work.[24] It was a return to the Victorian idea that the unemployed themselves were wholly responsible for their situation. Probably the biggest surprise was that the Government did not try to reintroduce workhouses. They would have been full to the gunwales with all the unemployment being caused by Thatcher's doctrinaire policies.

Not only was the pursuit of deflationary policies causing high unemployment, Thatcher's government also did nothing to stop the closing of manufacturing industries; in fact, they positively encouraged it. Partly, this was due to Thatcher's hatred of, and desire to destroy, trade unions.[25] Another reason was that, over the decades, most of these industries, especially Britain's traditional heavy industries, had become unproductive. The laissez-faire policies of Thatcher, which left everything to market forces, meant that there was no chance of any government money to save these industries and the jobs that went with them. Of course, everyone knew who was to blame for these industries' decline: the unions.

During the 1980s, Conservative Party-Political Broadcasts frequently harped on about how the frequent strikes in the 1970s had weakened British industry irreparably. In the run-up to the general elections of 1983 and 1987, there was always some snooty, old besom in the Question Time audience that asked, 'If Labour get back in, will it be beer and sandwiches at Number 10?' This patronising expression was meant to bring back the frightening prospect of the trade unions returning to the supposed power they had held in the 1970s.

Then there were the so-called 'restrictive practices' that unions insisted upon. This meant that one worker was not allowed to do anything that was the job of another worker. This is often portrayed as being petty, as this character's story demonstrates:

> As a trainee engineer in 1976, I remember changing a toilet roll when on secondment to our Sheffield factory and being seriously worried that someone might find out and accuse me of doing somebody else's job. My predecessor had almost caused a strike by helping to sweep up some rubbish. The union's grip was total, and the atmosphere was poisonous.[26]

This character does not realise it, but there was an important reason why unions insisted that everyone stick to his own job. It was something that I discovered for myself and something, which I also discovered, that not a lot of people are aware of. It concerns the rules that employers have about which tasks you can and cannot do.

Most teachers do a lot more than just teach and there is usually a physical aspect to their job. Back in my teaching days this could involve wheeling TVs on trolleys around and doing the same with PCs with those old-fashioned, heavy monitors. It was while pushing one of these PCs into a cupboard that I put my back out. The thing had wheels like a supermarket trolley, with a mind of their own, which made it extremely difficult to manoeuvre. Luckily, my back was only sore for a couple of days. But what if it had been a long-term injury? That was when I made my discovery.

I cannot remember exactly *how* I found out but find out I did. It turned out that I would not have received sick pay from my employer, the Council, because I was doing something that was not in my job description. After that, I refused to put the computer away, leaving it to the janitor, whose job it was. The head teacher did not complain about my stance, especially after I explained what it was about.

The man above that helped to sweep up some rubbish would have been in the same position. If he had injured himself, he would not have received any sick pay since he was doing a job he was not supposed to. Even worse, if somebody had tripped over the brush that he was wielding, he would be personally liable for any compensation to the injured party. The unions were not being awkward; they were simply protecting their members, even from themselves.

But still, the myth was propagated that the unions were responsible for all the ills suffered by British industry. Derek Jameson, editor of the *Daily Express* at the time, admitted in 1979 about the Winter of Discontent,

> We pulled every dirty trick in the book. We made it look like it was general, universal and eternal, whereas it was in reality scattered, here and there, and no great problem.[27]

There are still those that believe this nonsense that the unions were out of control in the 1970s and were the main reason for the decline of industry in the UK. This opinion was reinforced by the miners' strike of 1984-85. All the media were against the miners and they received no support from either the Labour Party or the TUC.[28] The violence against the striking miners by the police was ignored, while every half-brick thrown by a miner was scrutinised fully.

Of course, since the miners were out on strike for a year, they got the blame for all the subsequent pit closures. None of the media could admit that the NUM had been in the right all along. Instead, stories did the rounds about mines being unworkable when the strikers went back. Considering that the pit closures took place over the next few years, the tales of flooded mines and the like were obviously a pack of lies. There are those, however, even in ex-mining areas, that still believe this rubbish.

At any rate, there was an air of relief around Britain when the NUM admitted defeat. Thatcher was a hero for 'standing up' to the unions. Her government had already shown this 'heroism' earlier in 1984, when they banned anyone working at GCHQ from belonging to a union.[29] Although there were many complaints from the Left, most people in Britain did not bat an eyelid. They swallowed whole the Tories' and the right-wing media's claims that unions at an intelligence-gathering facility were a major security risk.[30] After all, everybody knew that the unions were on the side of the Soviet Union, were they not?

In fact, the *real* Soviet agents were embedded within the Establishment, as we had discovered in 1979. Anthony Blunt, who had been art adviser to the Queen, was exposed as a Soviet spy. The security services had been aware of this since 1964, when Blunt had given information in exchange for immunity from prosecution.[31] He was part of the so-called *Cambridge Five*, who had all attended Trinity College, Cambridge and then worked for the British intelligence services, where they passed secrets to the Russians. At one time, it seemed that the main career paths for Cambridge graduates were either working for the KGB or getting their own comedy show on the BBC.

The media had plenty to say about Blunt and his associates, but it was soon forgotten as they agreed with Thatcher's idea of 'the enemy within'. The workers at GCHQ were given back their right to join a union in 1997 by Tony Blair's Labour Government, but there are plenty of people still prepared to believe that Thatcher did the right thing.

Besides all the propaganda that working-class voters were subjected to in the 1980s, and are still subjected to, there were also two powerful motivators for them to vote Tory. The basis of both of these motivators was fear, a fear engendered by the media and Tory politicians alike. The first is illustrated by something that Margaret Thatcher is reputed to have said.

There is no record of Thatcher having said the phrase, although it is often attributed to her. Apparently, a one-time Duchess of Westminster was the one that originally used the expression, although it has been said that *she* got it from a poet. Whoever said it, it certainly fitted in with Thatcher's philosophy. It went, 'Anybody seen in a bus over the age of 30 has been a failure in life.'[32] Often, the sentence is quoted as being 'over the age of 25', while another word sometimes replaces 'failure in life'. It was a word that had been around for a long, long time but, in the 1980s, took on a new meaning, imported from America. That word was 'loser'.

68

Before the 1980s, the word was normally prefaced by the definite article: 'the loser' or 'the losers' if it was a team. It was only used in the context of games or sports. Now, it was applied to life. Suddenly, people were just Losers, full stop. And, of course, if there were Losers, there had to be Winners.

So, how did you know if you were a Winner or a Loser? That was easy. It was all to do with how much money you had or seemed to have. Conspicuous consumption was the order of the day. You had to have the best flat or house, the best car, the best, preferably designer, clothes, the best hi-fi, the best everything. Of course, this was relative; not everybody had a salary that would have the bank manager sending you a Christmas card. The main thing was to be better than those around you.

Men that worked in offices started wearing red braces, imitating the yuppies that they saw on TV. Their female counterparts, meanwhile, did what was called 'power dressing', which basically meant wearing big shoulder pads. Everyone seemed to own a Filofax, even if they did not need one and sales of Perrier went through the roof.

Not everyone could work in an office but, more and more, as the Tories closed all the mines, shipyards and factories, people in offices, shops, restaurants etc. were the only ones with jobs. And all of them wanted to be perceived as Winners, even if that meant getting into loads of debt. And debt had never been so easy to get.

Credit cards and store cards were handed out willy-nilly with applications very rarely turned down. People that had once relied on Provident Cheques and places like Fisher's Warehouse in Glasgow,[33] could now use their flexible friend to shop wherever they liked. It was the same with mortgages. You used to have to save up a deposit in order to buy a house but now banks, which were taking over building societies as the main mortgage providers, were authorising 100% mortgages and sometimes even more.

House ownership rose, especially since the Tories brought in legislation in 1980 allowing people to buy their council houses, often with substantial discounts.[34] Council houses in better areas were snapped up, while those that could not afford to

69

buy, even with a discount, were stuck in large council schemes. Other folk took advantage of those 100% mortgages to get their foot on the property ladder. In Glasgow, people with decent jobs moved from areas like Castlemilk to cottage flats in Croftfoot and Kings Park. As the 1980s went on, council estates became more and more the preserve of the unemployed.

One of Thatcher's great plans was to foster a culture of self-employment in the country, wanting Britain to become a nation of entrepreneurs.[35] Probably the most successful of those that took up this particular baton were the gangsters that flooded council schemes with drugs. Prior to the 1980s, drugs were just something you read about in the Sunday papers. Only rock stars, movie and television stars and, of course, students took drugs. It did not take long for that situation to change. By the mid-1980s council schemes were awash with marijuana, pills of all descriptions and even heroin.

With very little to no chance of ever working again, being made to feel like the dregs of society by the media and folk despising them for being on the dole, it was hardly surprising that people got angry. Throw drugs into the mix and you have a recipe for disaster. Millions were just thrown on the scrapheap with no future to speak of. Vandalism and other forms of crime increased, while 'normal' people despaired of having to live among these types. There was no escape, however; all the council houses in better areas had been sold off.

Perversely, it was the Tories that benefited from this situation, even though they were the ones that had created it. As the party that was supposedly tough on crime and had zero tolerance for drugs, who else were the 'respectable' working classes meant to vote for? The Tories were returned with a huge majority in 1983 and, although this majority was reduced, the two subsequent elections in 1987 and 1992 saw them returned to government comfortably enough.[36]

While many working-class Tory voters were afraid of being seen as Losers, others were inspired by a more basic fear. The 1980s were a time of paranoia; the Tories were obsessed with the whole idea of Communist infiltrators. But the Tories were not the only ones that were paranoid; many people were and, as it turned out, they were right to be.

I was at university in the 1980s and rumours abounded that the police employed informers to infiltrate left-wing political groups. In the Students' Union you used to get undercover police officers from the drug squad, sitting nursing their pints of heavy all night as they looked around to see if anyone was selling illicit substances. They stood out like a sore thumb with their moustaches, short, neat haircuts and unsuccessful attempts to dress down. They did not speak to anyone and obviously knew nobody. They were easily spotted. Those infiltrating political groups, however, were a different matter entirely.

TV programmes like *Harry's Game* and *Operation Julie* showed what proper undercover operations were like, with the infiltrators completely becoming members of the groups they were spying on. Everyone suspected that somebody sitting in their Socialist/Communist/Anarchist meetings was probably a police informer; it was impossible to tell who, though. There was no point in investigating matters, especially since nobody, apart from the spy, had any detective skills. The big question on everyone's mind, however, was what did the police do with the information? Rumours abounded about that too.

It was suspected by many folk that some kind of blacklist was being compiled. If you happened to be on that blacklist, you would find it difficult, if not impossible, to get a decent job. Such ideas were dismissed as nothing but paranoia, but it was noticeable that not many students got involved in politics anymore. I had been at university in 1978, got kicked out and then got back in 1983. The difference was stark. From most students being involved in politics in 1978, by 1983 hardly any were. Fear played a great part in this change, though hardly anyone would admit it.

A new phrase was coined in the 1980s: *politically active*. This phrase cropped up in the press and on television in the news and in dramas. It was used almost as a slur, as if it were something to be ashamed of, especially so if the person in question happened to be black. Courtroom dramas constantly used it as a kind of shorthand for 'active in *left-wing* politics'. With a black person in the dock, being termed 'politically active' was tantamount to saying that the person was guilty. No wonder people were scared to get involved in politics.

And it was not just in university that such fears were prevalent; they permeated the real world as well. Left-wing newspapers speculated that anyone involved in socialist politics or that was even active in a union, could well end up on a blacklist. This kind of stuff only appeared in the likes of the *Socialist Worker* or the *Morning Star*, not in the *Daily Mirror*. It was easy, then, to dismiss it as paranoia or propaganda. That, however, did not stop people from being extra careful.

Such concerns were not widespread, but those in good and relatively secure jobs believed that their interests were best served by keeping their heads down. To such people, joining a union or even associating with somebody that was in one was a dangerous proposition. The best thing to do was just to do your job, maybe go out for a drink now and again, and go home to your owner-occupied house or flat.

As we now know, those people had every right to be paranoid. In the early 1990s, the scale of the Economic League's operations became known.[37] They had spent years, if not decades, compiling lists of undesirables, which they passed on to companies that paid for the privilege. Even ordinary union members' names found their way onto this blacklist. It seemed that those paranoid folk of the 1980s were not paranoid enough.

The police too were involved in widespread spying on political campaigners, just as had been suspected back in the 1980s. They even operated as agents provocateurs, instigating acts of violence and vandalism.[38] So widespread were these operations that it is going to take until 2023 for an investigation to go through all the evidence.[39]

There was another aspect to the paranoia of the 1980s and beyond. Not only did some people feel that they had to keep their heads down and not be politically active; it even affected the way they voted, or whether they even voted at all. It had to do with the voting slips that get handed to people before they go into the booth to put their X next to their desired candidate. It turns out that those voting slips are not as anonymous as they are supposed to be.

It cannot have escaped anyone's notice that there is a serial number on your voting slip and a corresponding counterfoil has your voter registration written on it by the polling clerk.[40] For anyone that had the time, resources and inclination, it would be a relatively easy matter to find out who you had voted for. In fact, it seems the security services did just that to keep tabs on who was voting for the Communists, Sinn Fein and the like.[41]

Back in the 1980s, some people were, understandably, paranoid about voting. There were those that decided that it was safer never to vote at all. Others, though, inspired by the rumours about blacklists, thought that voting Tory was the ultra-safe thing to do. Doing that was bound to keep your name off any blacklist!

And so, working-class people had one more reason to vote Tory, albeit a tinfoil-hatted one. Then again, maybe they were the smart ones. They probably held onto their jobs until retirement age, or even got promoted.

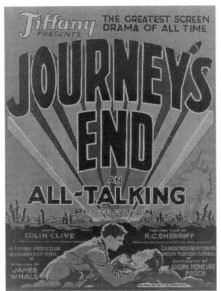

Fig.13 Poster for movie of Journey's End 1930.

Fig.14 Poster for movie All Quiet on the Western Front 1930.

Fig.15 Poster showing a still from Peace on the Western Front
1930

Fig.16 Captain Hurricane.

Fig.17 Miriam Karlin about to call everybody out in *The Rag Trade*.

5
Tally Ho!

We saw, in Chapter 2, how the BBC loved to show historical dramas that were essentially propaganda, with an upper-class gentleman usually stepping in to clear up a mess caused by some heartless member of the bourgeoisie. This was, and is, a standard theme of BBC dramas. There is, however, a further element of propaganda in these programmes.

These BBC dramas showed not only the paternalism of the landed gentry, but how easily they mixed socially with ordinary workers. This is not as mad, or unhistorical, as it sounds. There was a long history of upper- and lower-class men mixing, especially when it came to certain pursuits.

Horse racing was a thoroughly disreputable sport in the middle of the 19th Century and beyond. The races attracted all sorts of undesirables, like pickpockets, gangs of thuggish robbers, drunks, crooked bookmakers and folk running crooked sideshows. A race meeting was a dangerous place and you had to keep your wits about you. All that drunkenness and gambling was enough to give middle-class people apoplexy. It was hard for them to put a stop to it, though, when so many of the gentry, and even aristocracy, were involved.

The telegraph meant an increase in off-course betting, with bookmakers springing up in working-class areas everywhere. Results could be relayed almost immediately, meaning bets could be settled on the same day they had been placed. The railways, meanwhile, allowed more people than ever to travel to race meetings, even when they were some distance away.

By the late 19th Century, middle-class morals had spread to all levels of society, even if they were exhibited hypocritically. Respectability was the overriding concern of everyone of whatever class. This made cleaning up horse racing a lot easier. A more professional police force helped too. The sport remained, though, the preserve of the upper classes and working classes.

A slight triumph for the middle classes came with the 1853 Betting Act, which made off-course betting illegal.[1] Unfortunately, there were plenty of bookies prepared to risk jail by operating illegally. Upper-class punters could quite lawfully put their bets on at on-course bookies or even, in later years, do it by telephone. Middle-class moralists might tut-tut but they did nothing to restrict the betting habits of their 'betters', only those of the working classes.

In modern times, there has still been that involvement of upper-class and working-class people in horse racing. Every working-class area has its fair share of bookies, which are perfectly legal now. Go home to watch the racing on the telly and, until recently, the races would be previewed by, commentated on and examined by the likes of Brough Scott, Lord John Oaksey, Clare Balding, Julian Wilson; upper-class types all. Brough Scott and Clare Balding are still around, I believe.

Kellow Chesney's book, *The Victorian Underworld*, has details of all the sports that united the upper classes and the lower orders. There was *The Fancy* – bareknuckle boxing, which was championed by many of the aristocracy and gentry. Unlike horse racing, the upper classes lost interest in organised boxing toward the end of the 19th Century. It was no longer considered respectable, even with the introduction of boxing gloves. The mad, thuggish and syphilitic 9th Marquess of Queensberry defied the opprobrium of his peers to stay involved in boxing. He even took time out from stalking Oscar Wilde to lend his name to the rules that are still followed today.[2]

There were those *nostalgie de la boue*[3] types among the upper classes that frequented pubs in working-class areas to attend things like rat-baiting competitions. They frequented low-class brothels and cheap opium dens and liked to mix with the *Swell Mob*.[4] Such folk still existed in the 1960s and were to be seen mingling with gangsters at the nightclub belonging to the Kray Twins. Historically, though, such mingling of upper-class and ordinary people took place in the countryside.

Something we are all familiar with from films and TV programmes is the local squire drinking in the village tavern, buying rounds for all the ordinary folk there. He knows everybody's name, all about their families and is ready to step in and solve any problems they have. Whether this actually ever did, or does, happen is debatable; it probably did here and there. It is an image of England that has been portrayed so much that it has become *accepted* as real.

It is the same in Scotland, where the myth of the clan system has developed a strong hold. All the happy Highlanders lived and farmed in the shadow of the Chief's big house or castle and could feel safe and secure under his protection. They would wear their clan tartan with pride and follow their chief into battle against other clans or against the English, brandishing their claymores. Unfortunately, this 'Golden Age' never existed. It was simply a medieval-type feudal system and the 'caring' chiefs thought nothing of later throwing their 'family' off the land and filling it with sheep and deer.

Throughout Britain, the Industrial Revolution changed everything and almost wiped out this bucolic bliss. Huge towns and cities grew, where different classes lived in different areas. The common people lived in houses and flats clustered around the places where they worked. The prevailing winds in Britain go from west to east, so those that could afford it lived in the west of the cities, away from the stink. People lived separate lives according to which class they belonged. Now that much of Britain's industry has disappeared, class distinctions in housing are still in evidence, with the working classes living in peripheral schemes.

Of course, not everyone lives in cities; there are still plenty of working-class people living in rural areas and small county towns and villages. The BBC, and ITV for that matter, have constantly shown us that the countryside is a better place to live than in a city. Whether it is in the near past, like *Dr Finlay's Casebook*, *All Creatures Great and Small*, *Heartbeat* or *The Darling Buds of May*, or more modern times, like *Last of the Summer Wine*, *The Vicar of Dibley* or *The Green Green Grass*, living away from the city is paradise on Earth. Even the County of Midsomer in

Midsomer Murders seems like an idyll, despite the fact that half the population has been wiped out by killers.

In all these programmes, the sun always shines in a perpetual summer and there is no mention of how tough living in the country can be during the winter. Often people can be stuck in their own homes for days at a time, while in the cities the gritters have been out, making sure the roads are clear. There are pros and cons to living in the country as well as in the city. The problem is that we are told all the cons of the city, never any of the pros. It is the opposite when it comes to the country. None of these programmes ever mention the dark side of rural areas.

City folk would balk at having to kill something, even if they were absolutely starving. When it came to it, they would have to draw lots to see who was going to be landed with the task of chopping the head off a chicken or killing a rabbit. Meat is an anonymous entity in the city, bought in a packet at the supermarket or from a butcher. Even a whole chicken is practically unrecognisable when it is already beheaded, plucked and wrapped in cellophane. City people understand, though, where their meat comes from and are grateful to country folk for doing the necessary.

Apart from vegetarians and vegans, city folk know that it is necessary for those in the country to kill things. Fox numbers need to be kept down to stop them killing livestock, while deer and other herbivores need to be culled to keep them from destroying crops, trees, shrubs etc. Those in the city might be squeamish about it but they accept that these things have to be done if they want food on the supermarket shelves. There is, however, a world of difference between shooting a fox and having a pack of hounds tear it to pieces.

Fox hunting was banned in 2005 and, ever since, there have been moans and groans about how unfair the ban is and how it should be repealed. The *Countryside Alliance* is one group that has been campaigning for hunting to be made legal again. The arguments put forward for the ban to be abolished seem to be that fox hunting is a 'fundamental part of their (country folk's) way of life' and that the ban is based on class hatred.[5] Besides, as the *Countryside Alliance* explains, it is a monumental waste of money.

> Meanwhile the police are spending hundreds of hours investigating allegations of illegal hunting and thousands of pounds of your taxes are being wasted on pointless prosecutions.[6]

Actually, has anybody heard of the police investigating hunts or prosecutions taking place? That assertion is a complete lie. As for it being a 'class' issue, that is rather a specious argument. Even before Victoria came to the throne, laws were enacted to make illegal the cruel treatment of animals.[7] These laws were bolstered by subsequent acts of Parliament, but it is notable that upper-class blood sports were constantly excluded. The 2005 Act can be seen as getting rid of this anomaly, which was, manifestly, based on class.

Various arguments have been put forward saying that fox hunting has been beneficial as an effective pest control and for the environment.[8] Both arguments can easily be refuted by the fact that this 'pest' was deliberately introduced to Australia simply for posh people to hunt. It has proven to be an environmental nightmare ever since.[9]

The other popular 'sport' among the upper classes is shooting. Not for them the shooting of wild ducks, which can fly and duck and weave, making difficult targets. Their preference is for grouse and pheasant; birds that cannot fly and that are beaten out of their hiding places into the path of the shotguns. This delightful practice is having a negative impact on rural environments.[10]

Back to fox hunting and, despite the ban, the 'sport' has been going on unabated. The League Against Cruel Sports have been monitoring hunts and have gathered evidence that loopholes are being employed to allow 'traditional' hunts to go ahead. Furthermore,

> A hunt (the Belvoir Hunt) broke the neck of a charity worker working for an animal welfare organisation

operating within the law to monitor potential illegal hunting activity.[11]

The trial of the perpetrators of this crime turned out to be a complete travesty. George Grant was the leader of the gang, which comprised his son, Thomas, and four masked men. The Grants beat up Roger Swaine, stole his camera and broke the memory card, while the masked men attacked Darryl Cunningham, throwing him into a ditch and stamping on him. It was attempted murder in anybody's book. The Grants refused to divulge the names of the masked men, as did everybody else involved with the hunt. Meanwhile, the joint hunt master, Lady Sarah McCorquodale, eldest sister of Princess Diana, gave a character reference for George Grant. She said that he was 'very hardworking, good at his job,'[12] We were not told, however, what his job was.

If this crime had been carried out by a gang of drunken football hooligans, the two leaders would have been looking at some serious prison time. This assault, however, was premeditated, with a determined purpose in mind. Unbelievably, the Grants were given thirteen-month suspended sentences, 200 hours of community work and were ordered to pay £500 each to Darryl Cunningham.[13] It looked as if country criminals were being treated far more leniently than those in the cities.

This practice of having thugs around to 'protect' the hunt is long-standing. In the 1970s and 1980s, Hunt Saboteurs used to turn up at hunts, blowing bugles and laying false trails to distract the hounds. Invariably, they would be beaten up by hired thugs, who often employed blunt weapons to achieve their purpose. These gangs have become a regular feature of fox hunts.

Just like fox hunting, other cruel sports have carried on illegally ever since they were outlawed. Badger baiting,[14] cock fighting[15] and dog fighting[16] are still prevalent in the UK and are so secret that the RSPCA and the SSPCA find it next to impossible to infiltrate them. It does not take any great stretch of the imagination to suggest that the thugs that act as bodyguards for the fox hunters are the same ones that organise these disgusting spectacles.

Whenever such matters are raised in television dramas, it always tends to be 'outsiders' that are involved, city folk, of course. The press, meanwhile, put it down to Gypsies and, believe it or not, Asian immigrants.[17] The media, however, cannot really be blamed as they have good grounds for this bias; prosecutions of country folk for these crimes are few and far between.

As we have already seen, Gypsies tend to get the blame for any animal cruelty that takes place in the countryside, while fingers get pointed disproportionately at folk in towns and cities. An example is one particular character,[18] described in the article as an 'urban hunter'. He lives in Wishaw, which is hardly a metropolis but probably just qualifies as urban.[19] Despite that description, the man probably is not 'urban' at all.

He was charged with taking part in badger baiting, which is scarcely what one would call an urban pursuit. A badger is not the kind of brute you find just wandering along the High Street; in fact, badgers tend to avoid people altogether. Even if you live in the country, it is a rare occurrence indeed to spot one. If you want to get your hands on a badger, you have to go out actively hunting one and you have to know where to look. It is not the kind of thing a confirmed city boy would know anything about.

Like many towns, residential areas in Wishaw are on the periphery, abutting the surrounding countryside. So, the character in the article is not an 'urban' hunter at all. And badger baiting is not a solitary activity; it would be well-nigh impossible to accomplish on one's own. Besides, even if you could, what would be the point? Badger baiting has always been a crowd activity, with spectators betting on the outcome. Such a crowd would find it extremely difficult to operate in secret in the middle of town, again making badger baiting, of necessity, a rural activity.

Still, the media insist on talking about 'urban hunters', even to the extent that a new breed of dog is described as used for 'urban hunting'. These hulking brutes, known as bull lurchers (Fig.18), bred and trained to kill deer, foxes, badgers and anything else they can clamp their jaws round, are reported as operating in urban environments.[20] That conjures up pictures of herds of deer rampaging along Paisley Road West, while motorists on the Kingston Bridge at night have a hell of a time dodging all the badgers. The truth is that most of this hunting takes place in ex-mining villages, which are all in the countryside.[21] The phrase 'urban hunting' was not invented by the media but seems to come from the Scottish SPCA and the RSPCA.

The RSPCA was founded in 1824 and was simply the SPCA until Queen Victoria allowed it to add the word 'Royal' to its name in 1840.[22] It cannot be a coincidence that the cruel sports it boasts of being involved in banning were those participated in by the lower orders.[23] The ones enjoyed by the upper classes were conspicuously allowed to continue unmolested.

Even more ironic was the granting of a Royal Charter to the Society for the Protection of Birds by Edward VII in 1904.[24] Edward and his son, the future George V, were renowned as experts at bird shooting and were frequently to be seen blasting away at anything with a pair of wings. In fact, only eight years before giving a Royal Charter to what became the RSPB, Edward apparently shot an owl, a protected species.[25]

Edward seems not to have taken part in fox hunting; perforce, probably, since it would have to have been a particularly sturdy beast to carry his bulk around the countryside. He did enjoy big game hunting on trips abroad; a practice indulged in by future royals as well. For example, Prince Phillip, the Duke of Edinburgh, shot a tiger, a crocodile and six mountain sheep on a trip to India in 1961 (Fig.19).[26]

But that was a different time, you might argue. The truth is, though, that the Duke was a complete hypocrite. When he was slaughtering those animals in India, he happened to be President of the UK branch of the World Wildlife Fund.[27] The current UK President is Prince Charles,[28] who tried to convince Tony Blair that banning fox hunting was a bad idea.[29] That hardly sounds like the actions of someone trying to protect the natural world!

The World Wildlife Fund for Nature, as it is called nowadays, does not seem to be interested in saving species anymore, but concentrates mostly on climate change and associated

85

campaigns.[30] It is quite handy that this is something that can be blamed on us commoners, rather than rich people doing their best to wipe out endangered species. Even in Scotland, it is farmers that are in the firing line. Land managers are mentioned in passing, but there is no condemnation of how grouse moors are destroying the natural environment.[31]

National organisations behave in the same way, with the RSPCA and the RSPB often turning a blind eye to crimes in the countryside. In a way, however, it is difficult to blame them as the judiciary constantly hand down extremely lenient sentences. Google the phrase 'Gamekeeper fined' and lots of instances are thrown up. Click on any of the links and you will discover just how lenient judges are. Gamekeepers appear in court for killing birds of prey and merely receive fines, which are probably paid by their employers, to whom a couple of thousand pounds means next to nothing.

It is the same with other crimes. Remember the derisory sentence handed down to the Cunninghams for being involved in attempted murder?[32] And then there was our young friend the 'urban hunter' from Wishaw. A sheriff sent him to prison for twenty-one weeks, but that was quashed by the Sheriff Appeal Court in Edinburgh and changed to community service.[33]

Understandably, country folk have a vested interest in maintaining the status quo. After all, the judiciary seems to be on their side, while the media and organisations against animal cruelty blame townies for everything. And, of course, the great upholder of the status quo is the Tory Party.

English counties and shires, especially in the south, are the bedrock of Tory support. And there is no way those counties would keep returning Tory MPs if the working classes were not voting for them. Even in Scotland the Tories are strongest in rural areas. (Especially in terms of MPs.)[34] That seems to apply to ex-mining towns and villages as well.

Remember those monstrous brutes that were bred and trained to kill practically anything that moved? They belonged to a character that lived in Lochore, a small ex-mining village in Fife.[35] It is part of the Kirkcaldy and Cowdenbeath UK Parliamentary constituency, and the figures show that the Tory vote has been creeping up during the past decade or so.[36] The vote for the Conservatives in the Scottish Parliament elections has been increasing as well.[37]

There was a time when it was hardly worth the Tories' time to field a candidate in a mining area. Those areas, however, have changed considerably. The mines closed a long time ago, many of them have been shut for nearly forty years. A lot of people have grown up with coal mining just a story told by their fathers and grandfathers, something they need to visit a museum to find out about. In many of these towns and villages unemployment has simply become a way of life.

As the old adage goes, the Devil finds work for idle hands to do and that is certainly true in the case of the old mining communities. Living in the country, where they could earn a bit of cash in hand as bodyguards for fox hunters, they would become inured to blood sports. But why should the posh folk have all the 'fun'? They could not afford horses, but there were other blood sports they could indulge in.

And so, a symbiosis was born. The upper-class fox hunters relied on country ne'er-do-wells to guard the hunts and deal with nosey anti-blood sport people, journalists and the like. To keep these thugs onside, upper-class judges and magistrates make sure that working-class blood sports are punished extremely leniently. Voting Tory is seen as the best way to preserve this system.

An extension of the Tory Party is the *Countryside Alliance*, whose board reads like Debrett's Peerage.[38] It describes itself as 'politically non-aligned',[39] but its behaviour suggests otherwise. One of its avowed aims is to get decent broadband into the countryside. In the 2019 election, Labour promised to extend broadband throughout Britain. Not only that, but they were going to make it free by renationalising part of BT. The *Countryside Alliance* ridiculed this idea, with arguments straight from Conservative Campaign Headquarters.[40] So much for being politically non-aligned!

The *Countryside Alliance* has over 100,000 members[41] and even more supporters. In 2002, over 300,000, or perhaps even 400,000, converged on London to demonstrate.[42] As the BBC website put it:

> And while many protesters carried banners proclaiming: "Buy British food", "Save our farms" or "Town and country not town over country", these were far out-numbered by pro-hunt slogans.[43]

And that is the thing. The *Countryside Alliance* bangs on about farmers, small, rural businesses, post offices and broadband, but its main concern is demanding the right to brutally kill wild animals. As one demonstrator said,

> I want to go on the march because it's important to me to defend our freedom of choice, our way of life. If the government gets its way and bans fox hunting, then where will it stop? Will they ban shooting and fishing? We should be able to choose whether to do these things or not - not because government says that you can't.
>
> Steve (her husband) goes fishing and shooting; I go hunting, and I'd like Daisy, our daughter, to have the choice to do those things when she's old enough to decide.[44]

This woman demands freedom of choice and questions the right of government to make laws that curtail that freedom. It is doubtful that anyone would want to stop folk hunting and fishing, especially if they are going to eat what they catch. Unfortunately, people like this woman see no difference between catching a trout and hounds ripping a fox to pieces. And demanding freedom of choice is a dangerous road to go down. Libertarians want that freedom for everyone, including paedophiles. Furthermore, if hunting is not to be limited in any way, then where will the line be drawn? Maybe they would like to hunt human beings with hounds!

That demonstration in 2002 was against Tony Blair's Labour Government introducing the ban on fox hunting. Since then, the *Countryside Alliance* has managed to convince itself, and others, that Labour is the party of 'urban snobbery' against rural inhabitants.[45] They point to the fact that, as of 2020, Labour holds only '17 of the 199 rural seats in England and Wales'.[46]

This strange alliance between the upper classes and the working classes in the English counties was going to come in extremely useful for the former. It was going to be in a lot of the upper classes' best interests to leave Europe. To achieve this, they were going to have to convince those working-class allies that it would be to their benefit as well.

6
I Expect to See Mexicans

In 1970, John Christopher published a children's book called *The Guardians*.[1] It is set in a future where only working-class people live in urban areas, known as *conurbs*, while upper-class and middle-class folk live in the rural *counties*. Despite it being a children's story, the book is actually quite subversive. The protagonist, a boy from the *conurbs*, manages to sneak into the *county*, where he has to blend in with the inhabitants. That is where the subversiveness comes in.

Christopher points out all the little details that the boy has to learn in order to fit in. He needs to know, for example, when it is okay to use the electric light and when oil lamps are the preferred option. The story might be set in the future but knowing how to fit in is reminiscent of how the class system works today. Just as Christopher explains, members of a particular class have grown up learning all the little peculiarities, traits and quirks that let them recognise other members of their class. It is extremely difficult for anyone of a different class to infiltrate.

Most definitions of class concentrate on money, but it is far more than that. There are tradesmen, who work with their hands, that earn more than a teacher does. A tradesman, however, would consider himself working-class, while the teacher might see herself as middle-class. In fact, it is even more complicated than that. There are many teachers that think of themselves as working-class as well. Class is a state of mind.

There are teachers that are happy to buy and live in an ex-council house and send their children to the local school. Others, though, scrimp and scrape to buy a house in an area like Jordanhill or Scotstoun in Glasgow and to send their offspring to fee-paying schools. They have certain standards to maintain. Actually, some of the teachers that see themselves as working-class go down the same route, keen to give their children a 'better' life.

One of those well-paid tradesmen could also buy a house in a middle-class area for the same reasons as the working-class teachers. They will not fit in with their middle-class neighbours, but their children might. Even if those children fail to make the cut, then *their* children have a good chance. It only takes a couple of generations for a family to move into another class. The generations after that might well forget that their family was ever working-class at all.

The same goes for working-class and middle-class people that wish to join the upper classes; and they most certainly do. Just as they did in the Nineteenth Century, the super-rich make sure they buy a country pile and try to become members of the upper class. It does not matter from which class they originally came; they desperately want to be part of the country gentry.

Film stars, TV stars and pop and rock stars all have to buy a large country house. None of them can fit in with the local gentry, though the latter are friendly enough; everybody wants to be friends with a celebrity! As you may have guessed, it is the offspring of those celebrities that end up being accepted as upper-class. A prime example is the son of Bryan Ferry, Otis: fox hunter, thug and leading light in the Countryside Alliance's campaigns against the fox-hunting ban.[2]

Be that as it may, it is doubtful that the working classes in the countryside notice any real difference between the local gentry and the celebrity *parvenus*. Rich rock stars especially act as if they are upper-class. Trashing hotel rooms and driving Rolls-Royces into swimming pools might be termed 'Rock 'n' Roll', but it is no different from the behaviour of the Bullingdon Club. And like the upper classes, the celebrities have no need to work, having already made millions. Of course, some of them still *do* work, but they do not have to. Of the others, fame does not last forever but investments can make sure the cash keeps coming in.

One thing that all these rich folk have in common, apart from having lots of money, is that they do not see why they should pay tax. Tax is for little people. They will do anything to stop the Government getting its hands on their cash and there are umpteen banks and investment companies prepared to help them do it. One of the most popular ways is to hide the money in offshore accounts in places like the Cayman Islands.

For years, the European Union has sought to stamp out tax avoidance, concentrating mostly on multinational companies that have tortuous schemes in place so as not to pay their fair share. As the Panama Papers were to show, tax avoidance schemes are so convoluted that it is difficult to tell which money is whose.[3] The EU's plans to pass laws forcing companies to reveal what money they had and where it was certainly put the wind up the rich in Britain. They were going to have to get out of Europe.

There were already those that wanted the UK to leave the EU, though they appeared to be in a minority and considered extremist nutters by most people. There were the Eurosceptic Tories, John Major's famous 'bastards', desperately trying to cling to Thatcher's legacy.[4] The Referendum Party, financed by James Goldsmith's millions, folded in 1997 when Goldsmith died.[5] Then there was UKIP, a bunch of right-wing extremists that went through the usual splits and divisions that such parties go through.[6] Nobody normal took them seriously at all. Then, in the second decade of the 21st Century, people actually started voting for them. What happened to make these clowns more popular?

As we saw above, the super-rich in Britain wanted out of the EU, but they would get nowhere by telling anyone the real reason why. Even the forelock-tuggers in the country would baulk at letting their lords and masters dodge paying tax while they themselves still had to. Instead, an appeal was made to the well-known xenophobia of country folk. That might sound unfair, but people that live in country areas are notoriously wary of strangers. There are even places in the Scottish Highlands where you are not welcome unless you are wearing tweeds and carrying an open shotgun in the crook of your arm.

All over Britain there are small, country areas where even folk from the next village are considered foreigners. Of course, the heavy mob will be around if there are fox hunts, or other illegal, blood-spilling activities going on. As you might have gathered, places where such activities are rife will be especially unwelcoming, not to mention dangerous. And God help you if you happen to be brown or black!

In June 2020, the BBC's *Countryfile* did a piece on a DEFRA (Department for Environment, Food and Rural Affairs) report that said BAME (Black, Asian and Minority Ethnic) people do not feel welcome in the countryside and spoke of 'barriers' to visiting.[7] Country folk were incensed and showed their anger at being labelled racist by...er...being racist. Look at some of these comments on the *Sun*'s article about the story.

> If I go to Mexico I expect to see Mexicans. If I go to Japan I expect to see lots of Japanese. If I go to the British countryside I expect to see...Somalians?[8]

> Barriers - like the Grand National? Hope the local Hunt group gives them a decent head start.[9]

> Our countryside is all we have left. Look how the beaches have been treated. Just please leave us alone. Why do BAME hate the uk so much? What's the real bbc agenda? Hatred provoking. They want the uk to be BAME because they're the ultimate sheep. Define irony.[10]

> There's not as many chiggun shops and benefit offices in the countryside.
> And it makes grooming a lot harder for them than the towns when houses are spread out more.[11]

> The countryside with nice areas is mostly made up of white people as say somewhere like east London, Brixton, north London and those areas have a lot of trouble and dirty and run down. There is a reason some places are nice and some places are horrible go visit them and you'll see why![12]

After reading those little gems it seems like parody when the *Fieldsports Channel* website tries to counter the *Countryfile* report by claiming, 'Famed for its moderate politics and tolerant society, the British countryside reacts angrily to Fields' (Dwayne Fields, who presented the *Countryfile* piece) report.'[13] There is not much in the way of moderation or tolerance in those comments in the *Sun*!

The 2011 Census showed that black and Asian people mostly lived in urban areas; in fact, the vast majority of them did.[14] This could, of course, be put down to the support provided by family and others that come from the same country of origin as new immigrants. Also, there is the cheapness of rented accommodation in urban areas and the lack of accommodation in rural ones. This, however, does not tell the whole story.

There are people in Britain that came from the West Indies, Pakistan and India in the 1950s and early 1960s. Their children and grandchildren grew up speaking English, going to British schools, following British football teams etc. *Ethnically* they might be black Caribbean, Pakistani or whatever, but as far as nationality was concerned, they were British, English, Scottish or however else they saw themselves. Still, extremely few of them moved to the country.

The usual way for immigrants is to live together in one community and then gradually become part of the general population. It took a long time for the Jews and the Irish to do this, mainly because of prejudice; the general population refused to accept them. In these, supposedly, more enlightened times, though, you would expect sixty or seventy years to be enough for ethnic minority people to be absorbed into the general population.

Right-wing observers put the blame on people of colour themselves, claiming that they are unwilling to integrate. That, however, is a lie since BAME people have no problems integrating in urban environments, the more prosperous buying property in the suburbs. The countryside, however, still seems to be pretty much a no-go area for people of colour.

Meanwhile, UKIP's star finally appeared to be rising, gaining more than 150 seats in the 2014 local elections[15] and winning 24 seats in the European Parliament.[16] Comedians on TV joked that every time there was a scandal about racism in UKIP, their vote seemed to rise. And there were certainly plenty of racist scandals in the party.[17] Many former BNP voters were turning to UKIP, which, despite Nigel Farage's denials, showed that UKIP *was* a racist party.[18]

The Tory elite, who wanted out of the EU, had been scared to play the racism card, but now they did not have to; UKIP would do it for them. The super-rich were finally ready to hold a referendum on the UK's membership of the EU. This referendum was to be held in June 2016. The country geared up for a vote that the REMAIN side was expected to win. The Empire was long gone, and Britain was not the major player that it used to be. It was a big, cold, unfriendly world out there and everybody knew that the UK was better off as part of the EU. It was hardly necessary for everyone to get out and vote; only the terminally stupid would be choosing to cast the UK out on its own.

The whole campaign on the LEAVE side was full of dirty tricks, cheating and lies, not least of which was that the referendum was binding; in fact, it was only meant to be an advisory poll.[19]

In 1979 a referendum was held in Scotland to decide if there should be a devolved Scottish parliament. 52% voted in favour but, and it was a big but, the turnout was 62.9% of the eligible electorate. That meant that only 32.9% of the total electorate had voted for devolution.[20] Contrary to the subsequent outraged statements, it had been decided before the referendum that 40% of the electorate would have to vote in favour for devolution to pass into law.[21]

The argument for imposing a threshold was that it was an important constitutional measure, which was going to be passed into law providing enough people voted for it. The same reasoning was used in the 2011 Referendum on the Alternative Vote, where the same threshold of 40% was used.[22] Again, though, this meant that, if enough people voted, it would pass straight into law.

No such restrictions were placed on the Brexit Referendum because, as pointed out above, it was just an *advisory* vote. The result turned out to be remarkably similar to that of the 1979 Scottish Referendum. Nearly 52% voted to leave the EU,[23] which came as a huge surprise to everyone. The turnout, however, was 72.2%,[24] which seems like a respectable figure until you realise that just over 37% of the total electorate voted in favour of Brexit. That was better than the Scottish Referendum, but still not 40%. Amazingly, though, the Referendum was treated almost as a plebiscite and preparations began to be made for the UK to leave the EU.

So, why did people vote for Brexit? For many, including in the media, it was the 'little people' voting against the elite; those without power rebelling against those that had it. This was the picture that Nigel Farage painted,

> We have fought against the multinationals, we have fought against the big merchant banks, we fought against big politics, we fought against lies, corruption and deceit.[25]

A report by the Joseph Rowntree Foundation confirmed this view, saying that,

> The poorest households, with incomes of less than £20,000 per year, were much more likely to support leaving the EU than the wealthiest households, as were the unemployed, people in low-skilled and manual occupations, people who feel that their financial situation has worsened, and those with no qualifications.[26]

Arguing that the vote reflected deep-seated antagonisms of the dispossessed, however, does not tell the whole story. That description from the Rowntree Foundation could apply to members of different ethnic minorities, most notably those of a black Caribbean background.[27] And yet, that particular ethnic group, as well as others, mostly voted REMAIN.[28] The report by the Rowntree Foundation needs to be qualified; the word *white* needs to be added to its descriptions.

During the Referendum campaign, many of those that were going to vote LEAVE were asked why on various television and radio programmes. None of them could give an answer, relying on glib statements about EU regulations. When asked which regulations they meant, silence ensued. In fact, the best they could do was *ad hominem* attacks on REMAIN campaigners while completely avoiding the topics in hand. It was something they still resorted to long after the Referendum was over.[29]

If pressed, with each 'reason' for voting to leave the EU countered with facts, those intending to vote that way eventually admitted that their main concern was immigration. The leaders of the LEAVE campaign, especially UKIP members, hammered this point home, implying that the EU was totally in charge of Britain's borders and allowing almost unlimited immigration. Nigel Farage unveiled a poster showing masses of migrants and refugees queueing as if waiting to get into Britain[30] (Fig.20) while he spoke of 'mass uncontrolled immigration'.[31] The *Sunday Express* joined in, talking of 12 million Turks ready to come to the UK once their country became a member of the EU.[32] Essentially, the public was being told that the EU was planning to flood Britain with 'darkies'.

Certain commentators have highlighted the fact that country areas were the ones that mostly voted to leave.[33] This, however, is still expressed in terms of a sort of revolt of the dispossessed. Comparisons have been drawn with the political split in the United States, where Donald Trump was elected by mostly rural areas.[34] Just like other experts, though, these commentators miss the central point.

The USA has long been split along a countryside vs big city divide. It was a confusing divide, however, since both political parties historically appealed to different interests in different areas. In the cities, the Democrats became the party of the moderate left, while in the rural states it was the party of segregation, states' rights and the Ku Klux Klan. That changed dramatically when the Kennedy brothers began to enforce integration. It started to look as if the Republicans were a safer bet.

Things are still complicated as far as the electorate is concerned; some country folk in the south, while waving their Confederate flags, still vote Democrat because 'muh grandaddy did'. Donald Trump threw a spanner into things, appealing directly to people's racism with his plans for a wall along the Mexican border and his anti-immigration rhetoric. Everyone knew exactly what he meant by 'Make America Great Again'; it was all about a return to the old days, when white people dominated and the 'coloured folks' knew their place and were lynched if they stepped out of line.

Equally, the rural versus urban split evident in Brexit had nothing to do with the sort of political divide normally seen in America. Just like the vote for Trump, it was simply about racism. It was notable that arch-racist Stephen Yaxley-Lennon, aka Tommy Robinson, was one of the leading lights of those complaining that Brexit was taking too long. Among those attending his rally were members of the BNP, while swastikas were brandished by sections of the crowd.[35]

The BNP is just one of many right-wing groups active in Britain, albeit one of the more well-known ones. It has become, like the National Front before it, riven with arguments and splits, making it less of a force than it used to be. Erstwhile members and leaders have gone into, and founded, other groups, which all believe in pretty much the same things. One of the things they all believe in is *White Genocide*.

The *White Genocide* conspiracy theory is all about the white population of the world gradually being replaced by black and brown people. Apparently, a global elite is behind it all; most adherents to the theory blame the Jews. Since black (and brown) people are inferior to white in terms of intelligence, they are more easily dominated, which is why the Jewish elite prefers them. Immigration and mixed-race marriages are encouraged in order to breed out white people.[36] It is an attractive theory to your average racist, since it encompasses most of the people they like to be racist toward.

The theory is popular all over the world, wherever there are discontented white people: America, Europe, even Africa. In Britain, one of the leading exponents of the theory is Mark Collett, a former member of the BNP.[37] He has his own channel on YouTube, where he rails against the replacement of white people with black throughout Europe. He even argues that white Europeans are being written out of their own history.[38] His 'proof' is a series of cartoons, television dramas and Shakespeare plays; hardly what you would call 'hard' history. Probably his most ridiculous piece of evidence is the inclusion of a black soldier in a group of Victorians on Mars in an episode of *Doctor Who*!

Actually, Collett is not complaining about the black soldier *per se*; it is the way black people are presented as a normal, everyday sight in Victorian Britain and other periods of history. Obviously, *Doctor Who* is part of the global conspiracy! Maybe Collett is unaware, but there were many black slaves in Britain for a few centuries before Victoria came to the throne. Slavery was abolished in Britain in 1833; does Collett imagine that all those black people vanished into thin air?

An individual called Shaun made a video to refute Collett's arguments.[39] Although he makes some valid points, he misses out on a lot of fairly obvious counter-arguments. Italians and Greeks are quite swarthy, but representations of the Ancient Romans and Ancient Greeks are always of the Anglo-Saxon variety. Part of the reason for this is that surviving statues are invariably in white marble. The fact is, however, that the Ancient Romans (and Greeks) painted their statues to look lifelike. Over the centuries, this paint wore off.[40] Murals of Ancient Romans show the truth about their skin colour (Fig.21).

The big problem the followers of Mark Collett have with Shaun's video, though, is that he resorts to *ad hominem* attacks.[41] Normally, this would be a valid argument, but when you wander into the realms of History, all bets are off. One of the things a History student learns at university is to take into account the political views of a historian before totally accepting his thesis. A prime example of this is E.P. Thompson, who happened to be a Marxist. His book, *The Making of the English Working Class*, was influenced by his politics, meaning that many (including me) think that he exaggerated the numbers involved in the events and organisations he described. It is entirely reasonable to consider Collett's background in politics before taking on board his presentations.

Another whose life outside of academia is relevant is the man from whom many right-wing groups take their cue: David Coleman (no, not that one!). Coleman is Professor of Demography at Oxford University and his claim to fame is that, back in 2013, he predicted that white Britons would be a minority in their own country by 2066.[42] Well before he came out with this bombshell, Coleman co-founded pressure group *Migration Watch* and was a member of the *Galton Institute*, previously known as the *Eugenics Society*.[43] It is clear where his political sympathies lie. Of course, Coleman refuted any charges of being a right-wing bigot and he defended the *Galton Institute* vigorously. He said,

> Most of the Galton Institute's research fund at present is spent on a big reproductive health project in Ethiopia.
> The pressing need to help women in the poorest countries such as Ethiopia to avoid unwanted childbearing was emphasised very recently in the report of the All-Party Parliamentary Group on Population and Development.[44]

That seems fair enough, you might think; after all, it is a humanitarian issue, is it not? An article he wrote for the *Galton Institute Newsletter* in 2001, however, puts a different, more sinister, slant on things. It is worth quoting his words, along with what the *Guardian* said about them:

> At the same time, Coleman argues, in an article in the Galton Institute newsletter of March 2001, that European women should be helped to have more babies: "The root cause of excessive population ageing is very low birth-rates. An effective response must make the workplace, the tax and welfare system and gender relations as a whole more favourable to women, so they can fulfil ambitions, repeatedly stated, to have more than one child." This chimes with a classic argument of the eugenicists: "better" stock should have more babies, "worse" stock should have fewer.[45]

Chillingly, this was also a major tenet of the Nazis in Germany in the 1930s and 1940s. It was not the only bit of Nazi policy and propaganda Collett's followers lifted. One piece on their website, *Patriotic Alternative*, likens Muslim immigrants and asylum seekers to stink bugs invading the UK.[46] This is reminiscent of the way Jews were depicted as a plague of rats in the Nazi propaganda film *The Eternal Jew*.[47] The *Patriotic Alternative* organisation, meanwhile, offers camping and outdoors activities for young people, which conjures up pictures of the Hitler Youth![48]

Incredibly, the *Daily Mail* went down the same route in 2015 with a cartoon showing Muslims walking unimpeded into Europe, surrounded by rats doing the same thing.[49] (Fig.22) This was bringing Nazism into the mainstream, instead of being the preserve of insane, extreme right-wing pamphlets, although many would argue that is precisely what the *Daily Mail* is.

In 2018, Nigel Farage quit UKIP, citing its appointment of Tommy Robinson as an adviser and the party's 'fixation' with Islam as his reasons.[50] He did not acknowledge his own part in encouraging racists to the party with *that* poster. He went on to throw his weight behind a new party, the *Brexit Party*, whose leader, Catherine Blaiklock, had to resign after the disclosure of her numerous retweets of posts by Tommy Robinson and Mark Collett.[51]

Even worse were the revelations that members of the Conservative Party showed support online for Islamophobes and *White Genocide* conspiracy theorists. The Chairman of the Conservative Muslim Forum, Mohammed Amin expressed concern, saying,

> It (the Conservative Party) needs to hold a serious, independent inquiry both into its processes for dealing with issues like this and whether they are adequately transparent, and the even more fundamental question about the image the party is projecting to the British people, which makes people with racist and bigoted religious views believe that the Conservative party is the party for them. The people posting on Facebook certainly do believe that.[52]

So, there it was, confirmed by members of the Tory Party itself; racists voted for the party, seeing it as 'on their side'. It makes one wonder who funds all those tin-pot, right-wing organisations that encourage people to be racist and then, ultimately, vote Tory. The fact these organisations helped the Brexit cause, to the benefit of Britain's super-rich, allows one to reach one's own conclusions.

Of course, the Tories benefit because not many people like to be branded racists, even if it happens to be the truth. The Tory Party provides a good cover. At the General Election of 2017, and afterwards, voters deserted UKIP in droves.[53] It was better to admit to being swayed to vote LEAVE by the message on Boris Johnson's Brexit Bus[54] (Fig.23) rather than Nigel Farage's racist poster.

Meanwhile, more revelations came to light about the tax-dodging of the super-rich. The Paradise Papers showed that even the Queen had money stashed away in an offshore account.[55] Interestingly, leading Brexiteers were named in the Paradise Papers,[56] betraying the reason for the whole referendum in the first place. Nobody in the media, however, bothered to put two and two together.

Business leaders in Britain and Europe had warned right from the start that Brexit was going to be an economic disaster.[57] The super-rich cared little for business, however; it was not something they sullied their hands with. They were prepared to destroy the British economy just so they did not have to hand their fair share to the taxman. Meanwhile, all the working-class dupes that had voted to leave the EU would get their wish too. No immigrants would be coming to 'steal their jobs'. There were going to be no jobs to steal!

Of course, all of that was the case in England, but there were two other countries, and a bit of one, that were part of the UK as well. Wales voted LEAVE, although the turnout of 71.7% meant that only 37.6% of the electorate was actually in favour of Brexit.[58] One analyst suggested that it was the English living in Wales that carried the vote for LEAVE. Apparently, about a fifth of the Welsh population is English.[59] Much of this English population is retired[60] and it does not take a lot of imagination to figure out that they mostly live in small towns and villages in rural areas.

The problem with that analysis, however, is that a predominantly Welsh-speaking area like Anglesey[61] voted LEAVE, albeit by a narrow margin.[62] Comparatively large cities like Newport and Swansea, meanwhile, recorded victories for Brexit.[63] So, the Welsh were just as much to blame for voting Leave as the English in their midst.

In Scotland, the raw figures showed REMAIN winning by 62% to LEAVE's 38%.[64] With a 67.2% turnout,[65] this translated as 25.5% of the whole electorate voting for Brexit, while 41.75% voted to remain in the EU. According to Westminster, though, the Scottish vote counted for nothing; only the overall UK vote mattered. This meant that Scotland was being dragged out of the EU, against the will of its people, by a minority (37%) of UK voters. It hardly seemed fair.

Fairness, though, scarcely came into it. The working classes in the English counties had been duped into thinking that leaving the EU would make a difference to immigration. Meanwhile, the true reason for leaving did not seem to occur to any of them, even though it was obvious. The super-rich were ensuring that they would pay very little, or even no, tax, while everybody else still had to hand over a portion of their hard-earned.

Fig.18 Bull Lurcher. A beast bred for attacking any size of wild animal.

Fig.19 The Duke of Edinburgh and family pose with the corpse of a tiger shot by the Duke 1961.

Fig.20 UKIP's Brexit poster about immigration.

Fig.21 Mural of a Roman husband and wife. Note how Italian they look – a far cry from what we usually see in films and on TV.

Fig.22 The Daily Mail's Nazi-inspired cartoon about immigration.

Fig.23 Boris Johnson's infamous Brexit Bus. It was not the only lie told to Brexit voters.

7
A Racist Endeavour

In 1986, *Eastenders* had only been on TV for about a year, but it had already established itself as a favourite among viewers. Unlike previous attempts by the BBC to broadcast a rival to *Coronation Street*, this one had turned out to be a success. So popular was it that the papers were full of stories about the actors that appeared in it. Scandals were what sold papers and there had already been the story about the actor that played Dirty Den, Leslie Grantham, who had once been in prison for murder.[1] Now, there was another scandal for them to concentrate on.

A new character was introduced to the programme in August of that year. He was a graphic designer, a middle-class yuppie; he also happened to be gay. There had already been gay characters on television, mostly of the limp-wristed, feminine-sounding variety. That, unfortunately, included the character Gordon Collins in *Brookside*.[2] This new character in *Eastenders*, Colin, was nothing like that. He was just an ordinary bloke, who could easily pass as 'normal'. The right-wing press took an almost immediate dislike to him.

This dislike was fuelled by the character's very ordinariness, which right-wingers saw as an attempt to normalise homosexuality. This was a big deal among Tories and their friends in the press. There were stories about left-wing councils encouraging schools to teach even young children that homosexuality was completely normal and even preferable to heterosexual relationships. It was a pack of lies, of course, but many people were convinced that it was really happening.[3]

Colin, in *Eastenders*, was viewed as part of this left-wing propaganda to promote homosexuality as acceptable. The right-wing press, therefore, were overjoyed to discover that the actor playing Colin, Michael Cashman, was himself gay. The Sunday scandal sheets, like the *Sunday Mirror* and the *News of the World*, made up stories about Cashman having AIDS and printed the full address that he and his partner shared.[4] Bricks through his windows and death threats followed,[5] which is no doubt what those papers expected and wanted to happen. They even tried to fit him up as a paedophile![6]

Cashman went on to become a 'Rebel about a Clause' when the Tories' infamous Clause 28 came into effect. He helped to found Stonewall and became a Labour MEP for years. He is now in the House of Lords as Lord Cashman and those papers that printed lies about him now fawn over him as a member of the Establishment. Even Piers Morgan has apologised for calling his character on *Eastenders* a 'yuppie poof'.[7]

But it was not only Michael Cashman that the right-wing press lied about in the 1980s; they were at it with anyone they did not like. What they especially hated was Socialism and anything they deemed to be associated with it. In essence, that meant anything to do with equality and social inclusion. We have already seen how they reacted to a gay television character being portrayed as ordinary, instead of another Mr. Humphries from *Are You Being Served*. They were horrified when some Labour-controlled councils, especially in London, practised such social inclusion in real life.

Equality for women, ethnic minorities, the disabled and gays and lesbians is taken for granted nowadays, except among those on the extreme right; in the 1980s, however, it was a different story entirely. It was something that the Tory press saw as a threat to our way of life, and they fought tooth-and-nail to prevent it. It was Communism by the back door.

Ted Knight, Ken Livingston and Derek Hatton, all prefaced by the term 'Red', became well-known far beyond the limits of the councils they ran. They were branded the 'Loony Left', and the tabloid press revelled in tales of their profligacy. As one observer put it,

> The tabloid newspapers are, in general, not the slightest bit interested in what councils do or don't do about council housing or social services, but let

> any council give a few pounds to a gay or lesbian
> group and it becomes front page news.[8]

According to the tabloids, however, it was far more than a 'few pounds' that were handed out. There were jokey stories about black, one-legged, feminist lesbian collectives being handed thousands of pounds of ratepayers' cash. Other tales concerned manholes being renamed 'personholes', Manchester being renamed 'Personchester' and the word 'black' being removed from school dictionaries. All of these were either complete inventions or exaggerations, like the story of *Baa Baa Black Sheep* being banned.

A private, parent-run nursery in Birmingham and another in Hackney, London, banned the song, thinking it had racist overtones and referred to slavery. A Hackney Council spokesman refused to condemn the nursery and, indeed, supported it. This led to claims that Hackney Council had instituted the ban. As the story spread, other Labour-controlled councils were accused of banning the nursery rhyme.[9]

This nonsense was believed at the time and ever since, even though it has been debunked on numerous occasions. I have met more than a few teachers that swore blind that they were instructed to exclude the song from their classes. One nursery nurse claimed to have received a letter from the old Lothian Council, explicitly ordering the song to be banned. She could not produce the letter, which I thought was strange since it is the sort of thing one would keep. Tellingly, other staff had never heard of such an epistle.

Even years after the events, the press was still going on about councils wasting money on 'lesbian and gay committees, nuclear-free zones and red flags'.[10] The Tory Government brought in rate caps to stop these 'Loony Left' councils raising money to spend, resulting in a stand-off, which, eventually, the Government won.[11] Right-wing papers and other observers love to recount the stories of 'Loony Left' prodigality even in the 21st Century.

One website gets a bit confused about what to include in its catalogue of 'Loony Left' spending and policies. One group of stories, under the heading '1986, September, Scottish Crime Sheet,' tells about unscrupulous landlords in Edinburgh.[12] What that has to do with the local council they do not explain. In fact, it is more a condemnation of greedy capitalists, which one would expect to find on a left-wing website. It is notable that the site provides no sources for its stories, which is probably why it falls into the old trap of ascribing blame to the wrong people.

For example, in the section titled, '1986, November,' it is claimed that 'Two Labour councillors and two Manchester City Council officers flew to Nicaragua for a £3,000 'friendship visit' at the expense of the local taxpayers.'[13] This story has appeared before in various guises and is usually about 'Red' Ted Knight of Lambeth Council.[14] It makes one question the veracity of the Manchester story and, by extension, all the other stories on the website.

These attacks on the 'Loony Left' were calculated to make the Labour Party unelectable. Various such attempts had been made in the past, with varying levels of success. There was the *Zinoviev Letter* of 1924.[15] This was a purported letter from the head of the Communist International (the Comintern) telling British Communists to get ready to rise up in revolt. The *Daily Mail* printed this letter four days before the 1924 general election, causing great embarrassment to the Labour Party.[16] (Fig.24) Historians still debate about how much harm this did to Labour in the election.

Then, in the 1945 general election, Churchill claimed, in a radio broadcast, that Socialism in Britain would lead to some kind of Gestapo.[17] This nonsense was repeated in the *Daily Express*, almost making a laughing stock of Churchill.[18] (Fig.25) Again, this was a desperate attempt to make Labour appear unelectable, albeit it was an abject failure.

The media stories about the 'Loony Left' were just the latest in a long line of attempts to undermine the Labour Party. There have even been allegations of MI5 involvement in plans to destabilise Harold Wilson's government.[19]

The right-wing press continued with this 'Loony Left' nonsense into the 1990s. Neil Kinnock was on a hiding to nothing; he could expel as much of the so-called Militant

Tendency as he liked but he was still a link to the Labour Party of old.[20] It was a strange situation where the Tories were following economic theories that were from the early part of the 20th Century, but it was Labour that were portrayed as old-fashioned! The Tories were able to play this card continually, holding the threat of powerful unions over everyone's head. This way of working, however, disappeared when Tony Blair took over the Labour Party.

In the 1997 election, so frightened were the Tories, now under John Major, that their advertisers, the Saatchis, made a film depicting Tony Blair as a Faust figure, making a pact with Satan, in the guise of Peter Mandelson. It was meant as a party-political broadcast but John Major, horrified, refused to let it be broadcast.[21] As well as being morally opposed to the film, Major thought that it would backfire. He was probably right as it was admitting that there was not much to choose between Conservative and New Labour. It certainly seemed that way.

Under Blair, Clause IV of the Labour Constitution, which committed the party to the 'common distribution of the means of production, distribution and exchange,' was amended to speak about equal opportunity and individual potential.[22] Meanwhile, Labour distanced itself from the unions and Blair made it plain that he had no intention of abolishing Thatcher's anti-union laws.[23] No wonder the Tories had such a hard time against them.

The election campaign by the Tories appeared desperate, with posters showing Blair's 'Demon Eyes' and the slogan 'New Labour, New Danger'.[24] (Fig.26) The big problem with the campaign was that it admitted that New Labour was a new party, pretty much detached from the Labour Party of old. Instead of being able to talk about 'beer and sandwiches at Number 10,' the Tories were obviously floundering about looking for anything to counter this new threat. They failed miserably. Their friends in the press could not even publish any salacious stories about people in New Labour. Considering the scandals in the Conservative Party under John Major, nothing short of mass murder would have sufficed.[25]

Let us fast-forward past thirteen years of New Labour government and five years of a Tory-Liberal Democrat coalition to the 2015 election. The right-wing press was able to go back to its old 'Loony Left' campaigns since the new Labour leader, Ed Miliband, had helped shift the party back to the left, albeit slightly. This caused a rift with the Blairites, which the newspapers exploited mercilessly, calling Miliband 'Red Ed'.[26] That, however, was not the only method of attack used on Miliband.

Miliband is the son of Jewish parents, both of whose families had fled to Britain to avoid the Holocaust. Could it be that all the bile being directed at him in the press was inspired by anti-Semitism? One observer certainly thought so, pointing to the way that he was constantly portrayed as 'other' and not one of us.[27] This had gone on ever since he had been made leader. A year before the General Election, in the campaign for the European elections, the press were already used to portraying him as hapless and out of his depth, as this headline shows: 'Ed Miliband fails to look normal while eating bacon sandwich'.[28]

A few months later, at the Heywood and Middleton by-election, Nigel Farage, the leader of UKIP, ate a bacon sandwich too. According to the *Daily Mail*, 'he did much better than Ed Miliband'.[29] The implication was pretty clear: what would a Jew know about eating a bacon sandwich?

Ironically, Miliband himself was accused of being anti-Semitic. This was due to his condemnation of Israel for its invasion of Gaza and the killing of many Palestinians, including children.[30] Such criticism of Israel was being called a *hatred* for Israel and, it was argued, stemmed from a deep-rooted anti-Semitism among left-wing groups.[31] This argument said that the Left in Britain was not only condemning the actions of the Israeli Government, but was against the very existence of Israel. This was anti-Semitic. The problem with this view is that it is a very narrow-minded one.

Many Jews in Britain and around the world are opposed to what is happening in Israel; many Israelis are unhappy about it too. So, is it wrong to express anger at what is going on as being 'against Israel'? Actually, this argument is simply an exercise in semantics. In the 1960s, there were protests outside U.S. embassies all over Europe due to the Vietnam War. There were plenty of Americans opposed to the war as well, but we still speak of 'America' being involved. Similarly, Britain and her allies fought against Germany in WWII, but not *all* of Germany. Socialists and Communists, along with liberals and churchmen were locked up in concentration camps and many of the Jews that died in the Holocaust were Germans too. Speaking of war or opposition to a country is simply a shorthand way of referring to the current government of that country.

But let us go back to David Miliband and the 2015 General Election. The portrayal of Miliband in the press as a useless geek is a Jewish stereotype, usually dominated by an overbearing mother.[32] While their friends in the media concentrated on this racist caricature, the Tories themselves were more concerned, or professed to be, with the SNP's offer to join a coalition with Labour to keep the Tories out. This was presented in posters as Alex Salmond having Ed Miliband in his pocket. (Fig.27) The campaign certainly frightened English voters, who baulked at the notion of Scotland becoming the dominant partner in the Union.[33]

After Labour's disastrous showing in the election, Ed Miliband resigned. The new leader would be elected by all members of the party, diminishing the influence of the unions and members of Parliament.[34] This was seen as a good thing, that is until the party faithful voted. Jeremy Corbyn, who was well-known for being on the left of the party, ended up winning convincingly.[35] The Blairites in the party were shocked and angry, while the right-wing press prepared for a new wave of 'Loony Left' stories.

What the right-wing press decided to concentrate on was Corbyn's support for Sinn Fein, Hamas and others that were deemed to be terrorists. The phrase 'terrorist sympathiser' appeared frequently.[36] There is a serious problem, however, with following this mode of attack. As Daniel Finn pointed out in the *Guardian*,

> If support for a united Ireland made Corbyn and Livingstone into fellow travellers of the IRA, by the same logic, those who defended the union with Britain shared a political objective with the loyalist paramilitaries responsible for hundreds of deaths

during the Troubles. The argument of guilt by association can easily backfire on those who deploy it.[37]

In fact, Finn goes further, pointing out the double standards inherent in British foreign policy, which condemns Muslim terrorists while maintaining friendly relations with the murderous regime of Saudi Arabia. And both Britain and America have been guilty of supporting, and even arming, allies of groups that they class as terrorists. Even Nelson Mandela was condemned as a terrorist by Thatcher and Reagan.[38] Since branding Corbyn a 'terrorist sympathiser' raised too many awkward issues, a different way of smearing him had to be found. The answer was staring the right-wing press in the face.

In 2016, a list was leaked to *The Times*. It grouped Labour MPs by five categories: CORE GROUP, CORE GROUP PLUS, NEUTRAL BUT NOT HOSTILE, CORE GROUP NEGATIVE, and HOSTILE GROUP.[39] It was a list of those for and against Jeremy Corbyn among Westminster Labour MPs. As you might expect, the CORE GROUP NEGATIVE and the HOSTILE GROUP, was comprised of Blairites, who saw any kind of lurch to the left as making Labour unelectable. Among those in CORE GROUP NEGATIVE was Liverpool MP Louise Ellman. Three years later she left the Labour Party.

Rather than accuse Corbyn of making Labour unelectable, she blamed him for tolerating anti-Semitism in the party. She went further,

> But this issue is no longer just about the Labour party – it is about the threat a Jeremy Corbyn premiership could pose to the country.[40]

That made it sound as if Corbyn was another Hitler and we could expect extermination camps to be set up if he became prime minister. Ellman was not the only MP to use this reason, or excuse, to leave the party. Ian Austin and Luciana Berger did so as well. Of course, it was sheer coincidence that both these MPs had been listed in the HOSTILE GROUP.[41]

According to the BBC, 'Anti-Semitism was generally not regarded as a big problem in the Labour Party before Jeremy Corbyn's election as leader in September 2015.'[42] Tell that to actress Maureen Lipman, who decided to withdraw her support for the party in 2014, when Ed Miliband was still in charge.[43] Claims of anti-Semitism in the Labour Party certainly pre-dated Jeremy Corbyn's leadership. Lipman's reasons for abandoning Labour were telling. It was prompted by Miliband's support for a Commons motion to recognise the state of Palestine alongside Israel. She then proceeded to voice what seemed to be an Islamophobic diatribe.[44] Unfortunately, she came across as nothing more than a bigot.

Various celebrities, including Eddie Marsan,[45] Tony Robinson and Tracy-Ann Oberman,[46] condemned Jeremy Corbyn's Labour Party as being anti-Semitic and either left the party or indicated that they would not vote for it. Ironically, nobody knew, or cared, which of these celebrities were Jewish and which were not, except when the likes of Oberman made a big issue of it. The right-wing press, of course, were there to publish every detail of these allegations.

The International Holocaust Remembrance Alliance, in 2016, came up with what it called a 'working definition of anti-Semitism.' It gave some examples of what might be considered anti-Semitism, including: 'Holding Jews collectively responsible for actions of the state of Israel.'[47] It also explicitly stated that 'criticism of Israel similar to that leveled against any other country cannot be regarded as antisemitic.'[48] It was not the Labour Party that were guilty of such anti-Semitism, but those that were accusing the party of it.

The leading light in the campaign against anti-Semitism in the Labour Party had nothing at all to do with the party. Rumour had it that Rachel Riley, of *Countdown* fame, had been meeting Jacob Rees-Mogg, who needs no introduction, to discuss her political future.[49] She was certainly doing sterling work for the Tories already with her frequent online attacks against anyone on the Left. She even smeared Noam Chomsky as being anti-Semitic![50]

Riley outlined the 'anti-Semitic' abuse she had received online.

> In the name of Labour I've been called a hypocrite, lying propagandist, tits, teeth and ass clothes horse dolly bird, weaponiser of anti-Semitism, fascist, right-wing extremist, Nazi sympathiser, Twitter cancer, thick Tory, brainwashed, an anti-Semite, white supremacist, hate preacher, Zio political trollster, not a real Jew, a child bully, conspiracy theorist, a paedo-protector minion puppet who my dead grandfather would be disgusted by.[51]

Nobody would argue that those insults are in any way pleasant, but they are far from being 'anti-Semitic'. And yet, Riley insisted that they were. She also claimed that the senders of such bile were identifiably Labour supporters. She provided no evidence for this, so we were simply meant to take her word for it.

Michael Rosen is a successful poet and was once Britain's Children's Laureate. He also happens to be Jewish. As such, he was upset and angry when Rachel Riley appeared on *Channel 4 News* to talk about anti-Semitism. She said that most people did not realise she was Jewish because, 'I don't look like a typical Jew or anything like that.'[52] This, of course, begged the question of what a 'typical Jew' looked like. This was more of an anti-Semitic statement than anything Riley was accusing others of using. Michael Rosen was furious that the usual suspects, like the *Jewish Chronicle*, conspicuously deemed Riley's statement not worth condemning.

Riley did not answer Rosen's questions, either directly or indirectly, but waited nearly a year before reacting in her usual fashion. She accused Rosen of being anti-Semitic and a Holocaust denier! This was just weeks after Rosen had published a book about the family members he had lost to the gas chambers.[53] Rosen was a left-winger and a Corbyn supporter. Clearly, Riley's attacks were politically motivated.

Michael Rosen was not the only person to be angered by Riley's antics. 2019 was a busy year for her as she lashed out at anybody and everybody on the Left. She posted an image of herself online, wearing a T-shirt with an image of Jeremy Corbyn being arrested in the 1980s for demonstrating against Apartheid in South Africa. He carried a placard, which said, 'Defend the right to demonstrate against Apartheid. Join this picket.' Riley had deleted this and replaced it with, 'Jeremy Corbyn is a racist endeavour.' (Fig.28) Many people were outraged at this.

> Just wow. Wowwww.
> Up there with the most arrogant racist shit I have seen in a while. A blue eyed blonde haired woman literally ERASING black struggle to centre themselves as the victim of racism.[54]

Just imagine Riley's reaction if someone had done that to a placard about the Holocaust! It seemed that the only racism that mattered to her was that against Jews. Quite what that racism entailed she did not appear to know. She attacked a Miners' Association brass band for playing Jewish song *Hava Negila*, comparing them to the Ku Klux Klan![55] It just showed how insane, and right-wing, her attacks were.

Meanwhile, both Rachel Riley and Tracy-Ann Oberman, despite complaining about trolls, were not averse to doing a bit of trolling themselves. Oberman attacked a Jewish woman online, who happened to support Corbyn and, for good measure, tagged the woman's mother in the tweets.[56] There have also been allegations that both Riley and Oberman trolled and viciously attacked a sixteen-year-old girl with anxiety issues, causing distress to her and her family.[57]

Most people would be unaware of these incidents since the mainstream media studiously avoided mentioning them. The right-wing media's agenda in this respect was obvious, but supposedly left-wing papers like the *Mirror* and Scotland's *Daily Record* were guilty as well. The explanation for this was simple;

they were Blairites who hated Corbyn and everything he stood for. It was only the online, alternative media that bothered to mention the dark side of the campaign against anti-Semitism in the Labour Party.

In July 2019, the BBC joined in the witch-hunt when its *Panorama* programme 'investigated' the claims. The *Guardian* published the views of four columnists about the programme, with three convinced it was a true reflection of the facts and one complaining that the programme was one-sided. Even reading the opinions of the three that believed the claims of anti-Semitism in the Labour Party, one is still left with the impression that the programme certainly was one-sided.[58] It portrayed the so-called 'whistleblowers' as 'brave' individuals, who had come forward to expose what was going on in 'their' party. Not included in the programme, however, was the other side of the story regarding these characters. As Jon Lansman, a member of Corbyn's National Executive Committee, who happens to be Jewish, put it,

> And while I have deep empathy with the Jewish people featured on the programme, many of the interviewees were former staffers with an axe to grind. Some of them, Iain McNicol for instance, were even the very staffers who resisted implementing Shami Chakrabarti's recommendations on how to deal with antisemitism, have reportedly delayed action on cases to undermine Jeremy Corbyn's leadership and left a complaints process behind them that was shambolic and not fit for purpose. They simply do not have any credibility on the subject of tackling antisemitism.[59]

Well-respected journalist and author, Jonathan Cook, agreed with this assessment, adding,

> Delays in resolving complaints were chiefly the responsibility not of Corbyn and his staff but of a

party bureaucracy that he inherited and was deeply and explicitly hostile to him.[60]

These 'whistleblowers', it appears, were not just part of the problem, but *were* the problem. While the party leadership was desperate to investigate claims of anti-Semitism, this clique in charge of the investigations deliberately dragged its feet. In fact, the much-vaunted 'interference' by the party leadership was to get things moving, not to hamper investigations.[61]

Meanwhile, the Constituency Labour Party of Liverpool Riverside, revealed that they had made complaints of their own about being branded anti-Semitic. Apparently, the accusations were copied wholesale from the blog of right-wing commentator Guido Fawkes! None of their complaints were followed up, instead they themselves were investigated. They were lied about on *Panorama*, where they were unfairly painted as anti-Semites and given no right of reply.[62]

Something that has probably occurred to a lot of people is where the loyalties lie of these folk shouting about anti-Semitism on the Left. It is common practice to question the loyalty to Britain of Muslims, but when it comes to right-wing Jews that are apologists for Israel nobody wants to know. It could well be that they are working for Mossad, the Israeli secret service; after all, who would benefit most from pro-Palestinian activists being branded racists? The International Holocaust Remembrance Alliance already had things covered in its Working Definition of Anti-Semitism. One of its examples of anti-Semitism is, 'Accusing Jewish citizens of being more loyal to Israel, or to the alleged priorities of Jews worldwide, than to the interests of their own nations.'[63] So, there you had it. Even suggesting that someone might be working for Israel would be considered racist.

With the overwhelming claims of Corbyn's Labour Party being full of racists and any attempts to counter these allegations stymied before they began, it was hardly surprising that Labour lost the General Election in December 2019. In fact, it was a disaster, Labour's worst election result since 1935,[64] with many deserting Labour to vote Tory.[65] Corbyn announced his resignation even before all the results were in.[66]

In October 2020, the Equality and Human Rights Commission published its report into anti-Semitism in the Labour Party. The Campaign Against Antisemitism claimed that the report 'had "utterly vindicated" British Jews who had been accused of lying to smear the party.'[67] Actually, that was not the case at all. The report mostly concentrated on the procedures for dealing with complaints. Concealed among the *Daily Mirror*'s general back-slapping and triumphant statements, was the following:

> "The Labour Party's practice or policy of Political Interference in antisemitism complaints amounted to unlawful indirect discrimination against its Jewish members," the EHRC said.
> Mr Corbyn today said, "I do not accept" all the EHRC's findings and claimed, "my team acted to speed up, not hinder the process."
> Alasdair Henderson, Board member lead for the investigation at the EHRC, said Mr Corbyn's claim that his team acted to speed up the process was valid, but still undermined the process.[68]

It looked as if the allegations that the 'whistleblowers' had been delaying the investigations were true. We have already seen how Jonathan Cook supported these allegations. He also had plenty to say about the EHRC report. He showed how the report found no evidence of 'institutional' anti-Semitism in Corbyn's Labour Party. In fact, they could only find two people 'guilty' of anti-Semitism and the evidence against one of those was decidedly dodgy.[69]

Incredibly, the Labour Party, now under Keir Starmer, sorry, *Sir* Keir Starmer, not only accepted the report, but seemed to accept the mainstream media's interpretation of it. This was confirmed when the party, to the disgust of Jeremy Corbyn, cravenly apologised to *Panorama*'s 'whistleblowers' and agreed to pay them £200,000 in damages.[70] Unite's General Secretary, Len McCluskey, tweeted,

> Today's settlement is a misuse of Labour Party funds to settle a case it was advised we would win in court.

The leaked report on how anti-semitism was handled tells a very different story about what happened.[71]

That leaked report, made for the EHRC enquiry, made it plain that the 'whistleblowers' were the ones that dragged their feet over investigations into complaints of anti-Semitism.[72] Of course, those on the right of the party dismissed this report out of hand. They said that online conversations had been taken out of context, which is ironic since that was exactly what had been done to 'prove' that anti-Semitism existed in the Labour Party.

It was left to the online, alternative media to report that the *Jewish Chronicle* had to apologise and pay damages to Labour Councillor Nada al-Sanjari. The *Jewish Chronicle* writer, Lee Harpin, had accused al-Sanjari of anti-Semitism.[73] There was probably more than a hint of Islamophobia involved in it. The mainstream media completely ignored this; it did not fit their agenda.

On the evening of September 27th, 2019, in New York City, the Jewish newspaper, The *Algemeiner*, held its annual 'J100' gala to honour the 100 people that had had a positive influence on Jewish life. Various right-wing politicians and activists were present, while Donald Trump and Benjamin Netanyahu sent messages of greeting. Previous recipients of honours at the event include Rupert Murdoch and Michael Gove, which tells you all you need to know about it. Among the winners this year was one Rachel Riley, who received the 'Warrior for Truth' award.[74] At a ceremony endorsed by Trump and Netanyahu, it was clear that Riley was being rewarded for services to the political Right.

8
Young Ones

There is a thing called Black Propaganda, which governments and their secret services have used throughout history to discredit enemies and political opponents. The Zinoviev Letter, which we encountered in the last chapter, was one such incidence. If you remember, this was a forgery that was supposed to be from the Comintern telling British Communists to get ready to rise up. This is what Black Propaganda is all about - inventing lies and pretending that they come from the source one wishes to discredit.

A prime example of Black Propaganda is *The Protocols of the Elders of Zion*,[1] a Russian forgery setting out plans for a Jewish takeover of the world. It was written as if it were by the Jews themselves, effectively fanning the flames of anti-Semitism. Incredibly, there are many people that still believe that *The Protocols* are true, which shows how effective it was.

In the 1980s, British television and radio channels were involved in what seems like, with the benefit of hindsight, Black Propaganda on behalf of the Tories. The participants in this Black Propaganda probably had no idea what they were involved in, but it definitely worked. Whether they ever did discover, they would be too embarrassed to say. The chances are, though, that they still do not know anything about it.

The BBC had long been fond of commissioning comedy shows starring Oxbridge graduates, mostly ex-members of the Cambridge Footlights. Such programmes included *That Was the Week that Was*, *Monty Python's Flying Circus*, *The Goodies* and *Not the Nine O'Clock News*. Of course, since the stars of these programmes had mostly been to university, they were overwhelmingly middle-class.

Much of the content of these programmes came across as being left-wing or, at the very least, liberal. They mocked Authority and the Establishment, everything the Tory Party stood for. It never seemed overly vicious, though. A lot of it was satire and the Labour Party did not escape their attentions either. Even Tories could laugh at it and there were rarely any complaints about the programmes, not from politicians at any rate. Then, along came Alternative Comedy.

The alternative comedians caused a great deal of a stir in the 1980s, not least because they used a lot of bad language and were fond of a swear word or two. This was toned down a bit for TV, but people were still shocked. Remember, this was a time when even films shown late at night had swear words overdubbed. For example, the film *Silkwood* had the word 'fucking' in it, which was replaced with 'screwing,' said by a voice that was completely different to the voice of the man that was speaking. There were many instances of this, all of them sounding just as ridiculous.

Sometimes it seemed as if the swearing was more important than the comedy to the alternative comedians. A lot of it elicited cheers from the audience rather than laughs. These new comedians made no secret of their left-wing leanings and were not shy about saying exactly what they felt about the Tories and the Establishment in general. It was often said that to be accepted as an alternative comedian all one had to do was walk out on stage and say, 'Margaret Thatcher – what a bastard, eh?' Nobody would laugh; they would just hoot and cheer, which seemed to be the whole point.

Right-wing newspapers, like the *Mail*, the *Telegraph*, the *Sun* and the *Express* were outraged at these attacks on *their* party and went on the attack themselves. They could not be explicit about why they were attacking the alternative comedians, i.e., for being left-wing, so they concentrated on the 'shocking' and 'disgusting' routines that these characters presented as comedy. Pretty soon, however, a much better mode of attack was found.

If you take the time to investigate the backgrounds of the alternative comedians, you will find, with the notable exception of Alexei Sayle, that they were all from a middle-class background and that most of them attended fee-paying schools. Sayle professed to be shocked when his co-stars in *The Young Ones* were all chummy with the Oxbridge types that appeared in an episode of the second series of the programme.[2] (Fig.29) He must have been walking around with his eyes closed; they were all from the same background. And *that* was what the right-wing newspapers used to attack them.

Although BBC1 still broadcast programmes like *Terry & June* and unfunny Carla Lane comedies, BBC2's main comedy output consisted of 'alternative comedians' like Rik Mayall, Adrian Edmondson, Dawn French, Jennifer Saunders, Stephen Fry and Hugh Laurie. This was as nothing compared to the new Channel 4, which had *Saturday Live* (later *Friday Night Live*), *The Comic Strip Presents...* and *Who Dares Wins*. BBC2, and Channel 4 became the channels of choice if one wanted to watch middle-class people making jokes about Thatcher and her government.

ITV tried its best to cater for afficionados of this 'new comedy' with the short-lived *Alfresco* and the spectacularly unfunny *Spitting Image*. In the main, however, ITV was the place to go for 'old-fashioned comedy', like Jimmy Cricket, Cannon and Ball, Russ Abbott, Bobby Davro and, of course, Benny Hill. This took on a class aspect, with the old-fashioned comedy being seen as the preserve of the working classes. The right-wing press encouraged this way of looking at things.

Gary Bushell, in the *Sun*, was continually complaining that comedians working the circuit of pubs and clubs were never seen on TV, while Oxbridge graduates seemed to just walk into their own show on BBC2 or Channel 4. Meanwhile, right-wing papers delighted in telling us how middle-class and posh Ben Elton and the rest of them were. They were also keen to let everyone know how much money these individuals were making.[3]

Let us fast-forward for a moment to 2013, when people were complaining about left-wing bias on BBC radio comedy shows. The woman in charge of the programmes responded by saying, try as they might, they simply could not find any right-wing comedians to balance things out.[4] The truth was, though, that such a thing never really existed. Certainly, there were comedians that supported the Tories, but this never entered their routines at all. That is why I have used the more apposite term, 'old-fashioned comedian'; the 'you don't get many of those to the pound' type.

124

At any rate, the left-wing rants of the likes of Ben Elton clearly showed working-class people in the 1980s that the Left was the preserve of the middle classes. Meanwhile, probably the most popular comedian among working-class folk was Roy 'Chubby' Brown. His shows were always sold out and his videos and records were snapped up as soon as they were released. And yet, you never saw him on the TV, even in a toned-down version.

In July 1987, a few days before the General Election, the Tories held what they called a 'Family Rally' at Wembley Great Hall. (Fig.30) In attendance were Bob Monkhouse, Jimmy Tarbuck and Ronnie Corbett,[5] all mainstream, 'old-fashioned' comedians from BBC1 and ITV. Also there, sharing the stage with her leader, was Janet Brown, whose anodyne impersonations of Thatcher were a favourite of the Prime Minister. If memory serves, I believe Max Bygraves and Bernie Winters were creeping about as well.

The class lines were drawn, and it was pretty obvious which party many working-class people were going to vote for. The 'real' comedians and entertainers were all on the side of the Tories, which, of course, meant that the Tories were on the side of those comedians. Conversely, all those middle-class, smart-arsed comedians on BBC2 and Channel 4 supported Labour, which meant that Labour was for middle-class smart arses.

Of course, the main people that felt like this were those from the south of England; white people that still had jobs. To add insult to injury, those lefty, alternative comedians were constantly making fun of those southern Englanders. There was that Harry Enfield, for example, with his 'Loadsamoney' character. He was taking the piss; or was he?

As the character became more and more popular, the people that it was meant to lampoon began to treat it as more of a gentle dig. It was like Russ Abbott's 'C.U. Jimmy' character, which Scottish people took to their hearts and were not in the least offended by. Realising that his character was becoming a bit of a hero, Enfield decided to kill him off.[6]

Of course, this could be looked at another way. Perhaps Enfield realised who his target audience was supposed to be, and it was not working-class *Sun* readers. It is interesting to

125

note that Enfield's working-class characters always tended to be grotesque caricatures, like Loadsamoney himself, Wayne and Waynetta Slob, the Scousers and the Old Gits. Other characters, like Tim Nice-But-Dim, were gentle parodies. It could well be suggested that Enfield was a willing participant in television's Black Propaganda. Anyone doubting he would be that cynical might be interested to know that before abandoning Loadsamoney, Enfield took the character on a lucrative tour and released a hit single.[7]

The divide between the audiences for the two different types of comedy, alternative and old-fashioned, was displayed mercilessly in a TV special in the 1980s to raise awareness of AIDS. (Unfortunately, I can find no mention of it on IMDB or anywhere else.) Amid explanations and debunking of myths, bands played and comics (alternative, of course) did routines. In among all the trendiness, one pair of comics stood out like a sore thumb – Canon and Ball.

Rik Mayall had always professed to be a fan of the duo, which is maybe why they were invited to take part. Fair play to them, though, for appearing in a programme that most old-fashioned comedians would not have touched with a bargepole. The routine they did was not exactly hilarious and involved dishes coming down a chute. If it had been performed by Rik Mayall and Adrian Edmondson, the middle-class, student-type audience would have at least uttered the odd, polite chuckle. As it was Canon and Ball, however, they sat with sneering expressions on their faces. That moment defined the whole character of the Black Propaganda. Canon and Ball were working-class comics for working-class audiences.

The class and political differences on television became, if anything, more pronounced during the 1990s. Many working-class people signed up to satellite TV, which, after November 1990, effectively meant Sky. It offered movies and coverage of sports that appealed widely. Almost immediately, middle-class, left-wing comedians on TV derided it. Programmes like *Have I Got News For You* ridiculed it, and its viewers, relentlessly. Of course, they could easily argue that Sky was owned by Rupert Murdoch, who also owned papers like the *Sun*, the *Times* and the *News of the World*. That, however, would have been a lie.

126

While denigrating Sky and its viewers to get cheap laughs, left-wing comedians also laughed at the ubiquitous shell suits that were popular among working-class people at the time. The opposition to Sky was snobbery, nothing more. As journalist Maggie Brown said of Sky in the 1990s, 'For years it was dubbed "council house television".'[8] This snobbery helped again to convince people that Labour was the party of the middle classes. After all, the middle-class comedians sneering at their satellite dishes and shell suits were Labour supporters.

In later years, the alternative comedians, as they were called in the 1980s, became mainstream and even part of the Establishment. Adrian Edmondson is a regular on ITV quiz shows and has made anodyne documentaries for the channel too. Rik Mayall, before his untimely death, made adverts against joining the Euro and against having an alternative voting system in Britain.[9]

None of this really mattered, though. Their role in making Labour appear to be the party of the middle classes had long since been accomplished. Whether this accomplishment had been done cynically and deliberately is still up for debate. We have already seen how Harry Enfield's actions could be interpreted in this way, but there was no question of the cynicism of Ben Elton. Not only did he slavishly follow the middle-class zeitgeist away from left-wing politics and into environmentalism, but he also co-wrote a musical play with the surviving members of fascist rockers, Queen.[10]

Strangely, the worst of the old alternative comedians to reinforce the idea of left-wing politics being the preserve of the middle classes, albeit unintentionally, is Alexei Sayle. Sayle is caught in the common dilemma of those on the Left that make enough money to live comfortably. Residing in a middle-class area leaves him open to charges of abandoning his principles, while, if he were to live on a council estate, he would be accused of affectation. It is a situation in which one simply cannot win.

Sayle lives in Bloomsbury, a fashionable, middle-class area in London's West End.[11] He is still angry at the injustices in the world and continues to rant and rave about them in his stand-up routine.[12] He was a staunch supporter of Jeremy Corbyn and was a vocal critic of the purges in the Labour Party, which accused those on the Left, like Corbyn himself, of anti-Semitism.[13] That is where his residential situation comes in. Living in Bloomsbury means that he is a middle-class leftist, a champagne socialist. Worse than that, he is also part of what right-wingers like to call 'the elite'.

One observer in America compares the 'elite' with ordinary, working-class people, talking of how the middle classes work out in the gym while common folk have to do hard, physical labour and points to the hypocrisy of the whole group in different areas.[14] He talks as if this 'elite' is running the country, although he omits to mention anything about politicians, other than to have a dig at Barack Obama. This right-wing description of the situation in the USA could equally apply to the UK. Nigel Farage, for example, rails against the 'liberal elite' that cannot see the problem with immigration, as the ordinary man in the street can.[15]

Another character has nothing but contempt for what he calls the 'London elite'. His talk of them calling those that voted for Brexit 'morons' at their dinner parties confirms that he means the middle classes. He goes on:

> They are desperate to Remain in the EU. They hate Brexit. They hate people. They sneer and look down at the people who voted for Brexit.[16]

He is manifestly trying to anger working-class Brexit voters by informing them that a snobbish, middle-class elite are looking down on them. His mention of the 'media elite' in London as being 'the absolute swamp' is rather telling. That is the language of Donald Trump, which has been amplified by the quasi-religious cult, QAnon.[17]

In any case, studies are showing that Brexit was not a straight divide between working-class Leave voters and middle-class Remainers. In fact, some investigators have concluded that it was the middle classes that swung the Brexit vote, although there are question marks over their methodology.[18] Whether most of the middle classes voted to remain in the EU or not, the truth is that a substantial number of them must have voted

128

Leave. The right-wing media, however, still maintain that Brexit was a purely working-class decision. The fact that many people believe this shows how far the stock of the middle classes has fallen.

Throughout the Nineteenth Century, the middle classes acted as the conscience of Britain. Men like David Dale, Robert Owen, George Cadbury and Joseph Rowntree were not only model employers, but agitated for life to be made better for the working classes. Some of them were even involved in the development of trade unions. Many of them were Nonconformists in religion and they saw it as their duty to improve the life of their fellow man. They provided the backbone of the Liberal Party in the last quarter of the century.

In fact, the middle classes influenced all sections of society in the last couple of decades of the Nineteenth Century. From the Queen down to the lowliest worker, everybody was concerned with appearing respectable. And that was the operative word: appearing. Late Victorian respectability was simply a façade, while vice and crime still existed, but hidden away as much as possible.

People speak of Victorian times as if it was the same all the way through, but when Victoria's reign came to an end in 1901, it was a different world from when she came to the throne in 1837. Even in the period during her reign, the country changed considerably. Britain in the 1880s was utterly different from the one observed and written about by Charles Dickens in the middle of the century.

Kellow Chesney, in his book *The Victorian Underworld*, uses various sources to describe prostitution in London in the middle of the Nineteenth Century.[19] It was quite an open affair, with high-class prostitutes on horseback parading in Hyde Park and streetwalkers of all descriptions openly displaying their wares. The age of consent was twelve, later raised to thirteen, which meant child prostitutes were openly available. Brothels did a roaring trade, offering drink and dancing along with their traditional services.

In 1885, public pressure caused the Tory Government to pass the Criminal Law Amendment Act,[20] which raised the age of consent to sixteen and cracked down on brothels. They still existed, of course, as did prostitution and the sexual exploitation of children continued. The difference was that now one had to know where to look; sex was no longer openly available. Neither was pornography, which was advertised in shop windows in the middle of the century but was later driven underground. Again, one had to know where to look.[21]

This hypocritical, middle-class morality persists to this day and manifests itself in some ridiculous ways. A few years ago, there was an advert on television for some kind of cold remedy, cough medicine or some such. An older, middle-class man explained that some condition, a bunged-up feeling, if I remember correctly, was caused by 'Snot.' As soon as he said the word, he immediately screwed up his face in disgust and exclaimed, 'Yuck!' It was as if the word itself had soiled his tongue and he had to do something to make himself feel and look clean again. It encapsulated, in two simple words, practically everything there is to say about the British middle classes.

As our man in the advert showed, middle-class people conform to a reluctance to use what they believe to be offensive words. Even if they are utterly exasperated, they would never react the way Prince Philip did when he told a photographer, 'Just take the fucking picture!'[22] What would people think? It is only fairly recently that the middle classes have decided that the word 'poo' is acceptable. Any other word for 'shit' is likely to give them severe palpitations. In fact, anything remotely scatological, or even lavatorial, will drive them into a frenzy.

I often wonder how such folk manage when they go to see the doctor. Then again, doctors, being middle-class themselves, are just as bad. I remember suffering from a severe bout of food poisoning and my GP asking how my 'movements' were. When I explained that my joints were a bit stiff and sore, he looked at me as if I were mad. Like others of his class, he could not bring himself to use even the word 'faeces'. And how many of us have been exasperated by doctors talking about your 'tummy' etc.?

As well as being careful with language, the middle classes also conform with the way they dress. Take a stroll through Edinburgh's New Town and you will be surprised at how similar everybody looks. They shop at different places from the rest of us, at establishments that cater especially for them. For example, I have not seen a pair of corduroy trousers in a clothes shop or clothes department for nearly forty years, and yet I have seen them on the legs of middle-class men. Where do they buy them, if not at some specialist shop?

The strange thing is that it is virtually impossible to find out who the influencers are that decide which clothes are acceptable and which not. They do not copy film or TV stars or pop stars or the like, as many working-class people do. Trends in clothing among the middle classes just seem to happen; I mean, who started the fashion of threading a scarf through a loop, as everybody that is middle-class does now? It is like football songs and chants; nobody knows who starts them. They simply appear.

When it comes to the question of taste, whether in films, TV programmes, art, theatre, literature, there are those among the working classes that slavishly emulate what the middle classes deem to be good. Sometimes, they just happen to enjoy the same things. This is much to the chagrin of middle-class people, who will immediately drop their liking for something when it becomes too popular. An example is Vic Reeves, whose programmes on Channel 4 and then BBC2 were well loved by the middle classes. I remember how excited my fellow students and tutors were at Moray House in the early 1990s when they discovered that Reeves was coming to do a show in Edinburgh. As time went on, however, their opinion of Reeves changed.

It must have been galling for those middle-class women, now teachers, to go into schools and discover that *Shooting Stars* was popular among their working-class pupils. The last straw was when Reeves starred in a remake of *Randall and Hopkirk (Deceased)*, which was shown on – gasp! – BBC1! Needless to say, Reeves is no longer the draw he once was.

Zeitgeist is everything to these people, while they appear to believe that the story of *The Emperor's New Clothes* applies to somebody else entirely. Have a look on *IMDB* and see some of the reviews of movies. Foreign films are always rated highly, while American remakes are sneered at. Also praised to the hilt are boring, pretentious movies where nothing happens. When such a film receives negative reviews, there is always some snooty individual around to tell them to go and watch *Transformers* or some other Hollywood blockbuster.

In 1990, I was working at what was then called the Nature Conservancy Council in Edinburgh. At the time, some large cinema chain, I forget which one, was looking to buy the Cameo cinema in Edinburgh, a venue that normally showed arthouse and foreign films. Some of my middle-class fellow workers were outraged; where else would they be able to see 'quality' films? One such 'quality' film they spoke of was about a man and his grandson living in a remote area in Scotland, where a dead whale was rotting on the beach nearby. Sounds riveting!

As you might guess, none of these people had seen *Batman*, *Indiana Jones and the Last Crusade*, *Back to the Future II* or *Ghostbusters II*, which had all been released the previous year. None of these were 'quality' films, you understand and were simply produced to entertain the common herd, none of whom had the intelligence to watch what the Cameo had to offer.

This snobbish attitude toward the tastes of working-class people was mercilessly parodied in the TV programme *Absolutely*. In one sketch Jack Docherty and Moray Hunter were sitting in some kind of waiting room. Hunter, portraying an ordinary, working-class man, starts humming *Nessun Dorma*, which, when questioned by Docherty, a middle-class individual, he describes as the *World Cup Song*. Docherty, visibly incensed, snaps, 'How *dare* you like that!'

As mentioned above, some working-class people try to emulate the middle classes and profess to like the same things. In the main, though, most working-class people are content to just enjoy the things they themselves like and view middle-class snobbery with undisguised contempt.

There is a simple reason why working-class people have come to hate the middle classes far more than they do the upper classes; middle-class folk are the only ones they encounter in their everyday lives. And it is not just middle-class teachers, doctors and social workers they meet. Council housing schemes have mostly been built out in the suburbs. This was in order to get working-class people away from the filth and squalor of the cities. Many of these housing schemes were left to rot for decades and it is only fairly recently that attempts have been made at refurbishment. Unfortunately, being in the suburbs, housing schemes are in close proximity to middle-class areas. This has meant that working-class people meet folk from more affluent areas even in the supermarket.

Another way that working-class people have come into direct contact with the middle classes is through what is known as gentrification. This has happened in cities all over the world as the well-to-do encroach on traditionally working-class areas, eventually displacing the working classes altogether. Like a desert gradually taking over arable land, the middle classes have, bit by bit, replaced the working-class residents to become the archetypal city dwellers.

Whether this is a good thing or not depends on one's perspective. If you are a holidaymaker in New York's Manhattan, you will be pleased at being able to wander through Central Park unmolested and walk back to your hotel from a bar in the early hours of the morning. Gone is the crime-ridden area that we are all familiar with in films and TV programmes. It is now a relatively safe place to stay in and visit. Meanwhile, however, all those working-class people, mostly ethnic minorities, have had to move out. Where they have gone to is unclear. Perhaps they went to Brooklyn, but they will soon have to move again as that borough is in the process of gentrifying too.[23]

In Britain, regeneration is hailed as an effort to make an area better, but better for whom? Many Londoners found themselves displaced due to preparations for the 2012 Olympic Games. Afterwards, they were practically homeless, having to rent in the private sector.[24] In other cities, apart from in council schemes, regeneration often means gentrification and the working classes being priced out. And this is not the only way that the middle classes impinge on working-class areas.

In July 2019, one of those rare creatures mentioned above, a right-wing comedian, Geoff Norcott (he is really just an old-fashioned comedian; a sweary Bob Monkhouse), presented a programme that supposedly exposed the hypocrisy of the liberal middle classes. Gentrification, of course, was one of his main areas of attack. Another was the way middle-class people played the system to get their children into the 'best' state schools, often edging out working-class children that live in the catchment area.[25] It all seemed pretty damning. There were, however, problems with his analysis.

For one thing, Norcott has nothing at all to say about fee-paying schools, neither does he question a system where one state school is considered 'better' than another. He is also rather simplistic in his arguments about class. The working-class activists he joins to protest against the regeneration of Deptford are not the Tory-voting, Brexit-supporting types he believes the working classes to be.[26] Equally, the middle-class ones exploiting the school system to their advantage are not the trendy-lefty Corbynistas he portrays. Their selfishness, which he himself portrays, belies such a label.

It is a common mistake to infer that just because middle-class people dominate the so-called 'caring' professions, like medicine, education and social work, that they actually do *care*. If they did, they would want everyone to have the same opportunities in life; it is pretty clear, however, that they do not. They ensure that their children have every advantage, not just getting them into the 'best' schools but helping to map out their entire school career and beyond.

It is always possible that intelligent, junior members of the working classes might do as well as, or even better than, those from a middle-class background. In the competition for university places and jobs, middle-class people need an edge, an advantage. This is provided in the 'Interests and Hobbies' section of any application form. This is where attending a fee-paying school, or one in a middle-class area, comes up trumps. Not only do such schools get pupils ready for their exams; they also pay attention to the need for a well-rounded CV.

At a school I worked at in Glasgow, most of the teachers lived in well-to-do areas, like Jordanhill, Scotstoun and Milngavie. It was around April that one of them came in with raffle tickets to sell. The proceeds from the raffle were going to help pay for her son's school's annual trip abroad to aid poor natives by digging wells etc. This is a common occurrence at fee-paying schools and state schools in middle-class areas. It is obvious what the intention is behind these ostensibly altruistic schemes; it is to provide something outstanding to put on a CV or the 'Interests and Hobbies' section of an application form.

I wondered out loud in the staffroom why it was that such opportunities were not available in *all* schools. Shocked that I would bring up such a subject, the women (I was the only male teacher) all opined that pupils attending most state schools would not be able to afford to go on such trips. When I asked if *their* children could afford it, the resounding answer was 'Yes!' They were none too happy when I pointed out that, if that was the case, they did not need me to buy a raffle ticket!

At university I met quite a few people that had gone on these types of trips while at school. One guy and his girlfriend, who had attended the same fee-paying school in Edinburgh, spoke of going on an archaeological dig at Knossos in Crete when they were in Fourth Year. Apparently, they hated every minute of it, not being remotely interested, and slipped off every chance they got. This made me feel quite angry as I would have killed to go to something like that when I was at school.

When it comes to employment, the middle classes also have things sewn up. Unlike their working-class peers, they can afford to do internships, working for no pay to get experience. Mummy and Daddy can finance their little darlings through however long this takes. When a paid position comes up, the middle-class candidate has an impressive CV, with those school trips abroad and lots of relevant experience. Any working-class applicant does not stand a chance.

This is all, of course, grist to the likes of Geoff Norcott's mill. It would be surprisingly easy to fall into the trap of agreeing with him completely, were it not for him completely ignoring the upper classes. They are just as selfish and self-serving as the middle classes; perhaps more so. So where did the idea of the middle class being 'the enemy' originate? Surprisingly, this was all part of a plan.

The *New Culture Forum* was founded in 2006 and incorporated in 2010 as an organisation committed to fighting leftist ideas. As *The London Economic* website says,

> The NCF has come to prominence in recent years, with its pro-Brexit, lockdown-sceptical stance. In response to Black Lives Matter, it has pushed identity politics via a Save Our Statues campaign and promoted on YouTube celebrities and talking heads, including singer-actor Laurence Fox, commentator Melanie Phillips, and historian David Starkey.[27]

Practically everyone is familiar with Laurence Fox, who has become ubiquitous on social media. The upper-class actor is one of the main exponents of the 'All Lives Matter' phrase, which aims to portray 'Black Lives Matter' as racist.[28] He even started up his own political party to fight against 'wokeness' and in favour of freedom of speech.[29]

Being 'woke' has come to mean being aware of social issues, especially social injustices.[30] As you might expect, those on the political right are never too concerned with social injustices, so the term has become associated with liberals and others on the left. In many ways, it has developed into a pejorative word, used by conservatives and other right-wingers to ridicule people that *are* concerned about social justice.

Phrases like 'virtue signalling' and 'political correctness gone mad' are repeated over and over until they have become part of nearly everybody's vocabulary. They signify that not everyone that expounds 'woke culture' actually believes in it. They simply want to look good in the eyes of their peers. Unfortunately, the middle classes, with their history of being mostly concerned with appearances, make themselves an easy target for these accusations.

Much of what 'woke' is concerned with is the use of language. There is no *Index Verborum Prohibitorum*; common sense and a bit of human decency lets one know which words are offensive. There are many people, however, that have no sense of human decency except when it comes to their own peer group. Such folk are easy prey for the demagogues of the

New Culture Forum. As *Guardian* columnist Ellie Mae O'Hagan puts it:

> Having spent so long feeling silenced by the liberal consensus, people in this group have been given a new lease of life by the right's new insurgents. Not only were they correct all along; they were actually victims, zealously persecuted by an oversensitive and censorious society.[31]

The only real problem faced by such people was, as O'Hagan explains, one of feeling that 'You can't say anything anymore!'[32] And it is obvious what it is they want to say. They want to be able to use good, old-fashioned words like *poofs*, *Pakis*, *spazzies* etc. The truth is, though, that they still use these terms in everyday speech among their peers. So, what is their difficulty?

Sometimes people can slip up and use their 'old-fashioned' language in places where it is considered offensive. They always apologise profusely, while the media call what they said a 'gaffe'. The truth is, however, that if they never used those terms at all, then making such 'gaffes' would be impossible. Their apologies, therefore, mean nothing since they are simply sorry for being caught.

Both upper-class and working-class people use these terms frequently, so the idea of fighting for 'free speech' against 'woke' individuals is really only aimed at one group. As we have seen in this chapter, the middle classes find even relatively innocuous words offensive and difficult to say. The problem is that this gives the 'anti-woke' brigade the excuse of arguing that *all* terms that the middle classes find offensive are, in fact, innocuous. Actually, some commentators take the argument even further.

Stephen Fry is nobody's idea of a right-wing, anti-woke campaigner; this, however, is a mistake. It is often assumed that if someone is gay, then they must be left-wing or liberal. This assumption is made about Freddie Mercury, causing everyone to ignore his fascist lyrics and his appearance at Sun City during apartheid. Fry benefits from the same assumption, while his being considered one of the 1980s Alternative Comedians also leads people to the conclusion that he is far from being right-wing. As I demonstrated in another of my books, he is a religious bigot.[33] And that is not all. Here is a quote from him, which I make no apology for using again:

> It's now very common to hear people say, "I'm rather offended by that", as if that gives them certain rights. It's no more than a whine. It has no meaning, it has no purpose, it has no reason to be respected as a phrase. "I'm offended by that." Well, so fucking what?[34]

Apparently, although he comes from a middle-class background, all that mixing with the aristocracy and swan dinners with royalty have led Fry to believe that he is upper-class. His swearing betrays that, as does his use of 'one' when speaking of himself.[35] At any rate, his little rant above would be music to the ears of those in the New Culture Forum.

Essentially, what Fry has done is to shift the blame from those making offensive utterances to those that *find* the utterances offensive. Others spin things the same way, although not as succinctly as Fry does. It is a rather twisted way of looking at things, but it fits in neatly with the notion that working-class bigots have been the victims all along, as Ellie May O'Hagan mentions in the quote above.

Of course, nobody explicitly names the middle classes as 'the enemy' but it is obvious who they mean when they talk about liberal elites. The online edition of the Encyclopaedia Britannica draws a distinction between 'political elites' and 'cultural elites';[36] a distinction that most right-wing observers conspicuously avoid. Although there are middle-class folk among the political elite in the UK, the real power, as it always has, rests with the upper classes. Being part of the cultural elite gives one no real power at all, other than in influencing the culture at large in terms of taste in music, literature and the visual arts.

So, through a mixture of propaganda, black propaganda, downright lies and the well-documented hypocrisy of the middle classes themselves, many people had come to believe that the Labour Party, especially its left-wing faction, was the party of the middle classes. Many among the working classes had been brainwashed into believing that the Tory Party had their best interests at heart. Moreover, the middle classes had become an 'elite' that tried to stand in the way of everything the working classes wanted.

What was it, though, that made Britain, and, more especially, England, susceptible to this kind of propaganda? Was there something special about the working classes, indeed, all classes, in this country that made it so easy to fall for a massive con? Actually, there was. It was called Anti-Intellectualism.

Fig.24 Daily Mail article about the Zinoviev Letter. 1924

Fig.25 The Daily Express prints Churchill's ridiculous
assertions about the Labour Party. 1945

Fig.26 Tory General Election poster. 1997.

Fig.27 Tory Election poster. 2010.

Fig.28 Rachel Riley's tee-shirt calling Jeremy Corbyn 'A Racist Endeavour.'

Fig.29 The Young Ones episode featuring comics from Cambridge.

Fig.30 Tory Party Family Rally. 1987.

9
Albion Shrugged

There is a long history of upper-class individuals siding with the common people against the so-called elites. In Ancient Greece there were the tyrants, a word that originally just meant men that had usurped power unlawfully. Men like Peisistratus had the support of the lower orders and took over the power of the state in their name.[1] Then there were the *populares* of the Ancient Roman Republic, men who solicited the support of the common people against the elites in the Senate.[2] The most famous of these *populares* was Julius Caesar, who, like the tyrants of Greece, seized power illegally with the backing of the *plebs*.

One more thing that all these men had in common was that they were aristocrats, members of the very elite they were supposedly against. It would never have occurred to these individuals that a member of the lower orders could ever hold power. The filthy, uneducated masses of Rome, crammed into their rickety tenements, needed somebody like Julius Caesar to stand up for their interests; God forbid they might do it themselves. That was the road to anarchy and chaos. Even gangsters like Clodius and Milo came from the ranks of the aristocracy.[3]

The good ol' US of A has carried on this tradition right up until the present day, with so-called *populists* versus the *elites*. Just like in the ancient world, it was virtually impossible to separate the populists from the elites. The most recent example of a populist is Donald Trump, who was elected president in 2016. The execrable Ruth Dudley Edwards said of Trump that he 'understood the plight of poor white Americans.'[4] Quite how a millionaire, and son of a millionaire, could come anywhere close to understanding the lives of the poor she does not explain.

What Trump did understand, and tapped into, was the seething resentment among poor whites, who were ready to believe that their jobs had been stolen by African Americans and immigrants. It is an easy thing to do, giving people scapegoats, which is why it has been done multiple times. In Britain, Nigel Farage was doing the same thing; no wonder the two men got on so well.

Farage and Trump were from similar backgrounds, growing up rich and attending fee-paying schools. Unlike Farage, Trump went on to university, although the fact that he threatened it, and his school, with legal action if they revealed his academic record points to him not doing very well.[5] Fortunately for both men, they were able to follow in Daddy's footsteps and work in the financial sector. Neither of them exactly struggled to make ends meet and had no idea what life was like for people mired in poverty. That, however, did not stop them from using such people for their own ends.

Just like the *populares* of Ancient Rome, both Trump and Farage claimed to be standing against the 'elite'. And, just like the *populares*, both of them, with their privileged backgrounds and inherited money, could easily be said to be part of that elite. Obviously, however, they meant something different when they used the word; something that was understood by both them and their followers. Ruth Dudley Edwards gives us a clue when she uses the term 'liberal elite' when talking of 'the plight of poor, white Americans'.[6]

In the USA, where even the idea of having a British-style National Health Service is viewed as opening the door to Communism, anyone criticising those on the Right is considered a liberal. Desiring equal rights for blacks, ethnic minorities or women marks one out as a liberal too. In fact, it is remarkably easy to be branded a liberal in America. There are those that are considered Right-of-Centre in our country that would be accused of being a 'Pinko' in the States. Obviously, the word 'liberal' has a quite specific meaning; one that has been divorced from its *original* meaning. One woman, an immigrant herself, had a huge influence on how this word was changed.

Ayn Rand (Fig.31) was born in Russia in 1905, so was still a young girl when the Bolsheviks took over in 1917. Her father's pharmacy business was confiscated, which caused her to be resentful ever since. Once safely ensconced in America, she turned

145

her resentment into a philosophy, which she expounded in novels like *The Fountainhead* and *Atlas Shrugged*. She also wrote extensively about her philosophy, which she called *Objectivism*, a mixture of Plato, Machiavelli and Nietzsche, among others. A huge difference between her philosophy and that of others is that, in her ideal world, social responsibility does not exist. The only responsibility anyone should have is to himself or herself.[7] Obviously, her ideas have become influential among right-wingers in America.[8]

Some observers point out how elitist Rand's philosophy is,[9] how ridiculous the characters in her novels are[10] and some even question her sanity.[11] The most damning indictment, however, comes from academia, which sees her works as not worth studying seriously.[12] In fact, the most obvious flaw in Rand's philosophy comes from one of its most basic tenets.

> Take responsibility for your own actions. Even if an excuse is valid, it still takes blame off of yourself. Blaming yourself, in any case of failure (or neglecting to accept failure), will lead you to improve when improvements are necessary and possible.[13]

Rand does not stick to her own philosophy when it comes to the heroes in her novels and the capitalists she idolises. Any failure on *their* part is put down to the common herd that is holding them back, with the connivance of socialists and liberals. Lisa Simpson got it right when she said of *The Fountainhead*, 'Isn't that book the bible of right-wing losers?'[14]

It is the criticism from academics, however, that sticks in the craw of followers of Rand. In fact, most people on the political right in America take a jaundiced view of academics. They constantly go on about how American universities are full of liberals, with conservatives ostracised for their political views.[15] This has been a consistent theme in American politics for decades: anti-intellectualism.

The New Deal of the 1930s[16] was seen by many as the brainchild of East-coast intellectuals, who finally got their comeuppance in the post-war McCarthyite purges. But it did not stop there; Republican candidates have always tended to emphasise that their learning came from the 'university of life' rather than at an Ivy League institution. Donald Trump, who has displayed all the intellectual ability of a bag of spanners, is only the latest in a long line of anti-intellectuals on the American Right.

Of course, such tactics are used in the UK as well. Nigel Farage, for example, has successfully cultivated a blokish image, appearing in the media with either a fag or a pint in his hand. Like his American counterparts, he railed against liberal intellectuals, who were responsible for allowing immigrants into the country. But anti-intellectualism is not the sole preserve of extremist bigots; it goes much deeper than that.

One observer points to the response he got when commenting on a social media story about Alfie Evans, who was the subject of a major legal fight between his parents and the hospital taking care of him.[17]

> During the tragic case of Alfie Evans, I posted a comment asking why people with no expertise, experience or qualifications in medicine thought they knew more than doctors and I received a flurry of anti-intellectual comments in response. Some of the most concerning answers included: "Doctors are morons" and "I don't need a medical degree, I have common sense".[18]

The writer's aim was to show how anti-intellectual the British are, in contrast to the French, who are proud of people like Jean-Paul Sartre, Simone De Beauvoir and Albert Camus. Ed Rooksby, of Ruskin College, Oxford, showed that such anti-intellectualism and love of the 'common-sense' approach, dated back to Edmund Burke and was a repudiation of the theories and ideas of the French Revolution.[19] Burke's writings became the foundation of British Conservatism.

In fact, it has been claimed that such notions of 'common sense' long predated the French Revolution, even going back as far as the English Civil War.

> The radical wing of the Parliamentarian movement – groups such as the Diggers and Levellers – made frequent reference to 'reason' in relation to their

demands for radical redistribution of land and wealth. It was in this period that the powerful came to associate rational abstraction and theory with dangerous levelling tendencies – 'ideas' were suspect since they could be corrosive of people's taken-for-granted acceptance of the established social order as 'just the way things are'.[20]

In this analysis the English, and later the British, ruling classes deliberately encouraged the 'common sense' approach to all subjects in order to keep dangerous ideas and hypotheses in check. It has to be said that this strategy, if that was what it was, was remarkably successful. The British working classes might have read and discussed Marx,[21] but a revolutionary spirit never really materialised. The British Labour Party, although leaning toward Socialism, was remarkably pragmatic and seemed to be infused with 'common sense' rather than idealism.

Not only were the upper classes encouraging a 'common sense' and anti-intellectual outlook among the lower orders; they believed in it themselves. It has long been the case among the British upper classes that one should be clever, but not *too* clever. Attending a top fee-paying school, you would have Greek and Latin beaten into you, so the chances were, unless you were an absolute dimwit, that you would learn something. At the very least, you would have the ability to discuss things that ordinary folk would know nothing about. And then there is Oxbridge.

For ordinary people and those that are middle-class, getting into Oxford or Cambridge is a difficult and even harrowing process.[22] For those attending expensive, fee-paying schools, however, entry seems to be a foregone conclusion. This is especially the case for those at Eton, from where most Conservative politicians appear to come. Whether the entrance exams and interviews are specifically geared towards Etonians, or whether pupils at the school are admitted automatically is unclear. It certainly seems, though, that being at Eton virtually guarantees one an Oxbridge education.[23]

Of course, not all Tories that went from Eton to Oxbridge were non-academics; Anthony Eden and David Cameron both achieved Firsts. In the main, though, they have tended to get Seconds or even Thirds. Mind you, even those grades are impressive when you consider that most of their time at university is spent at endless rounds of parties.[24] It makes one wonder if they have actually done the work required to get those degrees.

Anyone that has read Tom Sharpe's book, *Porterhouse Blue*, or has seen the TV series of the same name, will be familiar with 'Skullion's Scholars'. Skullion, (Fig.32) the Head Porter of Porterhouse College, Cambridge, organises for clever students to write dissertations and sit exams for upper-class students, leaving the latter free to enjoy all the social life the university has to offer. Everybody wins. Upper-class students get their degrees, while clever-but-poor students get some money in their pockets. I suspect that there is more than a hint of truth in Sharpe's story and that the degrees of many among the upper classes would not stand up to close scrutiny!

For anyone doubting the lack of integrity among the upper classes, studies in America have shown that the privileged in society care about nothing but themselves. They are prepared to lie, steal, cheat and even break the law to gain an advantage over others.[25] Since such people are prepared to behave completely unethically in any situation, it would hardly come as a surprise to find that they cheat to gain their degrees too. And yet, they despise the intellectuals that got their degrees for them.

Working-class people also have a long-standing hatred for intellectuals and intellectualism. An Irish labourer in Scotland, who had ambitions of being a writer, was told by his brother,

> If you'd just been a poof the priest could have talked
> to you or one of us could have battered it out of you.
> But what the hell can anyone do about a writer?[26]

During the Miners' Strike, in 1984, it was decided by the Stirling University Students' Union that NUM members would be allowed into student functions. There was no real Students Union place at the time; it was just the Allangrange

149

Student/Staff Club, known as 'The Grange'. This was not owned by the students' union, which is probably why I met no miners there. Discos at the Pathfoot Building, however, were a different matter.

It was at one of these that a character called 'Stan' introduced himself to the small crowd I was with. Stan was with five of his mates, who, as usually happened, did not have to put their hands in their pockets all night as students competed to buy them drinks. Stan decided to have a go at us, demanding that we show up for a planned NUM march. Feeling brave after a few pints, I asked him if he had been at the recent march to stop the Government introducing student loans.

'And why would I want to go marching to help a bunch of poofy students?' was his reply.

His mates growled aggressively, which was our cue to move elsewhere. I heard the next day that some idiots invited them to their flat on campus for a party. The students in the flat ended up having to barricade themselves in their rooms as the miners emptied the contents of the living room/kitchen through the windows. And I do mean *through* the windows. The fridge and cooker went first, creating a big enough hole in the windows and their frames to allow tables, chairs and couches to follow them. Somebody outside phoned the police, but the miners were long-gone by the time they arrived. Miners were not exactly welcomed with open arms from then on and, after a couple of weeks, we saw no more of them.

Whether Stan had children or not, I have no idea. It was obvious from his attitude that he would not want them going to university. Maybe his kids rebelled and did go on to higher education. That would have been in the 1990s and they would have racked up loads of debt from relying on student loans. Then again, they would have been luckier than today's working-class teenagers, who often cannot afford to go to university at all. University has gone back to being the preserve of the middle classes.[27]

Attempts have been made to remedy this by introducing quotas, something the *Daily Mail* railed against, claiming that bright, middle-class pupils from independent schools were losing out on university places.[28] Despite these attempts to

150

balance things, and the *Daily Mail*'s hyperbolic scandal mongering, it remains the fact that university students are overwhelmingly middle-class. This, of course, adds to working-class hatred of intellectuals.

One individual, a lawyer from a working-class background, is full of this hatred toward what he calls 'elites'. Although he calls these middle-class people that want to stay in the EU 'snobs', his own snobbery toward such people comes through clearly.

> In June 2016, the train was de-classified and millions of 'gammon' plebs invaded the quiet, middle-class comfort of the elites. They have still not recovered from it. It has driven them half mad with fury. They are overwhelmed by spite and malice. Their response has been brutal and swift, and we haven't seen the last of it yet.[29]

The same sort of line was trotted out in The *Guardian*, with a reporter complaining that a left-leaning journalist, Ian Dunt, had Tweeted,

> Sick and tired of sending out cash to the rest of the country so they can whine about London and the immigrants who made it for them.[30]

The reporter goes on to blame the whole of middle-class London, which had voted Remain, for the snooty, and mistaken, opinion of Dunt. She trips herself up somewhat, however, by stating,

> In conversations with leave voters, I've found that the cost of EU membership, unnecessary regulations and lack of democratic accountability are cited almost as often as immigration as primary concerns.[31]

Perhaps she was unaware but, as we saw earlier, whenever Leave voters were challenged on these 'concerns' they could give no examples at all. The main thrust of the reporter's article, however, was not on Leave voters but on 'metropolitan elites'. Quite who those 'metropolitan elites' are, she does not say. That is left to others to explain.

Right-wing journalist, David Goodhart described the 'metropolitan elites' as people that opine, 'We've done it. We've gone off to good universities and become middle-class professionals, why can't you do it?'[32] Again, it is an attack on intellectualism; those 'metropolitan elites' have all been to university.

Another right-wing journalist, Andrew Doyle, interviewed American Peter Boghossian, assistant professor of philosophy at Portland State University, on his podcast.[33] The subject was the 'legitimation crisis' in higher education – the 'fact' that nobody trusted academics anymore. Of course, Boghossian concentrated on American universities, which, he claimed, were overrun with folk that subscribed to left-wing ideologies. The consequence was the abandonment of truth.

According to Boghossian, academics in America, and elsewhere, published books and papers in journals that were full of ideas and hypotheses with no real evidence. (We encountered this antipathy to 'ideas' earlier in the chapter.) Other academics would quote from these works, which would in turn be cited by the original academics as well as others. This goes around and around, building a smokescreen that masquerades as fact, when it is evidently not.

Strangely, this describes exactly the way the right-wing media, both in the UK and the USA, behaves. In Doyle's podcast, he and Boghossian show remarkable hypocrisy. They criticise members of the American Civil Liberties Union for suggesting that a book written by yet another right-wing journalist, Abigail Shrier, should be banned. Shrier's book, *Irreversible Damage: The Transgender Craze Seducing Our Daughters*,[34] discusses the issue of Rapid Onset Gender Dysphoria. Unfortunately, this phenomenon has no basis in medical science and there is doubt in many quarters that it exists.[35] Shrier merely uses ideas broadcast by others without any real evidence and, by Boghossian's own criteria, should be under attack by him.

Andrew Doyle uses the same methodology as Shrier in his criticism of anti-racism being taught in British schools. Even private schools are supporting Black Lives Matter,

> ...despite the fact that this explicitly anti-capitalist movement objects to their existence and would happily see these institutions razed to the ground.[36]

This is the usual, right-wing opinion of the Black Lives Matter movement, which has no basis in fact. Doyle is just regurgitating the ideas of others with the same political prejudices as his own. He even calls new curricula, which downplay colonial triumphalism, 'brainwashing' and 'indoctrination', ignoring completely that the same charges could be levelled at the learning of the greatness of the British Empire.

In that podcast with Peter Boghossian,[37] Doyle mentions a report by the Adam Smith Institute, which says that only 12% of academics at British institutions of higher learning supports right-wing or conservative parties. Whatever the reasons for this 'ideological homogeneity', the report recommends:

> raising awareness; being alert to double standards; encouraging adversarial collaborations; and emphasizing the benefits of ideological heterogeneity within the academy.[38]

That sounds suspiciously like the advocation of positive discrimination! I wonder how the *Daily Mail* would respond to that, given its hostility to positive discrimination in favour of children from poor backgrounds. With its usual hypocrisy, it would probably be all for it!

One of the possible reasons given by the Adam Smith Institute for most academics being left-wing is that

> The left-liberal skew may be partly explained by openness to experience; individuals who score highly on that personality trait tend to pursue intellectually stimulating careers like academia.

> And within the top 5% of IQ, openness to experience predicts support for left-wing parties.[39]

If a right-wing organisation like the Adam Smith Institute can admit that intelligence might be a factor in academics being more left-wing proportionally than the rest of the population, then others should be able to as well. As you might expect, however, they do not. It hardly matters *why* intellectuals are mostly left-wing; to the Tories, they just are. That is why the Tories usually profess to wanting nothing to do with such people.

We have already seen how business leaders thought that Brexit was going to be a disaster. Top economists felt exactly the same way and gave out dire warnings prior to the Referendum.[40] The Justice Secretary, Michael Gove, when pressed on this on Sky News, replied that the British 'have had enough of experts.'[41] As usual, the Tories, just like their voters, preferred the 'common-sense' approach. This, unfortunately, was to cause difficulties in 2020, something we shall come back to later.

Anti-intellectualism can, in some sense, be considered a consequence of democracy. Rather, though, it is a twisted interpretation of democracy. In this scenario, everyone's opinion is of equal value; even somebody that goes online and spouts any old crap is considered as valid as an expert that has studied a subject for years. Anybody with any sense knows that this cannot always be the case. Somebody with a basic qualification in General Science cannot possibly know as much about, say, Quantum Mechanics as an expert that has spent the best part of a lifetime studying it. Not everyone, however, has sense, common or otherwise.

The internet is often claimed to be a great tool for democracy and equality. It is, but the downside is that it has opened a door for every tinfoil-hat-wearing lunatic to expound their insane notions. It is no longer a case of common sense versus intelligent theories; in fact, empirical evidence is often on the side of the experts. Crazy ideas, such as the Jews ruling the world, elites extracting chemicals from the brains of children for their own use and Donald Trump being the new Messiah have no evidence whatsoever to support them. Indeed, *real* common sense tells one that they are a load of rubbish.

The most common argument in the USA is that of fundamentalist Protestants against scientists. These Protestants believe that every word of the Bible is the absolute truth and will brook no argument otherwise. To their minds, God made the World and everything in it in six days, as it says in Genesis. Of course, they are perfectly entitled to believe whatever they want, but that is not enough for them. They want everyone to go along with their beliefs and, to this end, they want schools to give equal weight to Creationism and Evolution. Rather worryingly, it seems that 42% of Americans believe in Creationism.[42] Even more worrying is that fact that these beliefs exist closer to home.

In Northern Ireland a group called the *Caleb Foundation*, which also advocates Creationism in schools and a literal interpretation of the Bible, has a lot of influence on the Democratic Unionist Party.[43] This does not make a difference to everyone's day-to-day life (yet!), but the group's influence shows up occasionally. The National Trust's Visitor's Centre at the Giant's Causeway, for example, includes references to Creationism and the Earth only being 6,000 years old.[44]

Britain might not have influential religious fundamentalists, but it has a huge reservoir of semi-educated people ready to believe any right-wing nonsense thrown at them. This is Thatcher's legacy: all those she threw on the scrapheap in the 1980s brought up children that had no hope and no ambition. Such children are practically impossible to teach since their parents have raised them to believe that education is a waste of time, and that school is just there to stop you enjoying life. Those children grow up and have their own children, and so it has gone on for forty-odd years.

When they leave school, these characters realise that they are practically unemployable and look for someone to blame. Obviously, it was the fault of the teachers, who, they all insist, hated them and constantly picked on them. They pass these attitudes onto *their* children in turn. Such people, even those

155

that spend their time destroying their brain cells with drink and drugs, are easy prey for right-wing rabble-rousers.

One team of writers says that 'anti-intellectualism is evoked as a way to halt the acquisition of new knowledge that would undermine groups with power and privilege.'[45] We saw this happen with Brexit, where the upper classes, for their own ends, convinced many among the unemployed that European immigrants were 'stealing their jobs.' This belief was stirred up by characters like Nigel Farage but, ultimately, it was the Tories that benefited.

Exactly as the experts predicted, once Brexit went through and all the Europeans were thrown out, there was a massive labour shortage in many industries. Abattoir workers were in short supply, meaning livestock had to be culled, while a lack of lorry drivers reduced the supplies of petrol in petrol stations and goods in supermarkets.[46] Meanwhile, crops had to be left to rot in the fields as there were no workers to pick them.[47] What happened to all those that had claimed that immigrants were stealing their jobs? They should have been beating down the doors at the Jobcentre!

There is one final aspect of anti-intellectualism that is rarely, if ever, commented upon: comics. We saw in Chapter 1 how comics were used to sell the idea of Empire and even to keep racism alive when the Empire was all but gone. There was also a distinct anti-intellectualism inherent in most, if not all, comics. Practically every child character had a 'Swotty Simpkins' in their class at school.

In the 1960s and 1970s, and perhaps even into the 1980s, child characters always hated school and often played truant. This was presented as normal and the only ones that liked school were the Swotty Simpkins types. Children in real life that enjoyed school and learning would read these comics and realise that they were not *normal*. The only way they could become normal would be to play up in school, not bother learning and even play truant now and again. One cannot help but wonder how many children were affected by these stereotypes.

Only one character was allowed to be clever: Roger the Dodger. His intellect, however, was put to practical use as he invented ways to get out of doing chores and going to school.

He, like every other character, had no interest at all in using his intelligence to actually *learn* anything. And, just like every other misbehaving character, he gets his comeuppance in the end, usually by means of a slipper applied to his backside.

Another character that always ended up on the wrong end of a slipper was Dennis the Menace. In the 60s and early 70s, Dennis was a nasty piece of work. He was a bully, a thug and a hooligan. Dad was always on hand, though, with his slipper and the final frame usually had Dennis across Dad's lap, awaiting the raised hand holding the footwear to make contact. This all changed, though, as it had to.

As public feeling turned against corporal punishment, so Dennis's traits had to be reined in. He could not be seen to be acting the way he did without being punished; being sent to 'Time Out' simply was not going to cut it. Instead of behaving like a thug, Dennis started to have adventures. He also acquired a gang of friends, who were the fierce rivals of Softy Walter (Fig.33) and his friends, the Softies. Needless to say, Walter and his gang all loved school and learning. The fact that the Softies were all rather effeminate sissies showed how those that were intellectual were meant to be perceived.

Dennis took over as the Beano's mascot, replacing Biffo the Bear in this respect, even taking over the front page. Biffo was relegated to an inside page and was eventually handed his P45 in the 1980s. Dennis, the school-hating, softy-bashing anti-intellectual was being portrayed as a role model for children. The right-wing agenda behind this could not have been any more blatant.

But it is not just comics that have been used to indoctrinate children. Other methods and other media have been employed to make sure that children grow up to respect and revere the Establishment. We shall now look at some of these in more detail.

157

10
The End of Rock 'n' Roll

The idea that teaching children in a certain way will form a certain type of adult has variously been attributed to the Jesuits and Aristotle, but it is something that all of us should stop and consider. There is nothing truer than the first line of Philip Larkin's poem, *This Be The Verse*, 'They fuck you up, your mum and dad.'[1] It is not just parents to blame, though. Quite a lot of others have a hand in it too.

From an early age, children are told fairy tales, most of which are about kings and queens. The ultimate accomplishment for any young woman is to marry a handsome prince, as Cinderella did. All the kings, queens, princes and princesses in the stories are good as well as handsome or beautiful. Any that do not fit this profile are not *real* royals, but imposters, like the Evil Queen in *Snow White*, who is, in fact, a witch. The genuine, good kings, queens, princes and princesses are all loved by their subjects, which stands to reason since they are kind and caring.

This attitude carries on into adulthood and it is amazing how much people in Britain love the Royal Family and refuse to believe anything bad about them. Even when the evidence is nearly overwhelming, as is the case with Prince Andrew and the allegations that he had sex with a minor, trafficked by his then friend, Jeffrey Epstein.[2] Meanwhile, anyone that accuses the Royal Family of being anything but perfect, like Prince Harry and his wife, Meghan Markle have done, is vilified by all and sundry.

Even when it comes to the taxpayer handing over millions to one of the richest women in the world, folk make excuses. 'She works hard for that money,' they say. 'She's worth every penny!' They even argue that the Queen brings in more money than she costs, since she brings in tourists. Actually, far more tourists visit Paris's Palace of Versailles[3] than they do all

Britain's royal properties put together.[4] It looks as though getting rid of royals means more visitors to palaces.

Another aspect of fairy tales that influences adults' opinions is that anyone can become royal. The many young women applying to study at St Andrews University in hopes of meeting Prince William[5] was reminiscent of all the excitement in Cinderella's house about the ball. The fact that William ended up marrying a middle-class girl he met at the university only increased the fairy-tale excitem
ent. After all, William had a younger brother!

Becoming a royal when you are female is a competitive business both in Fairy-Tale Land and in the real world. For males it is well-nigh impossible. A king might offer his daughter's hand in marriage, but, usually, you have to slay a dragon to win that particular bride. In the real world, dragons tend to be in short supply, so any young man's royal ambitions are hamstrung right from the start. Besides, even in fairy tales, any lad looking to marry a princess has to have one characteristic; he has to be noble.

The word 'noble' crops up a lot in fairy tales and other children's stories. You can have a 'noble heart,' a 'noble bearing' and even a 'noble brow'! Having a noble heart means that you are full of goodness, whereas a noble bearing or a noble brow means that you look as if you are a member of the nobility. Both meanings come from the same source, the Latin word *nobilis*, which mostly depicted someone that was high-born. The use of the word 'noble' in children's stories reinforces the idea that aristocrats, not just royals, are all good. In fact, the very word 'aristocrat' comes from the Ancient Greek word *aristos*, which means *best*. Aristocracy means 'rule by the best'.

Speaking of the Ancient Greeks, the heroes of most, if not all, of their stories were kings or members of the nobility. A phrase usually employed to describe such a hero was *kalos k'agathos*, which means handsome and good. This description will be familiar to parents reading fairy tales to their children; the prince, or any other male aristocrat, is always handsome and good.

Sometimes, though, an aristocrat can be evil. This problem is usually solved by making such an aristocrat a count or a baron

(Fig.34), both of which tend to be used in foreign countries.[6] One cannot expect a foreigner, even a member of the nobility, to be good, can one? It usually takes a common lad with a noble heart to defeat this character.

As we have seen elsewhere in the book, many adults in Britain almost worship the Royal Family and the aristocracy and it is no accident. They have been subjected to what is essentially propaganda since they were toddlers. And it does not stop there. Films, especially those made by Disney, reinforce these propaganda elements.

Of course, many Disney films are based on the fairy tales discussed above, with beautiful princesses, handsome princes and lads with noble hearts. Little girls were taken with Elsa in *Frozen*, and she joined Cinderella and Snow White as beloved characters that they could dress up as. They all want to be beautiful princesses and it would be a heartless parent indeed that burst their bubble by telling them that they were too ugly and too lower-class to ever become one!

It is not just girls that enjoy these films about princesses; everybody probably has happy memories of seeing *Snow White and the Seven Dwarves*, *Cinderella* and *Sleeping Beauty*. It might well explain the myths that have grown around a real beautiful princess, Diana, one time Princess of Wales. Just like her movie counterparts, stories have circulated about Diana's goodness, kindness and noble heart. Quite how true the stories are has become irrelevant; she has been turned into a real-life fairy tale princess.

Then, there are religious stories, which some people believe are simply fairy tales as well. We all know about Solomon, whose wisdom, kindness and handsomeness could make him the hero of any fairy tale. King Herod is painted as decidedly evil in the Bible but then, he was a usurper, appointed by the Romans and not a *proper* king. And then we come to Jesus.

Although children know all about the Christmas story of Jesus being born in a stable and ostensibly coming from humble origins, they are also taught to sing *Hosanna to the King of Kings*. In fact, many references are made to Jesus being a king: King of Heaven, King of Angels etc. (Fig.35)

160

They might also learn that Jesus was descended from King David. It all helps to contribute to the idea that royalty and aristocracy are more special and more important than other mere mortals.

When children are a bit older, they are still bombarded by Tory propaganda. A prime example of this is the *Harry Potter* books and films. One commentor points out that the whole notion of Hogwarts's pupils being *chosen* sets those pupils out as being special, almost aristocratic. The *noblesse oblige* of the wizarding characters toward magical creatures like elves reinforces the idea that Harry Potter and his friends are aristocratic Tories.[7] There are other elements to the story that support these claims.

In the very first book, Harry discovers that he is to go to an old, exclusive, fee-paying boarding school. This is in stark contrast to where his uncle was going to send him – gasp! – the local comprehensive! Harry also finds out that he is stinking rich and, in the final two books, that he is descended from wizarding aristocracy. Meanwhile, the character he fights against, Lord Voldemort, is not a *real* lord.

As we saw in an earlier chapter, television plays its part in promoting this vision of the upper classes being almost superhuman. The BBC's famous Sunday serials were a case in point. As well as this, television, as well as films, is responsible for other types of Tory propaganda as well; different, but no less powerful.

Many adverts target children directly, and not just so they can guilt-trip their parents into buying the latest, must-have product. There is more to it than that. Adverts, as well as television programmes and films, can influence children in other ways; ways that are almost subliminal. The following is key to this kind of propaganda.

> Studies have found that children do not have the ability to skeptically (sic) view marketing messages or even identify advertisements as marketing messages until they are in their teens. This means that marketing messages can be perceived as truths,

and in many cases, those messages can stay with
them until they become adults.[8]

This quote comes from a website that is concerned with the
negative effects that advertising has on children. It concentrates
on unhealthy eating habits, negative body images and the
objectification of women, but there are other elements present
in adverts that nobody seems to have studied yet.

Everyone old enough remembers the advert that ran in the
1980s and 1990s for Milky Way: 'The red car and the blue car
had a race…'[9] When it was revived years later, they had to
change some of the words. They were no longer allowed to say
that Milky Way would not spoil your appetite. In terms of the
studies mentioned above, young viewers of the original advert
would grow up believing that the chocolate bar was
insubstantial, even healthy. But what else would they have
gleaned from it? Well, they would have learned that blue was
the colour of Winners, while red was that of Losers.

This might sound like some kind of mad conspiracy theory,
but advertisers frequently use colours to evoke different
emotions around products.[10] The weird thing is that these
colours are discussed as if the feelings they arouse are somehow
innate; something people are born with. This is countered
somewhat, though, by the revelation that purple is 'commonly
associated with royalty, wisdom, and respect in color (sic)
psychology.'[11] How could anybody be born with a sense of
'royalty' and its association with the colour purple? Obviously,
such associations are learned.

The idea that children learn which emotions are associated
with particular colours is supported by the fact that a colour can
mean different things in different cultures. For example, the
colour blue stands for sadness and melancholy in traditional
western culture, but in Hinduism it means love and joy.[12] Blue
is also predominantly associated with boys in the West, whereas
it is a feminine colour in China.[13] This, and other examples,
prove categorically that the association of a colour with a
particular feeling or emotion is learned.

So, what are children taught about colours? Well, that Milky
Way advert is not the only place where you see red and blue in

opposition. It is standard in cartoons for blue to represent good and red evil. In Disney's *Aladdin* (the cartoon one) Aladdin is almost always seen against a blue background, while Jafar stands before a red one. Meanwhile, in the *Star Wars* films you can tell the Jedi Knights from the Sith Lords by their light sabres; the Jedis' light sabres are blue, while those of the Sith are red.[14]

There are plenty of other examples out there, which I am sure you will be relieved to find I am not going to list here. Like everything else, once you notice it you will be surprised that you did not notice it before and at how ubiquitous it is.

Blue has been adopted as the colour of right-of-centre parties everywhere, due to the British Tories' use of it since the 19th Century.[15] Red, meanwhile, is the worldwide colour of Socialism and the Left. In America, red is often used for the Republican Party, but this has just developed because television has needed a colour to show which states have voted for which party.[16] If you were to walk through a backwoods, Trump-supporting area in the States waving a red flag, you would soon discover that Republicans do not see it as their colour. The phrase, 'Better Dead than Red' does not refer to the Republicans at all.

In the UK, these colour associations are practically brainwashing our children into believing that blue is good and red is bad. As stated above, what children learn from adverts stays with them into adulthood. New generations of Tory voters are being produced without anyone, least of all the voters themselves, even being aware of it. Even when children became, and become, teenagers, the long tentacles of the Establishment are still looking to influence them and control them.

Young people can be a worry for the British Establishment as they tend to be unruly and not very fond of authority. This is especially true of working-class teenagers and always has been, even before teenagers were aware of themselves as a separate group. During WWII, gangs of teenagers that were not old enough to be called up for service terrorised Britain, looting, mugging and even raping. With most men away fighting, there was not a lot could be done about them.

In the 1950s, music engendered an almost exclusively teen culture. American Rock and Roll frightened the life out of the British Establishment, especially when Teddy Boys started ripping up cinema seats during showings of films like *Rock Around the Clock*. It seems incredible that people were frightened of the Platters and Bill Haley and the Comets, but the new music seemed scary, like youth culture itself. And worse was to come. The blatant sexuality of Elvis Presley, the wild onstage antics of Jerry Lee Lewis, the raucous performances of Little Richard and the sheer energy of Chuck Berry were enough to induce apoplexy in the older generation.

The answer was for Britain to have its own version of Rock and Roll. Impresario Larry Parnes signed up artists that he renamed Tommy Steele and Marty Wilde. He also signed Joe Brown, who insisted on keeping his own name. Another impresario and TV producer, Jack Good, was involved in promoting the careers of Adam Faith and Cliff Richard. What all these acts had in common was that they were pretty anodyne and inoffensive. They were also promoted not just as Rock and Roll singers, but as all-round entertainers. They were pale imitations of American Rock and Roll and posed no threat to the Establishment. So acceptable were they that most of them appeared in the *Royal Variety Performance*.

In the 1960s, Rock and Roll fell out of favour to be replaced in Britain by R&B, which took American Blues as its roots. Again, though, Britain's, and soon to be the World's, biggest band, the Beatles, saw fit to play at the *Royal Variety Performance* in 1963. To add insult to injury, any rebellious credibility they still retained died when they accepted MBEs in 1965.

Although bands and singers were no longer expected to be all-round entertainers, they were expected to appear on variety and chat shows and even comedy shows as part of the light entertainment. So it was that The Who could find themselves on the same bill as Jimmy Tarbuck,[17] while the Rolling Stones appeared on the TV comedy the *Arthur Haynes Show*.[18] It was difficult for such stalwarts of mainstream entertainment to be considered any kind of threat to the Establishment.

It was the same in the late 60s and early 70s. For all everyone seems to think it was a time of social unrest, that could hardly have been further from the truth in Britain. While teenagers rioted all over Europe and America, it was business as usual in Britain. The music reflected the total lack of revolutionary spirit. The psychedelic and hippy bands and the prog rock ones that followed sang about witches, gnomes and goblins. Their inspiration came from Tolkien rather than Marx.

Those were the so-called serious groups, who played album-oriented rock for bored, middle-class males. Of course, there were working-class teens that felt the same way and sat in their bedrooms listening to Emerson Lake and Palmer, Yes and Genesis. None of these bands had anything political to say, let alone try to stir up a revolution. The most popular band among these characters was Pink Floyd, who sang songs of middle-class angst for middle-class, male listeners. It was hardly exciting stuff. One song could take up the whole side of an album, only for the listener to discover that it was just the intro and the song continued on the other side!

Most teenagers, however, could not stand all the prog rock, album-oriented stuff and preferred the music played on the radio. *Top of the Pops* was a highlight in everyone's week as they looked to see if their current favourites had made it to Number 1 in the charts. At different points in the early-to-mid 70s, the charts were dominated by T-Rex, The Sweet, Slade, Rod Stewart, Gary Glitter, Elton John, the Bay City Rollers and others too numerous to mention.

None of these groups had anything even remotely political to say, but they still provided the younger generation with a feeling of rebellion. Not that teenage boys walked abroad wearing make-up and face glitter like their glam-rock heroes, but they did copy their clothes. Items like platform shoes and flared trousers looked effeminate to parents, so teenage boys could indulge in a bit of harmless rebellion. With boys as well as girls having long hair, and both sexes wearing the same clothes, adults complained that you could not tell them apart. They did not understand that that was the whole point!

The papers might rage about the androgyny of David Bowie, Marc Bolan and Steve Priest of The Sweet and of young people in general, but it was half-hearted shock. There was no challenge to the Establishment in any of the music or fashion;

165

on the contrary, it encouraged consumerism, which was what the Establishment wanted. It was all completely harmless and comfortably anodyne.

If somebody tried to rock the boat, as Paul McCartney did with his record *Give Ireland Back to the Irish*, it was a simple enough job to ban it from the airwaves. (It can come as a bit of a shock to discover not only that Paul McCartney once had something political to say, but that there was a time when young people bought McCartney's records!) It did manage to reach 16 in the UK charts,[19] even without airplay, but most people would not have heard it since it was not on the radio.

The same tactics were used at the end of the 1970s, when the Sex Pistols' *God Save the Queen* was banned from radio and TV. Like the Paul McCartney single, people still bought it and it ended up getting to Number 2 in the charts. There are even rumours that it was actually Number 1, and the BBC rigged the charts. At any rate, folk were stopped from hearing it, but the problem was that there were a lot more punk bands around; the BBC could not ban them all.

Bands like The Clash, The Jam and, although not strictly punk, the Tom Robinson Band spouted angry lyrics over angry music. They were angry about the whole system and even spoke of rioting. Unlike the bands of ten years before, none of these individuals would ever dream of taking some kind of medal from the Queen. Not that any OBEs or MBEs would be likely to come their way; they frightened the hell out of the Establishment.

After all the excitement of the late 1970s, the 1980s were something of a disappointment musically. The 'next big thing' turned out to be the New Romantics, who were about as far from punk as you could get. Bands like Duran Duran, Spandau Ballet, Visage and Adam and the Ants appeared to be empty vessels, interested in nothing more than 'looking flash and grabbing your attention.' Once they had our attention, they had nothing to offer but narcissism.

As the decade progressed, so the music seemed to reflect the political situation. The Pet Shop Boys sang about individual ambition, 'Let's make lots of money', while even Johnny Rotten seemed to be praising Capitalism in *This is Not a Love Song*.

Queen's fascist anthem, *We Are the Champions* had never been so popular, along with their other such songs, *One Vision* and *It's a Kind of Magic*.

Dance music became popular again, with House Music, Stock, Aitken and Waterman records and those God-awful medleys, like *Stars On 45*. It was like the mid-1970s again, with some good tunes but nothing else. Where seven years previously everyone was excited by the Sex Pistols, in 1984, most excitement was generated by Frankie Goes to Hollywood. Morons everywhere stifled a titter as they pointed out to their friends that Holly Johnson was singing about 'cumming'.

Of course, there were still bands around that made political statements through their songs, like The Jam, The Specials, Style Council, Fun Boy Three and Heaven 17. In fact, two of these songs got to Number 1, namely *Going Underground* and *Ghost Town*. You have to wonder, though, if a lot of the people buying these records were actually aware of what they were about. I have heard *Ghost Town* played at children's Halloween parties, along with *Ghostbusters* and *Thriller*, which makes me guess that many people are unaware of its meaning. And Fun Boy Three's anti-Tory song, *The Lunatics Have Taken Over the Asylum* prompted floods of letters to newspapers complaining that they were making a fool of people with mental health problems!

Further proof that folk do not know what the hell they are listening to came in the shape of David Cameron. It was back in 2008, before he became Prime Minister, that he told a Radio 4 programme that his favourite song was The Jam's *Eton Rifles*. Paul Weller, lead singer of The Jam and the writer of the song, was outraged.

> Which part of it didn't he get? It wasn't intended as a fucking jolly drinking song for the cadet corps.[20]

> Not everyone reads the lyrics! Sometimes, it's just a nice sound in the background.[21]

Cameron, of course, attended Eton so was, perforce, a member of the Cadets. According to him, he and the other boys were big fans of The Jam, saying, 'It meant a lot, some of those early Jam albums we used to listen to.'[22] The single *The Eton Rifles* was released in October 1979, when Cameron was thirteen years old. Perhaps what he meant by 'It meant a lot' was that the albums were a comfort to the youngsters when their arses were being caned, or otherwise abused, by older pupils.

Another comment by Cameron that underscores Weller's fury was, 'I don't see why the left should be the only ones allowed to listen to protest songs.'[23] Protest songs? That conjures up images of Peter, Paul and Mary singing *Blowin' in the Wind*, rather than Weller's slice of working-class anger. But Paul Weller was not the only one that was pissed-off with Cameron's apparent love of music.

In 2010, Johnny Marr, who had been guitarist in The Smiths, lost it when Cameron announced he was a fan of the 1980s band.[24] Actually, though, it was hard to see what Marr was complaining about; The Smiths never had even one song like *The Eton Rifles* or *Going Underground*. Unless you count militant vegetarianism, they had about as much to say politically as Kylie Minogue!

Morrissey, The Smiths' singer and lyricist, was obsessed with the 'Angry Young Man' films of the late 1950/early 1960s.[25] Stills from the movies were used as cover artwork for The Smiths' singles and albums, while some of the dialogue made its way into their song lyrics.[26] But were those films not political? Well, yes and no.

As mentioned earlier, these films were not concerned with the lot of the working classes in society, but simply one man's preoccupation with his own place in that society. This rather selfish viewpoint came through in The Smiths' songs as well. There was always an element of 'I'll show 'em' in them. It was something that would appeal to the 'angry young man' in everyone, as well as those that felt like outsiders or picked on. It would also appeal to a millionaire's son having his arse shredded at Eton. Unlike those of The Jam, there was nothing in The Smiths' lyrics that excluded the likes of David Cameron, even if he was fond of a hamburger or two.

A lot of erstwhile fans of The Smiths are nowadays upset and nonplussed about Morrissey's support for the extreme right-wing group Britain First. He has also shown support for racists, which means that he is positioning himself as one of those racists as well.[27] Maybe nobody should be surprised about Morrissey's politics. After all, his obsession with the 1960s continued after The Smiths split up; he even sang about the Kray Twins. It was only a matter of time before he discovered Enoch Powell!

Back to the 1980s and Daily Record columnist Joan Burnie made an observation in the 31st of December 1989 edition of the paper. It was one of those 'looking back over the past year' kinds of thing, except this time it was a decade they were talking about. Joan Burnie said that the soundtrack of the 1980s was the rattling of the collection tin. She was right. The 1980s was when *Children in Need* started, giving Tory-voting individuals the chance to salve their consciences a little by handing over a tenner once a year.

It used to make you feel sick when denizens of Edinburgh's New Town dressed up as cartoon characters and the like, shaking a collection tin in your face when, if they paid their fair share of tax, there would not be any children in need in the UK. These well-to-do hypocrites also joined in enthusiastically with other charities, like *Comic Relief*. It was the Tory way.

Since the 19th Century, many among the upper and middle classes in Britain have resented having to pay taxes and local rates. They do not mind their money going on the police and the armed forces, but they hate having to support the unemployed and the low-paid. They would prefer that the poor relied on charity, to which they could contribute and pat themselves on the back for doing so. At last, they had a government that agreed with their outlook and there were plenty of charities for them to feel good about throwing the odd tenner to. And July 1985 provided them with the biggest back-slapping exercise ever.

The idea of helping the starving of Ethiopia originally resulted in the single *Do They Know It's Christmas*, with various pop stars contributing to a line-up called Band Aid. It had been organised by Midge Ure and Bob Geldof after they had seen news reports about the famine in the North African nation. Things did not improve into the new year and Geldof and Ure decided to mount a huge concert to raise even more funds.

A lot has been said about Live Aid, much of it not exactly complimentary. Adam Ant was to call it, 'The end of rock 'n' roll,'[28] while others point out the failure of the whole enterprise due to the naivety of the ones organising the actual relief. That, however, is not what interests us here. What is relevant is the way Live Aid promoted a Tory way of looking at the world.

The line-up said a lot about the ethos behind the whole business.[29] Both in London and in Philadelphia, the programme was mostly made up of old, white men. In America, the Temptations and Stevie Wonder were the only black faces on stage, while at Wembley, Sade was the only non-white person appearing. She was also one of only two women on stage at Wembley. There were only two in Philadelphia too, Chrissie Hynde of the Pretenders and Alannah Currie of the Thompson Twins.

This parade of old, white men was reminiscent of the good, old days of the British Empire. Folk could hand over their cash, secure in the knowledge that they were doing their bit to help those poor, starving natives. Their consciences clear, they could continue to vote for the party that had fast-tracked a British citizen application so that a white South African, Zola Budd, could take part in the 1984 Olympics. Speaking of South Africa, some of the acts appearing at Live Aid had connections with the pariah state.

The South African government, as part of its apartheid system, set up so-called independent homelands where blacks were crammed into ghettoes. The United Nations refused to recognise these 'separate' nations and had long instituted economic, cultural and sporting boycotts of South Africa because of apartheid. To hopefully get around these regulations, one enterprising individual set up a luxury resort, called Sun City, in one of the homelands, Bophutswana. It had the added advantage of being able to offer gambling and topless showgirls, things that were banned in the puritanical state of South Africa.[30]

Like Las Vegas, Sun City needed top entertainers to keep the wealthy, white crowds coming, and there were plenty willing to take the fortunes on offer. Among those big names appearing at Sun City were Elton John,[31] Queen[32] and Status Quo,[33] all of whom also played on the Live Aid stage. Elton John and Queen had played at Sun City prior to 1985, while Status Quo went there in 1987. It betrayed a rather colonialist attitude, which cared nothing for black Africans unless they were starving.

Broadcaster Andy Kershaw later said of Geldof that he 'appears not to be interested in Africa's strengths, only in an Africa on its knees.'[34] Kershaw goes further in the article, saying that Geldof knows nothing about Africa at all. It certainly seemed that way in 1985 or, rather, it seemed as if he simply did not care. Hypocritically, a few months after Live Aid, Geldof took part on the record and in the video for *Sun City* by Artists United Against Apartheid.[35] Geldof might have been saying that he would not play Sun City, but he was not particularly bothered if anyone else did!

The stench of old, imperial attitudes continued after the Live Aid concert was over. Bob Geldof was given an honorary knighthood, which, since he was Irish, was not like a real knighthood. That has not stopped everyone from calling him 'Sir Bob' ever since. Midge Ure, on the other hand, although he had done as much as Geldof, received no such honour.[36] Perhaps it had something to do with the fact that Geldof attended a fee-paying school in Dublin,[37] while Ure came from a distinctly working-class background.[38]

Adam Ant was probably right when he called Live Aid 'the end of rock 'n' roll'; it was when rock and pop finally became an integral part of the Establishment. Of course, there were bands that had nothing to do with Live Aid, either because they had not been asked or had refused to take part. Their anti-Establishment credentials, however, were eventually to be thrown aside.

The Stranglers' *Waltzinblack* was used in TV chef, Keith Floyd's programmes, the Clash's *Should I Stay or Should I Go* appeared on a commercial for Levi jeans, while Captain Sensible of the Damned wrote and sang the theme for Jim Davidson's TV show *Big Break*. Even John Lydon, Johnny

Rotten himself, appeared in an advert for butter and on the TV programme *I'm A Celebrity Get Me Out of Here*. It looks like everybody eventually succumbs.

Besides all that, there is an intrinsic problem with music being anti-Establishment and rebellious. It was illustrated perfectly in the Specials' song *Rat Race*. The song rails against rich students but sounds in places as if the band has a grudge against academics in general. Apparently, having a PhD means that you are working for the Rat Race. So, somebody sitting in the ivory tower of academia is part of the capitalist system. This from a band that was raking cash in for a large company like Chrysalis!

And therein lies the problem. Even buying that record was taking part in the system and working for the Rat Race. Bands obviously want folk to hear their records, and the bigger the record company they sign to, the more distribution and promotion they will get. To the record companies, however, the bands are just commodities, to be sold to a target audience and then dropped when they go out of fashion. As a line in the Clash's *White Man in Hammersmith Palais* puts it, 'Turning rebellion into money.'

There was not much in the way of rebellion in the 1990s. The decade started with young people attending raves, often illegal ones, to take ecstasy and dance. It was hardly a challenge to the Establishment, although more than a few landowners were unhappy about huge parties happening on their property. The music reflected what was going on, with the dreadful *Ebeneezer Goode* by The Shamen getting to Number 1.

As the 90s wore on, there was less and less in the way of politics to be heard in popular music. Boy bands, like Take That, Boyzone, Westlife etc. by their very nature were not going to indulge in any politics in their songs; it might put young girls off. None of them had much to say in interviews either. Neither did bands that looked rebellious, like The Prodigy, whose Liam Howlett said, 'We're not a political band, we're an escapism band.'[39] Actually, that, in itself, was a political statement. There is nothing more Tory than escapism, closing one's eyes to what is going on in the real world.

Britpop was not much better. There was the band Pulp with *Common People*, but that was about it. Despite Oasis being chummy with Tony Blair, there did not seem to be anything political going on with them either. If there *was* anything political in their songs, their audience appeared to ignore it. That audience seemed to be mostly composed of what in England came to be known as 'chavs' and in Scotland are called 'neds'. They would stand around in groups singing *Morning Glory* while giggling and laughing. It has been said that the song was about cocaine,[40] but the giggling neds were unaware of that. To them, the song was just about waking up with an erection and they reacted in the same way as folk did to *Relax* over a decade earlier. And then came the Spice Girls.

Girls went crazy for the Spice Girls and their 'Girl Power' slogan. Unlike other groups, the Spice Girls were open about their politics, even though none of their songs were even implicitly political. Ginger Spice, Geri Halliwell said that Margaret Thatcher was 'the first Spice Girl, the pioneer of our ideology.'[41] The other four expressed equally Conservative views and were Eurosceptics and supporters of royalty and the aristocracy to boot.[42] Although this all came out in an interview in The Spectator, it was widely reported in the media and was bound to have an influence on their young fans.

In the 21st Century, there are so many different types of music that it is difficult to know what it is that young people listen to. There are things called Grime, Nerdcore, Dubstep, Trance and Steampunk among many, many others. Most of us oldies could not tell you anything about any of those music genres. In fact, there are probably plenty of young folk that have no idea either.

Strangely, music does not seem to have the hold over young people that it once did. Radio 1's audience figures are way below its 70s and 80s heyday and most of its listeners are in their late thirties or older.[43] Back in the glory days Radio 1 regularly got audiences of 24 million and its DJs were as famous as the pop stars whose records they played.[44] The decline of Radio 1, though, is not about the music *per se*. As the BBC's David Sillito puts it, 'The problem for Radio 1 is that today's generation gap is more about the way we consume music than the music itself.'[45]

Unlike earlier generations, young people these days would rather listen to online music apps like *Spotify*, which offer continuous music without somebody prattling on in between the songs. The youth of today are not used to having to listen or view according to the clock. They will watch programmes on Netflix or on BBC iPlayer rather than having to tune in at a certain time, as folk used to have to do. And apps like *Spotify* encourage young people to explore different types of music instead of just hearing what the radio DJ decides to play. They are as likely to listen to old music as they are to listen to new. This has an effect on the charts.

With young people preferring to stream music rather than buy it, it means that not as many sales are required these days to get into the charts. To get into the Top 40 requires a paltry sales figure of 8,000![46] Sales like that would have been seen as abject failure back in the 70s and 80s. To win a Gold Disc used to require 1 million sales, but nowadays only needs 400,000, while a record can go Platinum with only 600,000.[47] Music is nowhere near as important as it used to be. Obviously, young people have moved on to other forms of entertainment.

Most of that entertainment is provided by the ubiquitous mobile phone. A group of teenage girls used to be a noisy affair, but not nowadays. They might be sitting together on the bus, or on a bench, but they are not speaking; instead, each is looking at her own phone. Teenagers' eyes are still glued to their phones as they walk along the street and, quite often, they will bump into things or other people because they are not looking where they are going. Although they will be checking texts from their friends, much of what they are watching is on *TikTok*, *Instagram* or *YouTube*.

Becoming a celebrity has never been easier. Up until a few years ago, a contestant on *Big Brother* would often turn up later on *Celebrity Big Brother*. Simply appearing on TV made one a celebrity. Now, online media have all but taken over. Upload a funny video to *TikTok* and you could be famous for a short time, fulfilling Andy Warhol's prediction. Other people become famous on a long-term basis, gaining millions of followers on *Instagram* or *YouTube*. Such people often become what are known as 'influencers' and can be paid by or receive free items from manufacturers whose products they endorse.

Influencers can rake in millions, like revolting child toy reviewer, Ryan Kaji.[48] It is notable that one influencer, Jeffree Star, packed in a budding musical career to promote beauty products on *YouTube*. He has become more famous and has made far more money than he ever would have as a singer.[49] And then there is Mrs Hinch, who has millions of followers. There used to be a time when, if your mother sent you to the shop to get disinfectant and you returned with *Zoflora*, she would send you back to get a *proper* disinfectant. Now, sales of the stuff are through the roof, ever since it was endorsed by Mrs Hinch.

There are guides that one can download giving advice on how to go about being a social media influencer; it seems to have become a career choice. Meanwhile, it is estimated that 30% of 16-24-year-olds bought a product in 2020 after it being endorsed by a *TikTok* influencer.[50] This is obviously a growth industry and more and more young people are getting involved, both in uploading videos and in watching those of others.

It sounds like a gross generalisation but it happens to be true that most young, working-class people are obsessed with having the best phone, the best clothes etc. This has been the case for a while now, but the influence of social media is increasing this slavery to consumerism. While their middle-class peers are interested in the environment and saving the planet, most working-class youths find the subject boring and they are simply not interested. This is not to say that middle-class youngsters are any better or more intelligent than their working-class counterparts. Being interested in environmental issues has as much to do with fashion and following the crowd as desiring the latest iPhone.

Since young, working-class people are obsessed with consumerism and wanting to be better than those around them, it stands to reason that they have no time for any egalitarian principles. They are being brainwashed into becoming Tory voters.

Fig.31 Ayn Rand.

Fig.32 Skullion from *Porterhouse Blue*.

Fig.33 Softy Walter. From his looks and his description, no child would want to be like him.

Fig.34 The evil Count Olaf from *A Series of Unfortunate Events*.

Fig.35 Christ the King.

11
Taking Bread to the Top of the World

The Desperate Bicycles were a DIY punk band, who issued a handful of singles and an album before splitting up. The lyrics of their songs were intelligent, often witty and usually political. As well as politics, they had some interesting observations to make about the human condition. One of their songs was called *Occupied Territory* (Fig.36) and was about how we trick ourselves into misremembering things. As one line puts it, 'Our memories are occupied, rebuilt to fit our lives today.' This is certainly true and, if you think about it, we are all guilty of what the song calls 'false nostalgia.'

Billy Connolly once observed that things were not really better when we were young; it is simply that we *were* young. Looking back, we had a lot more energy, did not have the aches and pains we have today, and life was an exciting adventure. It is hardly surprising that we embellish our memories a bit and remember all those long, hot summers and white Christmases. We are simply deluding ourselves.

An example of this sort of thing is the way that some people wax lyrical about the days of vinyl records. Apparently, vinyl is 'romantic', a 'sensory' experience and simply sounds better.[1] There are those that are almost poetic in the way they describe the feel of the single or album cover in your hands, the look of the picture on the cover and then the smell of the record when you get it home and take it out to put on the turntable. Digital media simply cannot give one the same experience. These nostalgic revelries, however, leave out a lot of facts.

While it is true that there was a certain excitement involved in getting a new vinyl record, that excitement often turned to disappointment when you put the stylus to it. It did not matter if it was a single or an album; the chances were that it would

179

jump all over the place, missing out huge chunks of the music. Unless you owned an expensive, state-of-the-art hi-fi with adjustable stylus pressure, you had to blue-tack a 10p coin or even a key to the end of your pick-up arm. If the record stuck in places instead, you had had it – there was no way to fix *that*.

The only remedy for a stuck record was to give the pick-up arm a nudge and many of us remember songs with that stuck bit in it. My copy of *Can't Stand Losing You* by The Police stuck on the line, *But to carry on living doesn't make no sense*, meaning I always remember the song at that part going, *But to ca... But to ca... But to ca... But to ca... But to ca...* etc. And it is not the only song I remember that way; there are many.

What was annoying was that a vinyl record that either jumped or stuck was not considered a faulty product. I never heard of anyone taking a record back to the shop and I imagine if anyone did, they would have been laughed at. Records that jumped and stuck did not qualify as faulty goods; it was just the luck of the draw. Rumours abounded that the best vinyl was used for classical music, while the rest of us had to make do with vinyl that was pressed as thinly and cheaply as possible. Whatever the truth of the matter, many people at the time moaned constantly about the poor quality of vinyl records. The alternative was no better.

Cassette tapes were not as popular as vinyl, except among a certain age group. When we were at school, we used to record songs from the radio on blank tapes. This was illegal and the record companies were always complaining about it, but they were the very ones that produced blank tapes. What did they expect us to do with them? Taping music from the radio, however, eventually got irritating. DJs just would not shut up and it was impossible to record your favourite tracks without some inane babble before the song had even finished. As soon as you could afford it, you switched to buying vinyl records.

In the 1980s, the Sony Walkman and its imitators increased the popularity of cassette tapes, whether it was buying them pre-recorded or taping your friend's albums. Quite often, though, the tape got chewed up by the machine and it had to be carefully and laboriously extracted. You then had to use a pen to wind the tape back into the cassette. This took ages and could easily end in tears. It was easy to miss a small bit of the tape being twisted as you wound it in, meaning that the cassette would not work. And so, you had to pull all the tape out again to untwist the twisted bit. (Fig.37) By this point you were usually cheesed-off and angry and an inadvertently hard pull on the tape would snap it. That was the death of your cassette tape.

Anyone with any sense can see that digital music is far superior to any vinyl or cassette tape. One character claimed that his computer had crashed and he lost all his music, arguing that he would still have had it if it were on vinyl.[2] That, however, was his own stupid fault for not backing up his files, something there is no excuse for in these days of widely-available, and usually free, Cloud storage. These facts, though, will make no difference to the nostalgia freaks, who will still insist that old is best.

Even when it comes to television there are those that argue that the old days were better than the present. Again, though, the mind plays tricks. Satellite and Cable TV stations have allowed us to revisit 'classic' comedies, like *On the Buses* and *Bless This House* and see what a load of garbage they actually were. Everyone remembers *Tales of the Unexpected* fondly, but currently (2021) Sky Arts are re-showing the programme and it is surprisingly bad!

The problem is that we all remember great shows, like *Only Fools and Horses*, but the 1980s were also responsible for *Comrade Dad*. (How many people remember that programme?) Some programmes, like *The Avengers* and *The Prisoner*, are nearly as good as we remember them when they are repeated. Others, like *Adam Adamant Lives* and *Blake's 7* make us wonder why we ever liked them first time around. The truth is that most television back in the day was rubbish and certainly no better than today's efforts. Yes, many of them got audiences of twenty million or more, but that was because we were trapped between three channels and often just two. (Not everyone could get BBC2.)

YouGov polls have shown that people tend to think nostalgically of the decade when they were a child or a young adult, often viewing said decade as better than today.[3] There are people in their thirties and forties that think the first decade of the 21st Century was better than the current one, whereas older people would be hard-pushed to see much of a difference. It seems incredible to those of us that will not see 60 again that there are people out there that are nostalgic for CDs!

Advertisers have long realised the power of nostalgia and have frequently employed nostalgic themes in commercials. Probably the most famous of these in Britain is the 1973 Hovis advert, directed by Ridley Scott.[4] It conjured up nostalgic feelings for a bygone time that was still within living memory for many people, and not just the elderly. Someone that was 12 in, say, 1935 would only have been 50 in 1973. It was, however, to borrow The Desperate Bicycles' phrase, false nostalgia.

For many, the 1930s was not the cosy, happy time depicted in the advert. It was a time of unemployment, poor, sub-standard housing, hunger, rickets, tuberculosis and premature death. There were children that would not have made it up that hill without collapsing, gasping for breath and maybe even coughing up blood. As in most people's childhood, there would have been happy times and it was these that the advert was evoking, manipulating the audience into forgetting all the poverty and misery.

In a sense, it was not only false nostalgia, but false advertising as well. Hovis might have been around in the 1930s, but nobody at the time would have admitted to eating it. Brown bread was a sign of poverty in those days and people would have been ashamed to let anyone know that they could not afford white bread. (I once saw a government film from the period, in which a woman complained that she could not afford 'good, white bread' for her children.) Anyone doubting that white bread was a symbol of affluence should listen to Billy Joel's *Uptown Girl*. A line in the song says, '*She's been living in her white-bread world.*' Even in America, white bread was a sign of being relatively well-to-do.

At any rate, the advert worked, as did others of the same ilk. Political parties, of course, tried the same thing, particularly the Conservatives, who were, after all, the party of tradition. The most blatant example of this was John Major's party election broadcast of 1992: *The Journey*.[5] This was an attempt to 'humanise' Major, who was often portrayed as a grey, boring character. It was a nostalgic journey through the places he grew up in.

A team of psychologists analysed the short film minutely, writing an article discussing how it conveyed a sense of Britain's history, as well as that of Major himself. In looking at the part where he buys some tomatoes and kippers, reminiscing about how he used to buy the same items at the same place many years ago, the psychologists remark,

> Discursively pulling together the nostalgic past and present in this manner helps to naturalize (sic) the timelessness of Britain as a nation.[6]

In the 1979 election campaign, nostalgia was part-and-parcel of the Tory message. One broadcast featured Margaret Thatcher, her voice changed from its erstwhile screech to a slow, quiet, comforting tone. She spoke directly to the camera, saying, 'Somewhere ahead lies greatness for our country again.'[7] Notice the use of the word 'again' to conjure up Britain's imperial past.

Another broadcast spoke of, 'The things that made Britain great,' while Thatcher herself appeared to talk about using tax cuts as productivity incentives so that, as she put it, 'Once again, Britain will be back in the race!'[8] Unfortunately, as we were all to discover, Thatcher's policies were based in the past as well and any notions about productivity were abandoned to the cause of Deflation.

Coming back to nearer the present and polls showed that far more older people voted for Brexit than young people.[9] Various reasons have been given for this,[10] but, as we have already seen, immigration played a huge part. Nostalgia had a role in this;[11] younger people are used to going to school with and working alongside people of different races, older people are not. In fact, many older people remember, and reminisce, about a time when all they saw were white faces. 62% of Conservative voters in one survey supported Brexit,[12] so it is quite feasible to extrapolate that most older voters are Tories, certainly in England.

Jokes are made about the age of Tory voters, as in the description of a Scottish Conservative conference in Troon in 2012, which mused about it being 'organised by Saga Holidays with catering by Sanatogen.'[13] The Tories, though, get the last laugh. Those old folk that turned up to see and hear David Cameron were not the same ones that fawned over Thatcher in the 1980s. This was a different generation of oldies. And that is the advantage that the Tories have; there are always new cohorts of old people to replace those that have died.

As we saw above, research has shown that almost everyone is nostalgic about the days when they were still young. As time passes, people naturally get older, and their nostalgia can be used to make them support the Tories and Tory policies. In twenty or thirty years' time, those that reminisce about the 1990s might be persuaded to be nostalgic about the days before we were 'flooded' with asylum seekers and refugees. Even today's toddlers could be moaning in the 22nd Century about those bastards from the planet Zog, who come over here, simultaneously steal our jobs and live off the state and look at our women funny!

Television programmes, as we have seen, play their part in evoking nostalgic feelings that drive people into the arms of the Tories. We saw how programmes set in the countryside always portrayed it as a better place to live than towns and cities. One aspect of this is the device of introducing a black character, or family, into the programme; just for one or two episodes. In programmes like *Heartbeat*, which were set in past decades, this helped the whole false nostalgia agenda. The black people were welcomed warmly and treated no differently from white people. Obviously, if black people had settled in the British countryside (not *too* many of them, though), they would have had a happier experience. These programmes also helped to foster the notion that the black immigrants themselves were responsible for racism being so pervasive in Britain. Sometimes, however, the TV people seriously miscalculated the impact these programmes would have.

Somebody at ITV decided, for some strange reason, to remake *The Darling Buds of May*. (As if the original was not bad enough!) It was called *The Larkins* and starred the ubiquitous Bradley Walsh. As the lights with the 2,000-watt bulbs were wheeled out again to create the illusion of a constant summer, whoever was in charge thought it would be a good idea to borrow from some of those other programmes set in the past and throw a few black people into the mix to show how friendly the Larkin family was. The idea backfired spectacularly.

The first episode aired in October 2021 and the critics were unanimous in declaring it a failure. The critics concentrated on the banality of the script; the audience, however, hated it for a different reason entirely. What they were annoyed about was the appearance of those black people. Phrases like 'woke' and 'box ticking' were bandied about, while many pointed out that there were no, or very few, black people in the English countryside in the 1950s.[14] It seemed that a major part of the nostalgia inherent in *The Darling Buds of May* was that there were no black or brown faces in it. (Fig.38) The audience did not care about how black people were treated in the past; they were nostalgic for a past that included no black people at all.

To remember what the 1950s were like, you would have to be at least in your seventies, but it is doubtful that all of those moaning about *The Larkins* are in this age group. So, how can you be nostalgic about a period in which you did not live? It obviously happens and psychologists have come up with a name for the phenomenon. *Vicarious Nostalgia*, as the name suggests, is being nostalgic about *other people's* younger days.

> Today, it is argued, we no longer need to have lived a past in order to feel nostalgic for it (Chase & Shaw 1989). Baker and Kennedy (1994) draw a distinction between 'real' nostalgia, nostalgia for some remembered past time, and 'stimulated'

nostalgia, a form of vicarious nostalgia evoked from stories, images, and possessions (Belk 1988; Stern 1992).[15]

This analysis, by Christina Goulding, is dated 2002. Unfortunately, more recent works are only accessible to academics and students. It is doubtful, though, that the essential findings have changed much, although some of the conclusions might. For example, Dr Krystine I Batcho, in 2013, saw the phenomenon in a positive light.

It is possible that vicarious nostalgia can help a person rise above maladaptive grief for the good qualities missing from his or her childhood. ... Feeling nostalgic rather than simply bitter or hateful provides the opportunity to transform adversity into more than survival. Longing for another's childhood can provide a sense of what might have been and, therefore, what life could be—if no longer for oneself—then at least for other children. The representation of what one wishes had been can form the vision that inspires one to make that dream a reality for others.[16]

Christina Goulding appears to see Vicarious Nostalgia as something harmless and neutral. She sees it arising from not only associating with those that are not of one's age group, but from socialising with others of one's peer group that feel the same. One of the participants in her study was a girl that loved everything about the 1960s and she found it relatively easy to find others that were fascinated, and even obsessed, with the same period. It all seems pretty harmless, but Goulding provides us with a caveat.

However, nostalgia depends on other factors apart from socialisation and available stimulus; namely nostalgia is an emotion that is usually instigated by feelings of frustration in the present, compared with an idealised image of a perfect past.[17]

And therein lies the problem. We saw how people in their fifties and above were manipulated into feeling nostalgic for the 1930s by that famous Hovis advert. They were not, however, the only ones.

Even people that had been born long after the 1930s felt nostalgic. Many of those that had lived through the decade forgot all the bad things about it. Those that were born later had experienced none of these things and were able to look at the decade through the proverbial rose-tinted glasses. As psychologists have said, such vicarious nostalgia is usually engendered by a dissatisfaction with the present. The dangers of this are obvious.

Thinking that the 1930s was some kind of Golden Age would lead one to think, or be easily manipulated into thinking, that *everything* was better then. That would include having no NHS, not much in the way of welfare and poor housing that was only starting to be remedied by councils.[18] It also meant government economic policies that deliberately encouraged mass unemployment. It is no coincidence that these have been the policies of Tory governments since the days of Thatcher.

Even that woman in Christina Goulding's study nostalgic about the 1960s was treading a dangerous path. It is clear from the text that it is the *early* sixties she is nostalgic about; the time of the mods rather than that of hippies and skinheads. It is an easy time to feel nostalgic about, with the music and fashion and young people having more money than they had ever had before. Social problems, however, were still rife.

Up until the age of 5, which was in 1966, I lived in a tenement, which has long since been demolished, on Glasgow's Castle Street at the corner of Royston Road. I remember my life then quite vividly and music of the period can immediately take me back, especially The Shadows' *Wonderful Life*. Apart from my personal and specific childhood memories, I recall how my aunties, uncles and grandparents all lived within walking distance. Also within easy walking distance were two cinemas and all kinds of shops. On summer nights the shows would be on the waste ground opposite, blasting Beatles songs and with their lights reflecting in the canal. I remember that there were cafes everywhere and steam trains travelled along the top of Cuddies' Brae. All these good memories, however, are more than balanced by the bad.

Everywhere seemed remarkably dirty. All the old buildings were black, coated with a century of soot and grime. If you happened to brush against a wall, the dirt came off onto your clothes. During the winter it was always foggy; not just a mist, but a thick, dirty fog that caught in the back of your throat. The tenements were infested with mice, and you could not eat in bed unless a mouse came up while you were sleeping to get the crumbs and bit you. Also scary was the stairhead toilet, which we, as small children, would not use. Instead, we did our business in buckets, which my mother then emptied down the toilet and washed, ready for the next time. We were excited and overjoyed when we got a flat in Castlemilk with a garden and a real, inside bathroom with a real bath!

It was also a time when I first discovered racism, even though I did not know the term. The café near us was run by folk that were Indian or Pakistani. The women wore beautiful clothes in bright colours; baggy trousers and tops and scarves that covered their heads and wrapped around their necks to hang down their backs, all looking as if they were made of silk. The woman downstairs from us got a job in the café and began to wear some of the beautiful clothes that her fellow workers wore. I remember being confused as adults, including my parents, talked about how disgusting it was that she wanted to look like one of *them*.

Now, I do not know what age the woman was in Christina Goulding's study, but it is entirely possible that she never experienced the 1960s at all. She would know nothing of vermin-infested houses, having to share a toilet with three or four other families and all the dirt everywhere. To a mind full of music, fashion and Vespa scooters, it would seem like a paradise. She might easily be convinced that subsequent improvements to people's lives were not improvements at all. In other words, she could be manipulated into voting Tory.

We already saw, in Chapter 3, how revisionists are re-assessing the First World War, claiming that we have all been indoctrinated by poets like Wilfred Owen. It is handy that those that remembered those days are long dead. All we have are second- or even third-hand memories, which can easily be dismissed as untrustworthy. Unfortunately for these revisionists, the horrors of WWI are so ingrained in all our minds that it would take a major shift in thinking to change our image of that war. The same, though, cannot be said about WWII.

The myths around the war began well before it ended. We have already seen, in Chapter 3, how Dunkirk was portrayed as a victory, even though it was a defeat, every bit as ignominious as the Germans' retreat from the USSR. Britain had been effectively chased out of Europe, leaving her French allies under occupation for the next four years. It also exposed another aspect of Britain that is ignored or forgotten. American journalist, William L Shirer could not help but comment on how different British soldiers looked from their German counterparts in 1940.

> The young in the Third Reich were growing up to have strong and healthy bodies, faith in the future of their country and in themselves and a sense of fellowship and camaraderie that shattered all class and economic and social barriers. I thought of that later, in the May days of 1940, when along the road between Aachen and Brussels one saw the contrast between the German soldiers, bronzed and clean-cut from a youth spent in the sunshine on an adequate diet, and the first British war prisoners, with their hollow chests, round shoulders, pasty complexions and bad teeth – tragic examples of the youth that England had neglected so irresponsibly in the years between the wars.[19]

It is necessary to point out that the Nazis were preparing for war almost as soon as they got into power. Everything was geared toward this preparation, including the economy, education and welfare. This does not excuse the British Government for leaving many working-class people to rot in poverty, poor housing and disease. As soon as war was declared, however, it could suddenly find money to clothe, feed, house and give free medical treatment to hundreds of thousands of those working-class people. Suddenly, everyone was to pull together, which begs the question of why they could not have done such a thing before. Obviously, the upper classes cared nothing for the lower orders until they needed them to fight in another war.

This idea of everyone pulling together and supporting one another during the war became a common, nostalgic theme. Older people loved comparing those days to modern times, with everyone just out for themselves and not caring about others. It was such a common comparison that it has been parodied many times. It also happens to be a load of rubbish.

We saw earlier how gangs of unruly teenagers ran riot during the war, mugging people and engaging in all sorts of illegal activity. They were not the only criminals at large during the war years. Reported crimes between 1939 and 1945 grew by 60% in England and Wales.[20] We are not talking about the odd opportunist bit of thievery here. There was an increase in murders and rapes, while armed robberies also increased, carried out with guns and ammunition stolen from Home Guard stores.[21] It was a boom time for organised crime, with the production of illicit liquor, known as 'hooch',[22] and large-scale prostitution.[23] Renowned London gangster, 'Mad' Frankie Fraser opined that it was,

> the most exciting and profitable time there's ever been… it breaks my heart that Hitler surrendered because the war was a criminal's paradise.[24]

Class differences, meanwhile, were still maintained. The system of rationing was meant to be so that everyone got their fair share of food. Alcohol and tobacco were not rationed but there were constant shortages. There was plenty, though, readily available so long as you had money. The Black Market thrived during the war and rich people never went without their booze, fags, meat and eggs. Of course, the Government tried to clamp down, but it is interesting to note *how*.

Those convicted of being involved in the Black Market faced fines of £500 (nearly £20k in today's money) and two years in prison, as well as having to pay three times the value of what they had been selling.[25] It is notable that there were no fines or prison sentences for those that were *buying* illicit goods. The working-class spivs faced massive fines and prison terms, while the rich customers, who were the ones driving the black economy after all, got off scot-free. Some London hotels were fined in 1941 for buying 150,000 eggs on the Black Market. We do not know how much they were fined, but the spiv involved got three months hard labour.[26]

On the other hand, working-class folk swindling the system to get extra food were dealt with harshly.

> One woman in Hartlepool was fined £160 (the best part of £6k in today's money) in 1940 after using four ration books to get food for her family of three. Her 15-year-old son had accidentally been sent a child's book and an adult's and she used both for six months to obtain extra supplies.[27]

Perhaps the most disgusting crime, and one that belies the 'Blitz Spirit' that old folk go on about, was looting. People could go to the air-raid shelter and emerge later to find their house bombed and all their possessions gone. A chief inspector told of what happened in Dover after one raid:

> In cases where there are several houses bombed out in one street, the looters have systematically gone through the lot. Carpets have been stripped from the floors, stair carpets have been removed: they have even taken away heavy mangles, bedsteads and complete suites of furniture.[28]

As darkly comic as this is, there were incidents that could only be described as horrific. In 1941 the Café de Paris nightclub was bombed, and rescuers were hampered in their efforts to find survivors by ghouls stripping the jewellery from dead bodies.[29] Looting was widespread and even firemen, air-raid wardens and other uniformed personnel were involved.[30] During the last four months of 1941, over four-and-a-half thousand cases of looting were heard at the Old Bailey.[31] Those were just the ones that were caught; there were no doubt many more that got away with it. So much for the Blitz Spirit!

The right-wing media, however, continue to propagate the myth of the Blitz Spirit with stories of bravery and stoicism during the bombing. One such article in the *Express* mentioned the looting but gave the impression that it was only hardened criminals like Frankie Fraser that were involved.[32] The stories of how everyone stood together against the Nazis have to be maintained, even though the evidence shows that the opposite was the case.

Of course, Vicarious Nostalgia comes into play with WWII too, with people that were born long after it finished comparing it to the present day.[33] And, as you might expect, Tory politicians employ this kind of thing for their own ends. As part of the efforts to get people to stop working at home and back into the office, one-time leader of the Tories, Iain Duncan Smith, had this to say about civil servants:

In the 1940s they kept coming to the office – even when Hitler's bombs were raining down.[34]

As people pointed out, the bombing happened at night, bombs are not contagious and broadband was pretty scarce in the 1940s. There would be many, though, that would completely understand and agree with Duncan Smith's comparison. They probably believe that all the stories about crime and looting in WWII are left-wing lies.

As well as Vicarious Nostalgia, another phenomenon has reared its ugly head. The novelist Douglas Coupland invented a term for it, *Legislated Nostalgia* – 'To force a body of people to have memories they do not actually possess.'[35] Writer and journalist Owen Hatherley refers to the term as he discusses an invented nostalgic object: the *Keep Calm and Carry On* posters (Fig.39) and assorted merchandise. It has become the archetypal WWII nostalgia item, even though it never saw the light of day during the war.

Owen Hatherley points out several uncomfortable truths about the original poster.[36] It was made by the Ministry of Information for use in the event of an attempted German invasion. Of course, this never happened so the poster was kept under wraps. More than sixty years later, specimens of the poster were found among a box of items serendipitously bought at auction by the owners of a bookshop. To the delight of the bookshop owners, customers eagerly bought the posters, which

192

prompted the owners to make copies. The rest is history. Or rather, it is not. It is invented history and nostalgia.

Even those that lived through the war would not have been able to remember the posters, since they were never used. And yet, everyone sees them as being part-and-parcel of the Second World War. It conjures up images of the Blitz Spirit, which, as we have seen, was itself an invention. It is evocative of a better time, a Golden Age, when everyone looked out for one another. Like the poster and the Blitz Spirit, this Golden Age was an invention too. So, we have a situation where a poster that was never used conjures up nostalgic feelings for a time that is mere fantasy. It cannot be a healthy way to look at the world.

As Hatherley says, there is a sinister ideological message behind the *Keep Calm and Carry On* meme.[37] It appeals to a certain, mythical characteristic, which, if one does not have, one cannot be really British. It is akin to taking some horrible-tasting medicine because you know it is good for you. It is about acquiescing in whatever our lords and masters in Westminster decree, no matter what. Alexei Sayle used to mercilessly pillory this mindset, summed up in the phrase, 'Mustn't grumble.' Most of the population, especially in England, have come to believe that this mindset is what it means to be British.

Even when upper-class Tories are allowing raw sewage to be pumped into English rivers, in the middle of a pandemic, no less, nobody grumbles, let alone rises up to say enough is enough. They are our betters, are they not? And they know what is best, even though it might not seem like it. Just keep calm and carry on!

12
C'mon the 'Mune System

It was in December 2019 that we first heard of Coronavirus, or Covid-19 as it came to be called. (Covid-19 stands for **Co**rona **Vi**rus **D**isease 20**19**.) The virus was similar to one carried by bats, leading scientists to believe that it had been transmitted by these creatures. Quite how it had passed to humans was unclear, although those that had seen the movie *Contagion* would remember bats dropping shit all over the pigs that people were going to eat. The outbreak had occurred in Wuhan in China, leading all the Brexity types to say that it was the Chinese's own fault for eating bats.[1] After all, Johnny Foreigner would eat anything!

By February, the virus had spread to other countries and the World Health Organisation was warning that it could develop into a full-blown pandemic,[2] like the flu pandemic that happened at the end of the First World War. People in the media and online, however, pooh-poohed the notion, expecting it to be another anti-climax like Bird Flu. And then, on the 12th of March, the WHO announced that Covid-19 *was* a pandemic.[3] The response in the UK was one of hesitancy and delay, as if nobody knew what to do. And yet, we had always been told that there were contingency plans in place for such emergencies; obviously, there were not.

It is clear that the UK Government was thinking in terms of 'herd immunity' in the early days of the pandemic announcement and before.[4] That was why the Cheltenham Festival was allowed to go ahead as well as European football matches at Anfield and Ibrox. Events, however, as well as public opinion, soon changed the Government's collective mind.[5] On March 23rd the Prime Minister, Boris Johnson, announced a nationwide lockdown. Pubs were shut, shops, other than those deemed essential, were closed also, as were clubs, cinemas and theatres.[6] Everyone was told to stay indoors as much as possible and only to go out for food, medicine or for short periods of exercise.

Officially, the lockdown ended in May 2020[7] but, in reality, restrictions stayed in place well into July. Folk had to get used to not meeting in groups, not going to other people's houses and wearing a mask when on a bus and when going to the supermarket. Everyone took things in remarkably good spirits and adhered to the rules quite well in the main. Well, not everyone. For some, the rules were unnecessarily draconian and impinged on their freedom. They would have complained to the European Court of Human Rights were it not for the fact that most of them happened to be Brexiteers!

In May, a small crowd of demonstrators on Glasgow Green railed against the 'totalitarian state' and about standing up for their 'human rights'. They also ranted and raved about '5G', a conspiracy theory that we shall encounter later. And then came the best bit, where one character showed his complete ignorance by saying that there was no need to wash your hands because we had an 'immoon system'. The cry of 'C'mon the 'mune system!' by a woman in the crowd was a classic piece of unintended comedy.[8]

There were plenty of these idiots all over the UK, shouting about immune systems, even though they did not have the first idea about how they worked. To find that out they would need to look up what the experts said, which was complete anathema to them. Had they not been told, time and again, that they should not listen to experts? And had the Tories not explicitly recommended this course during the run-up to the Brexit referendum? The Tories' chickens were coming home to roost now that they actually needed people to listen to what the experts were saying.

As the year wore on, there seemed no end in sight to the pandemic and to the rules and regulations that people had to stick to. Of course, it did not help that the UK did not follow New Zealand's example and close the airports, or at least quarantine anyone that arrived. Instead, travel to and from countries that showed a high infection rate was banned. As Boris Johnson's father's roundabout trip to Greece showed,[9] you could never be sure of anyone's *original* departure point.

Meanwhile, folk came and went through Britain's airports without a by-your-leave, helping to keep the virus spreading. The Government's ridiculous 'Eat Out to Help Out' initiative, encouraging people to eat at restaurants during August, probably aided the spread of the virus as well.[10]

As the deaths mounted up, there were questions to be asked about how the Government had been handling things. Not everybody asked questions, though. Instead, they knew better than everyone else what was going on: the whole pandemic was a fraud and there was no need for lockdowns or vaccines or anything else. Right-wing commentators made sure they provided plenty of grist to the mill of these clowns.

We met *The New Culture Forum* earlier and saw how it existed to counter left-wing ideas in the media and elsewhere. Lockdown scepticism was right up their street and, as early as May 2020, historian David Starkey was on the NCF's YouTube channel blasting the Government for its handling of the pandemic.[11] It was not really the Government's fault, however, it was all those pesky left-wingers to blame. According to Starkey, the Tories were pandering to erstwhile Labour voters, all the scum in the North of England, by almost deifying the NHS. It was the left-wing folk running the NHS that persuaded the Government that Covid-19 would affect everyone, rather than just the old and vulnerable.

Starkey did not believe that the virus was as bad as was being made out. He admitted that older people with underlying health conditions, like himself, were at risk, but nobody else. Since he was not an expert in diseases, he turned to history to justify his position. He spoke of the Black Death and the positive impact it had in raising the standard of living of European peasants and in leading to the end of feudalism. That would have been a great comfort to all those that had lost loved ones to the plague!

Starkey, obviously, did not see multiple deaths as necessarily a bad thing; it was only the aftermath he was concerned with. That was why, when he spoke of the earlier Plague of Justinian, which ravaged the Middle East from the 6th Century to the 8th, the only negative outcome he saw was the rise of Islam. That would have gone down well with his viewers, who were looking for justification for their own right-wing opinions. Some of the comments below the video are interesting.

> Covid is a massive, hysterical over reaction and a deification of the NHS, which has become a hotbed for left wing activists.[12]

> Common sense and facts from the marvellous Dr. Starkey and precisely what I have been saying from the very start.[13]

Common sense? That certainly sounds familiar. Essentially what this character was saying was that Starkey was not one of those muddle-headed 'experts'; he was just spouting some good, old-fashioned, *British* common sense. Actually, Starkey's arguments were as full of holes as a pair of fishnet stockings. Not the least of his errors was in comparing pandemics from centuries ago to the one we have all come to know these days. Nobody back in the Byzantine Empire or in Medieval Europe had any idea how to cope with such a thing. Even something as simple as washing your hands would have been beyond them. In fact, the only effective method of dealing with both plagues would have been to cram everybody into churches to pray to God for deliverance.

The churches were closed during the Covid-19 pandemic, to prevent the spread of the virus in accordance with modern medical knowledge. With everything known nowadays about viruses and how to contain them, it stands to reason that there would be fewer deaths than there were hundreds of years ago. The idea that hundreds of thousands had died, rather than millions, by May 2020 cannot be used as an indication that Covid-19 is not as serious as previous pandemics. Those that followed Starkey and his ilk, however, were convinced that they knew better.

Meanwhile, Toby Young, who revels in trying to stir up controversy, set up a new website called *Lockdown Sceptics*.

The intended audience could easily be discerned by his use of the phrase 'metropolitan elite'. He also opined,

> Most sceptics will be small 'c' conservatives because we believe in liberty and are horrified by the confinement of people in their homes and... well, because scepticism is at the core of our political philosophy.[14]

> Decisions of this importance (lockdown), affecting the UK's entire population, shouldn't be 'left to the experts', as some people believed. [15]

While the likes of David Starkey and Toby Young played the 'common sense' card, others were not shy about spreading crazy conspiracy theories. Unlike the Lockdown Sceptics, they had experts on their side.[16] Unfortunately, some of these 'experts' had been banging on for years about radiation from 3G, 4G, mobile phone masts and radio and television transmitters. Giving their opinions credit would mean covering yourself from head to toe in Bacofoil and never removing it; not even to go to bed. Also unfortunately, said 'experts' had long ago been caught up in academic disputes about being too close to the business world.[17] No matter who was in the right, grudges in academia tend to be long-held and these 'experts' certainly had axes to grind.

Speaking of tinfoil, the king of the tinfoil-hat brigade, David Icke, was a leading exponent of the 5G/Covid link.[18] He saw this as part-and-parcel of the machinations of the *New World Order*. The NWO is a phrase beloved by right-wing nuts everywhere, who believe that Jews or shape-shifting aliens or both are pulling the strings of governments all over the Earth. The fact that the theory had the Icke seal of approval, however, tended to make it unbelievable in the eyes of anyone with more than one brain cell.

There were, however, plenty of monocellular-brained individuals out there that were prepared to believe this stuff. They deluded themselves, and others, by couching their theory in pseudo-scientific terms:

> On your oxygen molecules, the little electrons, with 5G they start to oscillate. So 5G is absorbing the oxygen and then your haemoglobin can't take up the oxygen.[19]

The trump card in the argument, or so these folk believed, was that Wuhan in China, where Covid-19 apparently started, was one of the first places in the world to have 5G. They also delighted in pointing out that African countries, where 5G was virtually non-existent, had very few cases of Covid. Time, however, was not on the side of these clowns as, by April 2020, hundreds, if not thousands, of cases were occurring in countries with no 5G coverage at all.[20]

These stories were totally debunked in the media, using scientific explanations, but they could be quite easily countered using a more simplistic method. 5G is going to make going on the internet on a mobile phone a lot faster and more efficient.[21] It makes no sense at all for phone manufacturers, phone networks, retailers, internet providers, operating system developers etc. to put the lives of paying customers at risk.

Insane as this stuff was, it was not the craziest conspiracy theory out there, not by a long chalk. That dubious honour belonged to a theory that involved Donald Trump, Bill Gates, Anthony Fauci (Director of the American National Institute of Allergy and Infectious Diseases), Communism, the New World Order, the Antichrist and just about anyone or any organisation with whom extreme right-wingers had had problems. Like all the best conspiracy theories, it originated in the USA but was adapted as it spread to Europe and the UK.

As mentioned earlier, the New World Order had been an obsession of the political Right for some time. When Donald Trump appeared on the political scene, the narrative began to change. Trump's tirades against liberals, foreigners and other hate figures of right-wingers let all the extremists know that he was on their side. Now, Trump was their saviour and, since many right-wingers professed to take inspiration from the Bible, it all got rather messianic.

A quasi-religious organisation sprang up called *QAnon*, which we met in passing earlier. Actually, it was less an organisation than a collection of myths that American right-wingers of all descriptions could rally around. The essence of the myths was that Donald Trump, while president, was fighting a secret war against an elite cabal of paedophiles in government, the media and business.[22] Conveniently, all these paedophiles happened to be liberal supporters of the Democratic Party. There was, however, more to it than that. It seemed that this paedophile elite also tortured children to extract a drug, called adrenochrome, from them.[23] Apparently, the drug is produced in the body when a person is fearful.

As if that were not bad enough, this elite also practised Satanism. The Satanic rituals of this group involved child sacrifice and the use of adrenochrome.[24] It is easy to see where the religious aspect came into the beliefs of QAnon. Since Trump was fighting this Satanic elite, then it stood to reason that he had been sent by God for this purpose. You can perhaps understand why those Trump supporters stormed the Capitol when Trump lost the presidential election to Joe Biden; they simply could not believe that God's plan had been thwarted. There were videos and pictures online of people in tears, utterly devastated that Trump had lost. The Devil had won!

When the media were full of stories about the coming pandemic, it was a godsend for all the right-wing conspiracy theorists. When lockdown came in America, right-wingers, as they did worldwide, raged against this infringement of their liberties. Obviously, somebody was to blame and the QAnon lads and lasses had already provided that somebody. It was those damned liberal elites up to their tricks again. The QAnon myths combined with scepticism about Covid-19 to produce a brand-new story. Luckily, the liberal elite unsuspectingly provided a basis for this latest fantasy.

The *World Economic Forum* was founded in 1971 to promote more eco-friendly and people-friendly governments, businesses and industries.[25] The WEF has held annual conferences at the

Swiss ski resort of Davos, involving government representatives, top businessmen and prominent cultural figures. In 2020, of course, it could not hold the conference so had to have an online, virtual meeting, at which the main speaker was Prince Charles.[26] He was launching a new initiative; the rather unfortunately named *Great Reset*.[27]

The idea of *The Great Reset*[28] was to bring top people together to use the circumstances of the Covid Pandemic to make the world a better place. It was not just a question of doing something about global warming; poverty came into the reckoning as well. As Kristalina Georgieva, Managing Director of the International Monetary Fund, put it:

> The best memorial we can build to those who have lost their lives is a greener, smarter, fairer world.[29]

Now, that statement was more than enough to put a shiver up the spines of right-wingers everywhere, but especially in America. In the USA practically everyone has been brought up to be terrified of Communism and Socialism. Even opening a copy of *Das Kapital* in a library is probably enough to set alarm bells off in some government department. In such an atmosphere, Georgieva's words were hardly going to go unchallenged.

A new story emerged that the liberal elites were responsible for Covid, or, at least, for instigating all the measures used to control the spread. In some versions Covid simply did not exist. The virus doing the rounds was nothing more than the flu. Others admitted that Covid-19 was real but claimed that it had been created by Anthony Fauci, at the behest of Bill Gates. This was all part of the great masterplan.

Bill Gates co-founded Microsoft and became a multi-billionaire and one of the richest individuals in the world. He was a latter-day Andrew Carnegie, determined to do good with his money, whether it was ill-gotten or not.[30]

His interest in global warming and in lowering the world's population, however, marked him as the enemy of the Right. Such a well-known, high-profile individual obviously had to be involved in the nefarious schemes of the liberal elite.

Opinion was divided over what, exactly, Gates was up to. It had something to do with vaccines, since his and his wife's foundation had donated $250m towards the development and distribution of an anti-Covid vaccine, especially for use in low-income countries.[31] This led to conspiracy theorists joining up imaginary dots to lead to this conclusion:

Bill Gates admits plans to reduce population through use of vaccines.[32]

The sheer ignorance of the folk believing in this nonsense was shown in the comments under the video.

Please Africa, Never let this Man in Your Beautiful Country, We Love You All.[33]

Another video on YouTube showed the truth about Gates, vaccinations and overpopulation.[34] In it, Gates argued that improving the health of children so that it becomes normal for them to live longer, encourages people to have less children. Meanwhile, myth-debunking website, *Snopes* showed that the ones attacking Gates were guilty of lying or, at the very least, being easily confused.[35] There was, however, worse to come as far as Bill Gates was concerned.

Everyone on the extreme Right agreed that Gates and his NWO cronies were taking advantage of the pandemic, whether it was real or not. As usual, though, the QAnon mob took things too far. Their reasoning was that a technological wizard like Gates was hardly going to get involved in vaccines unless he had found some way of incorporating his computing knowledge in them. According to this particular conspiracy theory, he had.

Apparently, the Covid vaccine was going to contain a microchip, holding all your information, which could be easily accessed and uploaded to a central database using 5G. It could also be used to track you, so that some form of control could be exerted. Even though this type of technology did not exist yet,[36] that was not going to stop the conspiracy theorists. What did exist, however, was a chip that would let you pay in shops, like swiping your bank card.[37] Adding together the real and fantasy elements of what could be done with a microchip was enough to frighten anyone professing to be a Christian.

Even people that are unfamiliar with the Bible know something about the Book of Revelation; there have been enough films made about the Antichrist (or the Beast, as he is more properly called in Revelation). One thing is explicit in Revelation:

> And he (the beast) causeth all, both small and great, rich and poor, free and bond, to receive a mark in their right hand, or in their foreheads: And that no man might buy or sell, save he that had the mark, or the name of the beast, or the number of his name.[38]

You will notice that the *mark* of the Beast and the *number* of the Beast are listed as two separate items. And yet, most films depict the Antichrist a.k.a. the Beast as having the number 666 somewhere on his body. No film, as far as I am aware, shows anyone sporting the mark of the Beast other than the Beast himself, but it is generally accepted that 666 is involved in some way. Even those that see themselves as religious experts believe this.[39] The truth is, however, that the mark could be anything, including Bill Gates's microchip.

A more worrying development for religionists was the patent filed by Microsoft in 2020. The title of this patent was *CRYPTOCURRENCY SYSTEM USING BODY ACTIVITY DATA.*[40] Now, that sounded as if the conspiracy theorists might be correct. After all, that was what they were accusing Gates of planning.[41] That, though, was not the scariest part. The patent number was *WO/2020/060606*, which conspiracy theorists said stood for *World Order* (as in *New World Order*) *2020, 666*.[42] Cue the theme from *The Twilight Zone*!

As one commentor explained, the *WO/2020* bit was simply standard notation for patents filed in 2020. The *060606* part, meanwhile, could easily be explained as being allocated by somebody at the *World Intellectual Property Organization* with a sense of humour. Well, that makes as much sense as the 'Satanic conspiracy' idea. And, as the writer also said,

> None of this means Microsoft will ever build this device because companies literally patent things on a daily basis as a just-in-case.[43]

So, as pointed out earlier, it is doubtful that such technology existed. Furthermore, Patent *WO/2020/060606* mentioned nothing about chips, micro or otherwise. It was far more likely that it was intended to be used with a mobile phone, giving everyone a choice in the matter. Sadly for the conspiracy theorists, this patent was not proof of any great plan involving vaccines and Bill Gates. The religious aspects of the conspiracies, however, kept on coming.

We have already seen how QAnon was quasi-religious in its beliefs about Donald Trump standing against the forces of darkness. This fear was substantiated when a Vatican whistle-blower, a 'high ranking official,' wrote open letters to Trump explaining what *The Great Reset* would entail. Those that did not accept its terms would be locked up in detention camps. While decrying this 'global conspiracy against God and humanity' and urging Trump to greater efforts, the whistle-blower added,

> As is now clear, the one who occupies the Chair of Peter has betrayed his role from the very beginning in order to defend and promote the globalist ideology, supporting the agenda of the deep church, who chose him from its ranks.[44]

Oh dear! Even the Pope was involved in the *Great Reset*, along with Bill Gates and all the rest of them. Trump was certainly going to have his work cut out! But who was this whistle-blower and 'high ranking Vatican official'? His name was Carlo Maria Vigano and he had his own agenda to peddle. His is a tale of thwarted ambition, bitterness and internecine quarrels within the Catholic Church.

Vigano expected to be made a cardinal but, instead, he was sent to the USA as a papal nuncio, trailing a bunch of controversies behind him.[45] In America he joined with other conservative clerics that were disgruntled with the direction the Church was heading in, especially after the ascension of Pope Francis. Francis's liberal stance regarding homosexuality had angered many leading lights in the Church,[46] especially in the United States. Vigano wrote open letters, accusing Pope Francis of covering up for a homosexual clique in the Vatican, which, Vigano claimed, was responsible for all the child abuse in the Church. This was despite the fact that Vigano himself had been accused of covering up for child abusers.[47]

In 2016, Vigano resigned as papal nuncio after reaching the age of 75, or because Francis fired him, depending on whom you believe. So, despite the claims otherwise, by the time he wrote those open letters to Trump, he was not what could be called a 'high ranking Vatican official'. In fact, he was *persona non grata* at the Vatican and was simply using the opportunity to vent his bitterness and bile.

An indication of where Vigano's politics lay was shown in yet another of his open letters, this time addressed to 'American Catholics and to all Americans of good will.'[48] He was supporting Trump's allegations of electoral fraud and putting a religious angle on it by describing the Democrats as the forces of the Devil. That certainly put a different slant on his rants about *The Great Reset*. He was just another right-wing nut, with his bitterness over his own thwarted ambitions making his comments more barbed.

Although Vigano was ostensibly appealing to American Catholics, his open letters appeared in right-wing, online periodicals, not Roman Catholic ones. In fact, he probably knew as much as anyone that it was folk that were *anti-Catholic* that would believe anything about the Vatican, as long as it was something bad. And those that are anti-Catholic also tend to be racist, homophobic and terrified of anything displaying even a hint of socialism. Vigano made his appeal directly to the anti-Catholic and homophobic views of the extreme Right. Who else but a right-wing bigot would believe that all homosexuals are pederasts, as Vigano was implying?

While Vigano was venting his spleen about the Vatican, inspired by his spite and bitterness, he left the racism and anti-socialism to others. Picking up the anti-socialist baton was one Martin Armstrong, who described *The Great Reset* as 'The Final Battle Against Marxists.'[49] Quite why the 'elites' would want to bring about a Marxist society he did not explain. It seemed to be enough for his followers that he claimed that they were, even though it made no sense that the likes of Bill Gates, who benefited greatly from the capitalist system, would want to set up a socialist economy. Like Vigano, however, Armstrong had a personal axe to grind.

He was jailed for 11 years for fraud, a sentence which included 7 years for contempt of court when he refused to hand over some of his ill-gotten gains.[50] The tone of the article in the New York Times shows that the writer, and the newspaper, think he was hard-done-by. The comments too are supportive of Armstrong, comparing how he was treated to how the doyens of Wall Street constantly get let off scot-free.

Armstrong himself plays up the angle of the *Deep State* triumphing with the removal of Trump and betrays some of his bitterness at the same time. There is no doubting what his inspiration is for the following statement:

> They imprison small company officers under the pretense of security fraud yet NEVER prosecute even one banker – ever! MF Global stole their client's money and Federal Bankruptcy Judge Martin Glenn refused to comply with the bankruptcy law to protect the bankers.[51]

So, just like Vigano, Armstrong is turning his own bitterness into a political crusade. His was a small business compared to MF Global; something he is obviously angry about. Strangely, he makes no mention of the fact that Trump did not go after these bankers either. No doubt he was stopped by the *Deep State* and a Democratic Congress! Whether or not he is right about these bankers defrauding people and getting away with it is not the point. If true, then it is evidence of nationwide corruption. It is not, however, proof of the conspiracy he claims *The Great*

Reset to be. And, again, what benefit would these billionaire bankers get out of a Marxist system?

Believing in conspiracies often seems part-and-parcel of being an American. It probably comes from the country being founded by revolution. Such a state is necessarily paranoid; the Soviet Union was the same. This paranoia affects the media as well and is transmitted to most of the country's citizens. Throughout its history, there have been various conspiracy theories in the USA involving British agents, Freemasons, Communists and Islamic extremists among others. The big difference this time around was that the conspiracies about Covid-19 did not stay within American borders. They spread to other countries, including the UK.

As we know, there were those in Britain that already believed there was some conspiracy afoot, whether it be 5G radiation causing Covid or whatever. Demonstrations against lockdown were fairly common and, although illegal, some drew large crowds. Speakers included David Icke, no longer a figure of fun in a turquoise shell suit,[52] and, incongruously, Jeremy Corbyn's brother, Piers. Conspicuous among the various placards and banners carried by the demonstrators were various QAnon symbols and sayings.[53]

The QAnon mythology was not adapted for British consumption by its exponents but served up unchanged; Trump as the Messiah and all. At first sight it might seem as if QAnon had no relevance in Britain but, after all, it was meant to be a worldwide conspiracy. Those 'liberal elites,' were already familiar bogeymen to the British public.

Just as with Brexit, it was people that could well be classed as elite themselves that took up the QAnon baton in the UK. There was John Mappin, scion of the family famous for *Mappin and Webb*, the jewellers. He broadcasted online videos pushing QAnon agendas[54] as well as founding *Turning Point UK*, a branch of a pro-Trump, American, right-wing student organisation.[55] And then there was Jack Kidd, playboy and polo-playing brother of former model Jodie, who attended the ultra-expensive Harrow school.[56] These characters had huge followings online among people that were obviously too stupid to tell who was elite and who was not.

Getting new followers in the UK was relatively easy for *QAnon*. There had long been suspicions about powerful people in the UK being involved in a paedophile ring. A quick Google search throws up all manner of articles about Cyril Smith, Edward Heath, the Elm Street guesthouse as well as Jimmy Savile and his political and Royal contacts. It appeared that there was a great deal of truth in the stories, which made it easy for folk to accept the idea of there being a worldwide paedophile conspiracy, which was part of the *QAnon* doctrine.

A group called *Freedom for the Children UK* began to organise demonstrations throughout Britain. *QAnon* symbols were on display at these marches, (Fig.40) while the group's *Facebook* page expounded *QAnon* conspiracy theories.[57] The individual behind *Freedom for the Children UK* was one Laura Ward, who was also involved in *QAnon*.[58] Ironically, Ward's fellow *QAnon* conspiracy theorist, Jack Kidd, was a friend, and one-time business partner, of Ghislaine Maxwell,[59] who was allegedly involved in trafficking underage girls with Jeffrey Epstein.[60] Not surprisingly, Laura Ward's group had nothing to say about that!

A more sinister aspect of *QAnon* was the inherent anti-Semitism of the whole thing. Considering all the rednecks and KKK-types involved in the movement, this was hardly surprising. Practically every online exposition of the conspiracy theory mentions the Rothschilds and George Soros, a Jewish-American billionaire and philanthropist. There is also the fact that the whole conspiracy theory bears a remarkable similarity to known anti-Semitic forgery, *The Protocols of the Elders of Zion* as well as displaying echoes of Medieval *Blood Libel* stories.[61]

Considering the way *QAnon* was making inroads in the UK, one would have expected the people that had been going on about anti-Semitism for years would have something to say about it. The silence from the likes of Rachel Riley and Tracy-Ann Oberman was almost deafening. Presumably, they did not want to hurt their friends on the Right, particularly in the Conservative Party.

With Brexit, the ultimate beneficiaries in terms of votes were the Tories and it would no doubt be the same with all this stuff about conspiracies. To make sure, several Tory MPs, including

Home Secretary Priti Patel and Leader of the House of Commons Jacob Rees-Mogg, lent their names to John Mappin's *Turning Point UK*.[62] In fact, they were quick off the mark to do so.[63]

Meanwhile, Nigel Farage was still hanging around like a fart in a lift. There he was, among all those Tories, giving his support to *Turning Point UK*,[64] and giving fawning speeches over in America to the Trump faithful. Of course, that kept him in good standing with all the *QAnon* nuts. He decided the time was ripe for him to step into the British political arena again. The *Brexit Party* was to become *Reform UK* (Fig.41) with its main policy being the ending of Lockdown and all Covid restrictions, except for the most vulnerable. And, as usual, moaning about immigration was a huge part of it.[65]

Farage had put the wind up the Tories before and now he had done it again. Almost immediately after Farage announced his new party, a group of Tory MPs started up what they called a *Covid Recovery Group*. This group was only fifty strong, but it looked as if more would be joining. Its aim was, ostensibly, to stop Boris Johnson extending Lockdown too far and to make sure business did not suffer.[66] In reality, the obvious point was to pre-empt any desertion of Tory voters to Farage's new camp.

This *Covid Recovery Group* felt strong enough to make demands of Boris Johnson to bring Lockdown to a quicker end. In fact, they wanted all restrictions lifted by the end of April, claiming that there would be no need for them once most people had been vaccinated.[67] Johnson, however, was more cautious, although he was looking to re-open schools in March.[68]

Meanwhile, in America, there were moves in Congress to try to impeach Donald Trump for inciting the attack on the Capitol in January 2021. Most Republicans took Trump's side and voted against impeachment, allowing Trump to walk free. Boris Johnson was being interviewed on US television and, when asked about Trump's acquittal, called it, 'all the toings and froings and all the kerfuffle'.[69] This dismissive phrase would help keep the Trump supporters in the UK onside.

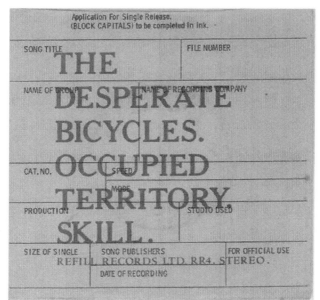

Fig.36 The Desperate Bicycles *Occupied Territory* single. 1978.

Fig.37. A familiar sight for users of audio cassette tapes.

Fig.38 *The Larkins.* 2021. In *The Darling Buds of May*, Mariette married the tax inspector Cedric Charlton. This time around, Cedric Charlton was being played by a black actor. The big worry among racists was that Marietta would marry Cedric in *The Larkins* as well.

Fig.39. The quintessential WWII poster, even though it never appeared during the war.

Fig.40 *Freedom for the Children rally* in Huddersfield. Note all the *QAnon* slogans on the placards.

Fig.41 Nigel Farage starts up yet another right-wing party.

13
__Cancelled__

'Woke' was an adjective that people used about themselves to signify that they knew what was going on around them, i.e., they had woken up. It was like people saying they were 'politically aware' in the 1980s and, just like in those days, the Right constantly denigrated such individuals until 'woke' became a pejorative word.

To the utter horror of papers like the Telegraph, the Daily Mail and the Sun, gay and lesbian relationships have largely been accepted as normal in British society. No longer can they print addresses and encourage their knuckle-dragging readers to attack people, as they did with Michael Cashman in the 1980s. They have even had to stand by and watch as gay and lesbian couples get married quite legally. A line has to be drawn somewhere to stop us all going the way of Sodom and Gomorrah and the right-wing media, and their readers have decided to draw that line at rights for trans people.

Most of us get quite confused with what 'trans' means, automatically assuming that it means 'transsexual' as in somebody that wants to have a sex change. Apparently, though, it can mean a lot of different things.

> By "Trans / Transgender" we are referring to all people who consider themselves to fall under the trans / transgender and gender variant umbrella. This includes, but is not limited to: trans women, trans men, transsexual men and transsexual women, non-binary, androgyne, polygender, agender, genderqueer, gender non-conforming, genderless, gender questioning, gender diverse, cross-dressing and transvestite people, and anyone who feels that the gender assigned to them at birth incompletely describes or does not at all describe their own

personal (a)gender identity. We also include those who reject the western division of cis/trans labels who are gender non-conforming.[1]

It can often seem amusing that folk can get all hung up about pronouns, calling themselves, and wanting others to call them, he/she/it/they. When it comes right down to it, however, most people just do not care. They might not understand and find it funny, but if somebody wants to be referred to as 'they' then why not? The majority of people just shrug their shoulders and comply. After all, what harm is it doing? Unless you are a right-wing Bible basher, it is not worth bothering about.

The right-wing media, therefore, had to find some other way to, as they see it, stop the rot. Their strategy was to stir things up by claiming that trans people, more specifically trans men, are dangerous. The *Daily Mail* ran a story in 2020 about how seven sex attacks were carried out in female prisons by male-born convicts that identified as women.[2] Buried away in the article is the timeframe in which these attacks took place. They occurred over a period of ten years. Altogether there were 124 sexual assaults in women's prisons, which means that 117 of those assaults were carried out by women.

The *Mail* gloried in telling us that, although trans women only make up around 1% of the female prison population, they were responsible for 5.6% of sexual assaults.[3] What is not pointed out, however, is that the *Mail*'s own figures mean that women are more than sixteen times more likely to be sexually attacked in prison by another female-born woman than they are by a trans woman.

Another aspect that the *Mail* ignores is that most of those seven sexual assaults might well have been perpetrated by one individual. Karen White, whose birth name was Stephen Wood, carried out a number of attacks when sent to a women's prison. She has also admitted to sexually attacking young children. Such an individual should not have been allowed to wander about unchecked in a women's prison, which was acknowledged by the Prison Service,

> We apologise sincerely for the mistakes which were made in this case.
>
> While we work to manage all prisoners, including those who are transgender, sensitively and in line with the law,

214

we are clear that the safety of all prisoners must be our absolute priority.[4]

As Jenny-Anne Bishop, a member of transgender rights group *Transforum*, said,

It is almost the exception that proves the rule, you've just got to look at what went wrong and make sure it doesn't happen again. No system is perfect.[5]

In other words, the Karen White case was an anomaly. The scare stories in the press about some huge, hulking brute with a face like Shrek planting a wig on his head and declaring himself a woman so he can go on an orgy of sexual assaults in a women's prison are patently untrue. There were even allegations in the right-wing press that female prison officers were raped by trans prisoners, taking their cue from former Tory justice minister, Rory Stewart.[6] According to Lord Keen, then spokesperson for the Ministry of Justice in the House of Lords, however,

There have been no reported incidents of any type of sexual assault against prison officers by transgender prisoners.[7]

Despite this debunking, many cling to the idea that trans women are simply predatory men in disguise. The *Mail's* story about female prisoners being raped was seized upon by American-based group *Women Are Human*, which exists solely for the purpose of fighting against trans rights.[8] The website Media Bias/Fact Check says of Women Are Human,

Overall, we rate Women are Human right biased and Questionable due to a lack of transparency with ownership and the consistent promotion of anti-transgender propaganda.[9]

There are quite a few of these types of groups around; all dedicated to the single pursuit of stopping trans women being treated as women. Although nominally feminist, these groups often have links with the religious right in America.[10] This is even true of such groups that are based in Britain. One of these is *Fair Play for Women*, which is, along with other, similar groups, incredibly secretive about where its funding comes from. Ostensibly, it uses crowdfunding, but many large donations come from anonymous sources.[11] Considering how close the ties are between the religious right and TERF (Trans-Exclusive Radical Feminist) groups in the USA, it is more than reasonable to conclude that the anonymous donations are by the religious right in America.

This secrecy explains why there are so many of these groups, instead of a single, united one. You would imagine that a single group would be more effective than all these organisations campaigning for the same thing independently. The truth is, though, that a single, large organisation would be required to keep public accounts, opening its funding up to media scrutiny. Small groups, however, are not so required, which is why the campaign is being pursued in this way.[12] Why would these groups be so concerned with secrecy if they did not have something to hide?

A damning indictment against these organisations is that, although professing to be feminist, they do not appear to be interested in anything to do with contemporary women's issues. For example, the most recent campaign concerning women in England and Wales was about Hormone Replacement Therapy (HRT), which many women take during the menopause. It was costing such women a fortune, but a high-profile campaign led to the Government changing the rules and saving women up to about £200 a year.[13]

There is no mention of this important campaign or victory on any of these so-called feminist websites. Neither is there anything about how young women are currently at risk of being injected with drugs at nightclubs.[14] No matter which parts of their websites you go to, there is nothing but hatred toward trans women. Often, this is couched in terms of men dictating who is to be termed a woman without taking into consideration the views of *actual* women. It is presented as a 'women's rights' issue,[15] but is that really the case? As one observer put it,

> Anti-trans have a hard time separating their perceptions
> of cis (*cisgender* – the gender you were born with) men as

sex-crazed, aggressive predators. They see transwomen as no different.

Transwomen are just trying to covertly invade girls bathrooms to... I dunno. I dunno what anti-trans think transwomen do in the toilets...[16]

This view of trans women as predators out to molest young girls is reminiscent of films made in the 1950s and 1960s in America, warning boys about homosexuals.[17] For some reason, everyone seemed to think back then that all homosexuals were pederasts. In the case of trans women, however, it would appear that these so-called feminists think that *all* men are looking for the opportunity to get their filthy hands on young women and even young girls. That, however, is all it is: appearance. The omission of one group shows that these women are not as concerned about predatory men as they seem.

Although you rarely hear them mentioned, there are people that are trans *men*. These are folk that are born as women but identify as men. Which changing rooms or toilets are these individuals supposed to use? Some of them take hormones that make them appear more masculine; hairier and bulkier. They would stand out like a sore thumb in a female changing room. On the other hand, would they not be at risk from all those sex-crazed, predatory men in a male changing room? This is never addressed on these pseudo-feminist websites, which makes one wonder who is actually setting their agenda.

The Lady Boys of Bangkok (Fig.42) is a show that first appeared at the Edinburgh Festival Fringe in the 1990s. Since then, they have been doing sell-out tours every year all over Britain. The show's audience tends to be predominantly female, which the promoters have recognised, targeting hen parties and office staff nights out.[18] Most men would feel distinctly uncomfortable at the show, questioning their own sexuality when they find the trans women on stage attractive. This is a fundamental problem for many men; does being physically attracted to a trans woman mean that one is gay?

There are several reasons why men are uncomfortable with the whole idea of trans women, but they all come back to the fact that there is still a stigma attached to being seen as gay. Although it stands to reason that gay men would not find a trans woman attractive, heterosexual men are confused about the whole business.[19] Today's society claims to be more open and inclusive, but it is *tolerance* rather than *acceptance* that is the norm. Most gay men still find it difficult to be open about their sexuality and heterosexual men are still terrified of their friends, neighbours and work colleagues thinking that they are gay.

Most heterosexual men would rather that trans women disappear altogether or, at the very least, not be accepted in society. In that way they would be spared their worst nightmare: picking up a girl, only to discover later that she has meat and two veg secreted about her person. Actually, it is not such a thing happening that is frightening, it is the possibility of others finding out about it. And it is not as if he can do a quick check in the nightclub or in the taxi. Doing so would soon lose him the chance of sex and he would be lucky to avoid a sizable prison sentence, especially if he persisted in this activity.

Given the fear and hatred of trans women by men and the complete absence of any current, highly publicised women's issues from the so-called feminist anti-trans websites, it is not too much of a stretch to suggest that the whole agenda is being set by men. And that agenda goes further than being just about trans women. Green MSP Patrick Harvie wrote an article for *The National* in which he said that there was a new anti-LGBT+ initiative by religious right-wing groups in America called, 'Split the T from the LGB.'[20] Whether he is right or not about who is behind this strategy, it certainly seems to exist and seems to be remarkably successful.

Stonewall has been the mainstay of LGBT+ activity in Britain for the past thirty years. It has fought for equality and justice for people that have faced discrimination due to their sexuality and/or gender identity.[21] Now, Stonewall faces the biggest crisis in its existence, and the threat comes from within. A breakaway group has been set up, calling itself *The LGB Alliance*.[22] This group is opposed to people choosing which gender they identify as and, consequently, has been labelled as anti-trans and even transphobic. Rather worryingly, that word 'Alliance' is a favourite of right-wing groups like the *Taxpayers Alliance* and the *Countryside Alliance*.

As well as sporting a right-wing name, the LGB Alliance has some dodgy bedfellows. The group has received support from homophobes and even neo-Nazis and, apparently, refuses to distance itself from them.[23] It has even shared a platform with ultra-right-wing organisation the *Heritage Foundation*.[24] The Heritage Foundation's own website says,

> Heritage's mission is to formulate and promote public policies based on the principles of free enterprise, limited government, individual freedom, traditional American values, and a strong national defense.[25]

In short, the Heritage Foundation is against everything the LGB Alliance is supposed to stand for. It certainly makes one wonder who is behind the LGB Alliance's transphobic agenda.

Patrick Harvie calls the agenda to split the LGBT+ cause a 'wedge issue,'[26] as in driving a wedge between erstwhile allies. There is another meaning, however, to it being a wedge issue. Right-wing Christian groups are overjoyed at this splintering of Stonewall, arguing that neither Stonewall nor the LGB Alliance are worthy of public support.[27] In their eyes, this transphobia and split in the LGBT+ ranks is the thin end of a wide, and long overdue, wedge. It appears that they see it as just the beginning of a way of taking us back to a time when same-sex relationships, let alone same-sex marriages, were illegal.

The sad thing about all this in-fighting is that the average *Sun* reader will just view it as a pointless argument among a bunch of poofs and weirdos. Those behind most, if not all, of those so-called feminist websites probably hold the same belief, although they would never voice it. The big question is, however, are these feminists dupes or are they a willing part of the agenda? It surely cannot have escaped their notice that all their supporters in the media are right-wing and hardly friendly to feminism. The fact that they feel the need to hide their finances suggests that they know exactly what they are doing.

One thing you will never see on any of these websites is the word 'woke'. Using this word would betray their right-wing sympathies, which they are desperate to keep under wraps. Their supporters, however, have no such compunction.

David Robertson (Fig.43) is a Scottish Evangelical now based in Australia.[28] As well as having his own blog, he writes for various Christian periodicals. In one such article, he joins other right-wing commentators in condemning the guidelines the Scottish Government has drawn up for schools. 'Children as young as four will be able to change their name and gender at school without their parents' consent!' he quotes from the *Telegraph*.[29] Actually, he, along with the others, is twisting the facts to suit his agenda.

For years now, teachers have been trained in how to deal with a child disclosing that they have been sexually abused. This, rather obviously, does not involve the teacher asking the class to put their hands up if they have been abused. In the same way, the Scottish Government guidelines[30] tell schools and teachers what to do *if* the situation arises. They are not demanding that a teacher goes into a Primary 1 class and ask, 'Hands up who wants to use the girls' toilet today!'

In his article in *Christian Today*, David Robertson expresses his support for the group *For Women Scotland*, another of those small, pseudo-feminist organisations.[31] Unfortunately, he lets the cat out of the bag somewhat on his blog, where he opines, 'The LGBT brainwashing of children is one of the most disturbing aspects of todays (sic) Woke world.'[32] Oh, dear! One wonders how For Women Scotland would feel about that little revelation.

As well as betraying one's right-wing sympathies, using the word 'woke' also aligns one with some rather unsavoury characters with rather unsavoury opinions. For example, when the BBC decided to commission a programme about the younger members of the Royal Family, outrage ensued. The programme was going to be written and presented by the BBC's media editor, Amol Rajan, who had been a vocal critic of the monarchy in the past. The assumption by many was that Rajan was left-wing and the word 'woke' was, of course, employed.

> The B.B.C. has never been fair and wont (sic) be until it removes its woke policy.[33]

As some commenters pointed out, the BBC is renowned for fawning over the Royal Family, so this notion of it being left-wing and 'woke' made no sense. Others took their political bile further.

> Why has this man been given the opportunity to say such terrible things about OUR repeat OUR royal family, you can say what you like in your birth country, but don't disrespect and verbally abuse OUR royalty.[34]

As we saw in earlier chapters, this kind of racism was encouraged by Brexit and went into overdrive when the Black Lives Matter movement came on the scene. The anti-woke brigade went berserk, not liking the fact that attention was being drawn to the more unsavoury aspects of Britain's past. They claimed that black people, in league with liberals and leftists, were trying to rewrite history.

Taking down statues and renaming streets were part of this rewriting of history and were seen as woke culture running mad.[35] In reality, street names have always been changed to suit contemporary sensibilities, such as the once ubiquitous *Gropecunt Lane*, which has long since disappeared from English towns. Even London's Rillington Place was renamed Ruston Close due to its association with the Christie murders.[36] There is no difference between these changes and calls for name changes to places in modern times. Current sensibilities are no less valid than those of the past.

Comments about this issue, as usual, show that most people on the Right simply do not understand it.

> Statue -wrecking etc is so much the easy banal option instead of focusing on really changing the lives of marginalised and impoverished people living NOW isnt it?[37]

> Live and work in the here and now. The pass (sic) is the pass (sic) you cannot change it.[38]

What these characters do not understand, or pretend not to understand, is that statues and street names do not represent

221

history but are a form of hero-worship. Nothing can be changed in the here-and-now while there are statues of slave traders and the like standing as testament to what Britain believes to be good and praiseworthy. Removing statues and changing street names will not erase these men from history.

When Communism collapsed, the people in former Soviet Bloc countries pulled down statues of Lenin and other Communist leaders. Perhaps they should have left them standing; after all, those characters are part of their history. It seems unlikely that any of the anti-woke brigade would ever have suggested this. And what about the statues of Saddam Hussein in Iraq? Should they not have been left where they were, with just a plaque on each of their plinths explaining who he was and what he did? That was what the anti-woke brigade was suggesting should happen in Britain.

Most of us, including the anti-woke brigade, are unaware of what the inside of a Cambridge college looks like or what adornments are visible. When news emerged about Jesus College's plans to remove a memorial to a past benefactor to the college from its chapel, the most common reaction would have been, 'So what?' It was surely up to the college itself to make such decisions. The anti-woke brigade, however, did not see things that way. The fact that the benefactor in question was linked with the slave trade, coupled with the Master of Jesus College being a black woman,[39] had them foaming at the mouth. Some of the comments betrayed the *real* thinking behind their complaints.

> Here we go again - she (Sonita Alleyne, the Master of Jesus College) would not be where she is if not for this chap however problematical his past - history can never be changed and his was a different age-no doubt he purchased slaves from other african tribes who enslaved their own and sold them.[40]

> Do we send back home all the ancestors (sic) of slave's alive today, they have obviously benefitted from their past.[41]

This commenter does not even know the difference between 'ancestors' and 'descendants'! As can be seen from these two

222

comments alone, it was racism, pure and simple, that was behind the pronouncements of the anti-woke brigade. But it is not just history and the presence of black people in 'their' country they are worried about.

> This is why the UK has fallen & taken over. UK history, culture, books, freedom of speech erased. Infiltration in Government & UK way of life. This country is run by Allah, Gandhi & the likes of Will I Am.[42]

They honestly believe that people of colour have taken over the UK, even though our Prime Minister being such a racist would suggest otherwise. To prove his point, the commenter above says, in another post,

> Our TV adverts contain 75% against 25% Caucasians. Who do they think they are?[43]

This character has probably sat making tally marks, counting all the people of colour and white people in adverts over a weekend, or even a week. There are not many around that are as sad as this, but the idea that there are far more black people in adverts these days is a common complaint. Actually, they do have a point; there certainly seems to be a racial imbalance in TV adverts currently. This, however, has nothing at all with the UK being 'taken over'. The truth is far more prosaic.

The BLM movement gave everybody a bit of a shake, including advertising agencies. They realised that the tokenism apparent in their adverts just was not going to cut it anymore. They obviously made a conscious effort to have more black people in the adverts they made; after all, black people eat pizza, buy lottery tickets, go shopping and celebrate Christmas just like white people do. Unfortunately, they have all had the same idea at the same time, so it looks like overkill when the adverts are shown on TV. The advertising agencies have, no doubt, cottoned on to this and things will sort themselves out soon enough. In the meantime, the anti-woke racists will just have to put up with all those black faces on their televisions.

One thing the anti-woke brigade rejoices in is pointing out how ridiculous woke culture is and how woke people complain about everything. Often, however, they succeed in only making themselves look stupid. In November 2021 there was an article online about a prudish individual, named Adrian Shann, who took offence at the words on a ketchup bottle at Pizza Hut. It said, 'Shake, Squeeze and Squirt' on the bottle and Mr Shann complained that the words were sexual in connotation, and it put him off his food.[44] The anti-woke brigade were straight in there.

> Lol ....Indicative of todays over Woke generation spoiling life.[45]

There was no way, by any stretch of the imagination, that anything in that article could be considered woke. It just showed that the anti-woke brigade were ready to apply the term to anything they did not believe in, whether it was apposite or not. And, of course, where there were anti-woke opinions, racism was never far away.

> I take it Mr. Shann is not C of E or R.M And would probably take offence if given a bag of (pork) Scratchings.[46]

Hand-in-hand with all the complaints about woke culture are complaints about *Cancel Culture*. Although those condemning Cancel Culture admit that such 'cancelling' can be done by the Right, they mostly see it as a left-wing phenomenon, closely tied-in with wokeness.[47] Those support it, on the other hand, view it as a way of bringing the powerful to book.

In this day of mass media, rich and powerful people can often say or do the wrong things. This results in outrage on the internet, where a boycott can be organised. Kanye West, for example, posed for pictures with Donald Trump and later said that 'slavery was a choice'.[48] He was boycotted online, and everybody thought twice about buying his records. Companies, too, can fall foul of Cancel Culture.

As its website boasts, Goya is 'the largest, Hispanic-owned food company in the United States'.[49] (Fig.44) In 2020, the CEO of the company, Robert Unanue, praised Donald Trump, asking Americans to pray for the then president and referring to Trump as 'a builder'.[50] Unfortunately, as everyone knows, what Trump was planning to build was a wall, running right along the Mexican border. Not only that, but he threatened to force Mexico to pay for it. He was hardly what one would call a good friend to Hispanics. Robert Unanue's words, not surprisingly, led to calls for a boycott of Goya products.[51]

What the right-wing media finds most objectionable, however, is the way that individuals can find themselves 'cancelled' for racist, homophobic or misogynistic statements, either online or out in the real world. The BBC railed against this aspect of Cancel Culture.

> For those at the receiving end of cancel culture, the consequence can lead to loss of reputation and income that can be hard to recover from…
>
> Letting go of an employee who has committed an offence may be the fastest way for a firm to quickly restore its reputation.
>
> But for the employee who was fired, moving isn't as easy and finding new work can be difficult.[52]

While the British media condemn Cancel Culture for its possible devastating effects on ordinary individuals, the same media had very little to say about the activities of the Economic League. If you remember, this organisation was responsible for making lists of union leaders, socialists etc. that companies could use to avoid employing 'undesirables'. Even after the Economic League closed in 1993, another such organisation, called *The Consulting Association* continued to supply blacklists, particularly to the building trade.[53] No doubt sometime in the future, we shall discover that a similar blacklist is being circulated at present.

The difference between being 'cancelled' and being on one of these secret blacklists is obvious. The 'victims' of Cancel Culture know exactly what they have done, and it is entirely up to them to apologise and mend their ways. Those that lost their jobs and could find no other employment because they were on a secret blacklist had no idea what they had done wrong. In fact, they had done nothing wrong except hold the 'wrong' political views, although they had no way of knowing that.

The online edition of the *Daily Mail*, in November 2021, had a list of tales of woe about those that had suffered because of Cancel Culture. The word 'woke' got a few mentions as well.[54] A year before, the same organ rejoiced in the fact that the Westminster Government was introducing new instructions for secondary-school teachers.

> As part of the Government's drive to protect freedom of speech, secondary school students will learn that people with controversial opinions should be respected.[55]

Of course, that all depends on what those 'controversial opinions' are. Every year, especially around November, the *Daily Mail* joins other right-wing media in condemning footballer James McClean for refusing to wear a poppy. Those connected with the paper almost succumbed to apoplexy when McClean turned his back on the English flag while *God Save the Queen* was playing at a pre-season friendly in America.[56]

McClean has explained his position on numerous occasions. As we saw in Chapter 3, the British Legion says on its website that 'Poppies are worn as a show of support for the Armed Forces community.'[57] Coming from the Nationalist Community in Northern Ireland, McClean does not feel it appropriate to show support for the British armed forces. He often cites Bloody Sunday[58] as one reason why he has no love for the British Army. He is still, however, castigated constantly. And he is not the only one.

Every November, and sometimes even in October, the right-wing press is inundated with angry letters about somebody appearing on television without a poppy. Folk even get stopped in the street to explain why they are not wearing one. It has got so that many people now wear one out of fear. A term has been coined for this climate of intimidation: *Poppy Fascism*. Some well-known names have taken a stand against it, but not everyone feels powerful enough to do so.[59]

Foreign celebrities appearing on British television probably wonder what is going on when a paper flower is slapped onto them before they appear on camera. Television companies are so frightened of a backlash that they probably employ somebody to make sure nobody goes onscreen without a poppy. This can sometimes end up being absolutely ridiculous, like the time Cookie Monster from *Sesame Street* appeared on *The One Show* sporting a poppy.[60] (Fig.45) Not only was this little stunt ridiculed mercilessly, but it also angered the Poppy Police, who considered it disrespectful.[61]

This Poppy Fascism shows that Cancel Culture is not solely the preserve of left-wing and liberal types in Britain. As far as can be determined, though, nobody has lost their job (yet!) for not wearing a poppy, much as many people would love it to happen. Neither, however, has any ordinary person due to 'woke' culture. The main 'victims' in Britain appear to be celebrities and academics.

Kathleen Stock was Professor of Philosophy at the University of Sussex. She was also a vocal critic of transgender legislation, leading many to brand her as transphobic. In 2021, she became a trustee of the LGB Alliance, a group we have already met. Her views caused students at Sussex to demand her removal, with posters appearing around the campus. According to the Times, she had to teach remotely due to 'fears for her safety'.[62] Many university and college lecturers, however, have been teaching remotely due to Covid, which makes you wonder how true this assertion is.

Despite receiving support from the University[63] and other Philosophy academics,[64] Stock decided to resign. She appeared on Lorraine Kelly's morning television programme, where Kelly pointed out that, contrary to what Stock was claiming, she was not a victim of Cancel Culture since she had resigned. Kelly also stressed that, far from being silenced, Stock had more of a voice now, appearing on various TV shows and in the press. Stock was also asked what it was she wanted to happen but refused to answer.[65]

It was just a couple of days later that a new organisation was announced called *The University of Austin*. It promised to offer students 'free speech' and 'forbidden courses'.[66] The institution was unable, however, to give students accreditation, meaning that it was just going to be a right-wing talking shop. Interestingly, Kathleen Stock was offered a position and accepted it 'with alacrity'.[67] That said a lot about Stock's political inclinations and also cast doubt on her reasons for resigning. She was not the only academic to be 'cancelled'.

David Starkey (Fig.46) is a prissy little man, who comes across as having an extremely high opinion of himself. He was a lecturer in History at the London School of Economics and would have remained unknown outside of academia if he had not managed to break into the media. He was, and is, rude, antagonistic, strident and, quite often, aggressive. The audiences lapped it up, leading to even more radio and television appearances.

Starkey's history programmes have been entertaining and informative and his enthusiasm for his subject shines through. The only thing that spoils his presentation is his pedantic tendency to pronounce every syllable in each word, like 'Par-lay-a-ment', which is intensely irritating. The problems that people have with him, though, are due to other programmes he appears in, such as *Question Time*. Unfortunately, Starkey has come to believe that he is an expert in everything, not just the Tudors.

This feeling of omniscience and infallibility he has developed has even influenced how he views history. He does something that most historians do their best to avoid doing and undergraduates are advised not to do, comparing the past with today to make a point. It is fine to look at, say, Victorian times and nowadays to see what is different and what is the same in order to show how history is a process. This, however, is not what Starkey does. He does things such as likening Brexit to Henry VIII's break with the Catholic Church and claiming that the EU is just like the Church of those days.[68] It is hardly surprising that he sets other historians' teeth on edge. In fact, 100 historians signed an open letter calling for Starkey not to be called a historian, other than on his specialist subject, the Tudors. They claimed that he was bringing the term 'historian' into disrepute.[69]

This open letter was occasioned by Starkey making racist comments on *Newsnight*. This was not to be the last time he would make such comments, not by a long chalk. The final straw came on a podcast with right-wing commentator and activist, Darren Grimes.[70]

(The offensive bit has been edited out, but there is still plenty there to be concerned about.) While discussing Black Lives Matter, he said, 'Slavery was not genocide otherwise there wouldn't be so many damn blacks in Africa or Britain would there?'[71] He later apologised for his remarks, but it was too little too late as far as many were concerned. His last chance had long gone.

Starkey was stripped of honorary titles from universities, sacked or forced to resign from various posts and dropped by his publishers.[72] He moaned to Nigel Farage on *GB News* about how he had no respect for all those universities that had 'cancelled' him. Although he claimed not to be a victim, he certainly played the part.[73] He called what he had said 'a slip of the tongue'. He obviously had no understanding of the ramifications of his statement.

As some people pointed out, Starkey's spurious logic could be applied to other genocides, especially the Holocaust.[74] One individual asked us to picture the furore if Jeremy Corbyn had said such a thing about the Jews.[75] (Not that he ever would.) Most other commenters were decidedly on the side of Starkey.

> Starkey has been accused of telling the truth, and not bowing down to all the Woke nonsense surrounding blm.
> The trouble is that so many are afraid to agree with him, as they to would be castigated by the 15% who seem to think they should be running the country.
> He is right about the universities, they are bending over backwards, and will soon disappear up their own back *****.[76]

> Good on you David, don't take any crap from the s.nowflake "woke" thugs.[77]

> What happened to Starkey proves, once and for all that there is no such thing as free speech in the UK.[78]

> the only reason he is disliked by the Woke society is he tells the truth and backs it all up with facts that they cannot dispute well done David.[79]

Actually, that is precisely the problem: Starkey offers no facts whatsoever to back up his statements. That is what those historians that signed the open letter were annoyed about. The other commenter, who, like many others, was concerned about free speech, might be interested in another academic that was 'cancelled'. Then again, he would probably be all for it in this case.

David Miller, Professor of Political Sociology at Bristol University (Fig.47), had long been accused of anti-Semitism in his lectures and in online posts. In October 2021, the University sacked him, saying that he 'did not meet the standards of behaviour we expect from our staff'.[80] So, was the University right to sack Miller? It all depends upon who you ask.

Before he was sacked, many academics worldwide signed an open letter decrying the attacks on Miller and calling for academic freedom.[81] Meanwhile, another international group of academics signed a different open letter condemning Miller's many statements about Israel and Jews in general. According to them, it was not a question of free speech, but dangerous nonsense that risked the safety of Jewish students and other Jews in Britain.[82] They did not explicitly call for him to be sacked, but such a course of action was certainly implied.

Bristol is a solidly Labour area, so Robert Halfon, Tory MP for Harlow, decided to step in. Along with other Tories, Halfon urged the Universities Minister, Michelle Donelan, to cut funding to Bristol University if they did not do something about Miller's anti-Semitism.[83] An internal investigation into Miller's statements, conducted by a QC, concluded that said statements (or *alleged* statements) 'did not constitute unlawful speech'.[84] The University, however, no doubt feeling under pressure, sacked him anyway. What happened to Miller was the very definition of being 'cancelled'.

Whatever the rights and wrongs of the case, one thing stands out clearly: none of those that ranted about free speech when David Starkey was 'cancelled' were anywhere to be seen, or heard, when the same thing happened to David Miller. It seemed that free speech was only to be practised by those on the Right. The *Daily Mail* ran an article about Miller in February 2021, right in the middle of all the controversy. One comment seemed to sum up the opinion of every Tory voter.

> Lots of comments here saying its OK as its just 'free speech'. (Actually, there were only one or two.) Not in this case. He is a Professor spewing his foul anti-semitic views on students - thats not free speech its indoctrination and brainwashing.[85]

14
Part of the Union

Although many of the reasons for members of the working classes voting Tory were the same across Britain, those in Scotland had, and have, their own particular reason. It all goes back to a split in the Liberal Party in the 1880s; a split that was never healed.

Scotland was a Liberal country, as can be seen in 19th Century election results. In 1880, the Liberals won 53 out of the available 60 seats, including one of the normally Tory university seats.[1] It was the same in the 1885 election, with an increased electorate and Scotland now having 72 seats at Westminster. The Tories only won 10 of those, including the two university seats. The rest were either won by the Liberals or by smaller parties that would vote alongside them.[2] Things were to change, however, when it came to the 1886 election.

The reason why there was another general election so soon was that Gladstone's government had been roundly defeated in the House of Commons. Gladstone had made no secret of his intention to introduce a Home Rule bill for Ireland. This he did in 1886, but he had underestimated the depth of feeling against Home Rule in his own party. A strange combination of old-style Whigs and radicals led by Joseph Chamberlain (Fig.48) joined the Tories in voting against Gladstone's bill. Even Parnell's 86 Irish MPs could not save it.

In the 1886 election, 45 constituencies stayed faithful to the Liberals, while 11 voted Conservative. The other 17 elected candidates from the new Liberal Unionist Party. An electoral pact had been arranged between the Tories and the Liberal Unionists, meaning that they did not stand against each other. Those 17 Liberal Unionist MPs, along with those elected in England, were going to be voting with the Tories in Parliament. Liberal seats were drastically reduced and, apart from a brief three years as a minority government, the Liberals were out of office for the next twenty years.

Joseph Chamberlain and others were often accused of 'playing the Orange card,' a charge Chamberlain vehemently refuted. There was no denying, however, that his political allies, the Tories, most definitely *were* playing such a card. Randolph Churchill spoke to Orangemen in Belfast in February 1886, giving them the rallying cry, 'Ulster will fight, and Ulster will be right.'[3]

In Scotland too the Orangemen rallied to the cause. It is notable that some of the constituencies that changed from Liberal to Liberal Unionist were, and are, considered to be Orange/Masonic areas, for example, the three Ayrshire constituencies.[4] In Glasgow, the two constituencies that changed to Liberal Unionist, St. Rollox and Tradeston, contained much of Glasgow's heavy industry, which were the preserve of Protestants.[5] They also happened to have large Irish Catholic populations, which many Protestants felt threatened by. Those Irish Catholics were unable to vote in elections until 1918.

Gladstone made another attempt to pass a Home Rule bill in 1893. This time it passed in the Commons but was thrown out by the Lords. When the Tories and Liberal Unionists came back into power in 1895, they decided that it was time to put an end to the demands for Home Rule in Ireland. The usual Tory method of dealing with Ireland was coercion, but the Liberal Unionists no doubt had a moderating influence. The new way became known as 'Constructive Unionism' or 'Killing Home Rule with kindness.'[6] It was thought that removing other Irish grievances might dampen support for Home Rule.

The Land Question had been a major problem in Ireland for decades. Landlords, often absentee, charged extortionate rents, which caused misery for many. There were rent strikes accompanied by mass evictions, which usually resulted in violence. The British Government of Tories and Liberal Unionists brought in measures to relieve this tension, culminating in the Wyndham Land Act of 1903. By the terms of this act, landlords were given incentives to sell their land, while prospective purchasers, erstwhile tenants, were given government loans at low rates of interest.[7] This helped to destroy the Protestant hegemony of land in Ireland.

Much more significant, though, was the 1898 Local Government Act, which organised district councils along British lines. Irish Nationalists won control of all these councils, save for those in some counties in Ulster.[8] It was the end of the Protestant Ascendancy in Ireland. Unionists were now concentrated in Ulster, which was to cause huge problems in years to come.

In 1912, the Liberal Unionists and the Conservatives made their alliance official, and, in England and Wales, candidates thereafter simply stood as Conservatives. The Tories knew which side their bread was buttered in Scotland, so they went by a different name there: Unionists.[9] Sometimes, they still went by the name Liberal Unionists or National Liberals, but they all took the Conservative whip at Westminster. (Fig.49)

Meanwhile, there was more worry for Unionists in Scotland and in Ulster. The Liberal Party had been returned with a huge majority in 1906, but this majority disappeared in the 1910 elections. To form a government, the Liberals again relied on the Irish Parliamentary Party for support. Home Rule legislation was inevitable and Unionists on both sides of the North Channel were soon up in arms.

In 1912, a total of 237,368 men and 234,046 women signed the Ulster Covenant. This was a document declaring that nobody, not even the Westminster Government, could force Ulster into a Home Rule Ireland.[10] In the same year, a paramilitary group, the Ulster Volunteer Force, was set up to resist, with arms, if necessary, any attempt to enforce Home Rule on Ulster.[11]

Edward Carson, the leader of the Ulster Unionists, then travelled to Liverpool to seek support there. There were plenty of Orangemen in Liverpool prepared to give him a hearing. Many of them were Ulster Protestants, who resented the Irish Catholics in their midst. Considering Carson's targeted audience, it was obvious where his next stop was going to be - Glasgow. Thousands of Orangemen turned up to hear him, along with Unionist politician John Ure Primrose.[12] The latter also happened to be the chairman of Rangers Football Club, which was rapidly becoming a focus for Orangeism and Unionism in Scotland.

Apparently, seven UVF companies were raised in Scotland,[13] while, in 1914, a British Covenant, in support of the Ulster one, was signed by two million people.[14] The Home Rule Bill was passed in 1914 and was awaiting Royal assent when a war got in the way, causing everything to be postponed.

The whole business of the Ulster Protestants defiantly refusing to be part of a United Ireland under Home Rule betrayed a lot about their feelings. The Irish Parliamentary Party, along with other supporters of Home Rule, were actually committed to Ireland remaining a part of the United Kingdom. What they wanted was a *devolved* parliament, with Westminster still ultimately in charge and able to amend or annul any Act passed in Dublin.[15] Furthermore, terms were inserted in the Bill to forestall any discrimination on religious grounds.[16] Home Rule was not going to be anything like 'Rome Rule,' despite what the Ulster Unionists said.

An even more significant part of the 1912 Bill was that elections in Ireland were to be held under the system of proportional representation.[17] This was to protect the Unionist Protestant minority. With all these safeguards in place, it is difficult to see why the Ulster Protestants were so intransigent. Their very name, though, of Ulster Unionists, rather than Irish Unionists, shows what they really thought about Home Rule.

Mention was made earlier of the Protestant Ascendancy, which was about Protestants having control over Irish land, local government, and even national organisations, like the police. As we have seen, this control began to erode at the end of the 19th Century. More and more Irish Protestants retrenched to Ulster, where they still had power. The whole idea of Irish Catholics being their equals filled them with dread. Demands were made, all the way up to the start of the war, for Ulster, where they still ruled the roost, to be partitioned from Ireland and to remain part of the UK.

Let us go straight to 1922, when the Irish Free State began. The terms of the Anglo-Irish Treaty of 1921 allowed Ulster to secede, but not all of Ulster did. Three counties, Cavan, Donegal and Monaghan, had far too many Catholics for the

Unionists' liking. And, of course, their bigoted opinion of Irish Catholics told them that they bred like rabbits, which would not bode well for the future. Only six counties made up the new statelet, which remained part of the United Kingdom.

Considering the whole *raison d'être* of the new statelet was to maintain the Protestant Ascendancy, it was surprising that it was not named the *Orange* Free State. The name was available, since the one in South Africa had ceased to exist in 1902. Instead, the boring and straightforward name of Northern Ireland was chosen. Right from the start, it was clear that Irish Catholics were to be second-class citizens in Northern Ireland.

Meanwhile, an unholy alliance of the Orange Order, the Freemasons, the Scottish Unionists and Rangers Football Club attempted to have a similar set-up in Scotland. In fact, they went further than the Ulster Unionists; they wanted Irish Catholics out of the country altogether. The Church of Scotland joined in enthusiastically with the publication of *On the Menace of the Irish Race to our Scottish Nationality* in 1923.[18]

This racist report blamed all the ills of Scotland, including drunkenness and crime, upon Irish Catholics. It warned that these people were infecting Scottish society, bringing good Protestants down with them. A distinction was drawn between Scottish Catholics and Irish Catholics, confirming that it was *racial* bigotry the Church was promoting. The Church later (much later) apologised for the report, but it is interesting to note that a group demonstrated outside the General Assembly, accusing the Church of 'betraying the faith of Reformation leader John Knox.'[19] Strangely, there is no evidence anywhere of Knox professing hatred of the Irish, so those bigots were acting on their own initiative.

When the Government refused to accede to the Church's demand to repatriate Irish Catholics, a new, more sinister, method of discrimination developed. Job interviews always contained the question of what school one had attended, adversely affecting anyone that was Catholic, not just the

Irish.[20] In this way, all the best jobs were kept as the preserve of Protestants. What really concerns us here, though, is how this affected the Scottish Unionist vote.

The 1929 General Election was the first one where the electorate was truly democratic. Everyone aged 21 and over now had the vote, both male and female. The result in Scotland was that Labour won 36 seats, the Unionists 20, the Liberals 13, while 2 seats went to other, minority parties.[21] That, however, does not tell the whole story. As is often the case, the First-Past-the-Post system throws up some irregularities when it comes to elections. Nationally (in Scotland), the Unionists won 35.9% of the vote, while Labour won 42.3%.[22] That puts a totally different slant on things.

In a straight percentages-for-seats PR system, the Unionists would have had 25 seats, Labour 30. In those terms, the Labour victory does not look so conclusive. In fact, the percentage of votes for the Unionists and their allies in Scotland held up pretty well, never falling below 35% until the 1970s.[23] Now, at no point during that period did the upper and middle classes make up 35% or more of the population, so a lot of those Unionist voters were working-class. So, what happened in the 1970s to change things?

As well as appealing to the anti-Irish element among Scottish Protestants, the Unionists had another advantage over other parties. While others, like Labour or the Liberals, were based in England, the Unionists could boast that theirs was a purely Scottish party. Never mind that they took the Conservative whip in Westminster, and participated in Tory governments, they were Scottish. That Scottishness came to an end in 1965 when the Unionists officially joined with the Tories to create the Scottish Conservative and Unionist Party.[24]

Although the name 'Scottish' was preserved in the new title, the party was controlled from London and was simply a branch office. That was not the only reason for disliking this new moniker. The Conservative Party in England did things that would have been unthinkable to the Scottish Unionists, like fielding – gasp! – *Catholic* candidates, such as William Rees-Mogg.[25] Unionist candidates had all, to a man, been Protestant and some, like John Gilmour, MP for Glasgow Pollok 1918-

1940,[26] Thomas Moore, MP for Ayr Burghs 1925-1964[27] and Archibald McInnes Shaw, MP for Western Renfrewshire 1924-1929, and candidate in two other constituencies in the 1930s, were all members of the Orange Order. In fact, McInnes Shaw was, at one time, Grand Master of the Orange Lodge of Scotland and then Imperial Grand Master of Great Britain and the Dominions.[28] Matters got even worse for erstwhile Scottish Unionist voters in the 1970s.

Anyone that grew up in the 1970s will be familiar with the way that comics seemed to be continually amalgamating. At the beginning of the decade, there were six popular comics called, *Buster*, *Lion*, *Valiant*, *Jet*, *Thunder* and *TV21*. These amalgamated to become three: *Buster & Jet*, *Lion & Thunder* and *Valiant & TV21*. Then the '&s' were dropped to leave us with *Buster*, *Lion* and *Valiant*. Further amalgamations took place between these and other comics until, eventually, they disappeared altogether.

Also in the 1970s, the Tories decided that the Conservative and Unionist Party was too much of a mouthful and shortened it to the Conservative Party. The Scottish branch also shortened its name and became simply the Scottish Conservative Party. This was especially the case after Margaret Thatcher became leader. People got used to hearing on TV that, 'There now follows a party political broadcast by the Scottish Conservatives.' Unionism no longer appeared to be a selling point.

Thatcher's Government proved to be somewhat troubling as far as the Orangemen and their ilk in Scotland were concerned. They certainly approved of her hard-line stance against the IRA Hunger Strikers, who were demanding to be treated as political prisoners. In fact, her hard-line stance against the IRA in general met their enthusiastic approval. Her economic policies, however, were problematic in the extreme.

As good right-wingers, The People (as we should perhaps call them since not all of them were Orangemen and that is the term they use for themselves) were happy to buy into the story that it was the actions of trades unions that had caused British industry to be uncompetitive. It was okay, though, to view the unions as some abstract concept, but the reality was that it was *their* unions that Thatcher wanted to destroy. That realisation must have come as a complete shock to them.

The People had maintained their hold on Scotland's heavy industries by dint of funny handshakes, the flash of a sash or good, old-fashioned nepotism. If all else failed, a job candidate could always be asked the question about his school. Even the unions were dominated by The People and Catholics were kept at bay. Of course, there were Catholics working in the shipyards etc. but only as unskilled or semi-skilled labourers. Tradesmen were all Protestant since no Catholic apprentices were taken on. Now, those heavy industries were disappearing and along with them was disappearing The People's dominant station in Scottish society.

Thatcher may not have personally destroyed Scottish industry, but her policies certainly did. Monetarism, the new Deflation, specified that government spending should be cut back as much as possible. Meanwhile, other nations lavished subsidies and cheap loans on their industries,[29] leaving British firms trailing in their wake. To Thatcher, though, the market was all, and British businesses had to make their own way in the world's unfair market. In the space of a couple of decades, Scottish industry was devastated and barely existed at all.

New businesses gradually took the place of heavy industry, such as computer firms and service industries. These new companies, however, had their headquarters abroad and they could not care less what school you went to. As long as you were qualified or skilled enough for the post, you got it without the need for handshakes or your father being the head of the local Orange Lodge. Another problem was that these businesses were hardly what you would call labour intensive, so they did not make much of a dent in the unemployment figures.

Unfortunately for The People, generations of job security had made them rather lazy when it came to education. When you could be guaranteed a job or an apprenticeship when you left school, then what was the point of learning anything more than the basics? This meant that when Scotland's heavy industry vanished, there were no jobs for The People's offspring. They were thrown out of school at the age of 16 with no job to walk into and no prospects. To make matters worse, they could not even sign on the dole anymore. Thatcher's Government had changed the law in order to massage the unemployment figures. Under 18s were no longer entitled to any benefits, so were not counted as being unemployed. The People now had to look after their idle offspring until they were 18.

With The People having every reason to hate Thatcher and her government, it was hardly surprising that they stopped caring about the way she stood up to the IRA anymore. In fact, in October 1984, when the IRA bombed the hotel where the Tory cabinet was staying, even some Orangemen were disappointed that Thatcher escaped unscathed. Rather than outrage, they expressed the opinion, 'Those stupid Irish can't do anything right!'

And then, in 1985, Thatcher confirmed herself as nothing less than satanic in the eyes of The People. She signed the *Anglo-Irish Agreement* with the Taoiseach of the Irish Republic, Garret FitzGerald, giving the Irish Government 'an official consultative role in the affairs of Northern Ireland.'[30] As if that were not enough to give The People apoplexy, Article 1(c) of the Agreement made their blood run cold. It specified that 'The two Governments...

> declare that, if in the future a majority of the people of Northern Ireland clearly wish for and formally consent to the establishment of a United Ireland, they will introduce and support in the respective Parliaments legislation to give effect to that wish.[31]

In Thatcher's next two elections, the Tory Vote in Scotland fell below 30% for the first time. Even her dismissal and replacement with John Major did not make a difference. In the first general election with Major as Conservative leader, the party could only manage 25.6% of the votes cast.[32] But worse was to come. In 1997, the year of the Labour landslide, the Scottish Tory vote fell to an all-time low of 17.5% and, for the first time ever, Scotland sent not one Tory MP to Westminster.[33]

For The People, it looked as if everything was gone, their political party, their places of work and even their lodges. The old areas in Glasgow that were hotbeds of Orangeism have almost disappeared, with most working-class people living in outlying council schemes. Of course, the lodges still existed, but not to the same extent as they used to. In fact, academic Tom Devine claims that the Orange Order in Scotland is in terminal decline.[34] His argument that only about 1% of Protestants are members, however, shows a remarkable lack of understanding of The People.

In 2020, a new book about the Orange Order and Orangemen in Scotland was released. It was by Dr Joseph Webster and called, *The Religion of Orange Politics*. Webster spent five years among Orangemen in an unnamed ex-mining town in North Lanarkshire. In a review of the book, Tom Devine had this to say:

> It is not surprising to read in his pages that Orangemen (all Webster's interviewees were men) remain fiercely opposed to Scottish independence, are Rangers supporters to a man (the bus for Ibrox leaves from their club), deeply loyal to the monarchy, proud of their Protestant heritage (despite the fact that few ever attend church) and strongly opposed to denominational schools.[35]

When you consider Devine's ubiquitous claims about the Orange Order being on its last legs (Google Tom Devine Orange Order and you will see how far his opinions have spread) the ignorant bigotry expressed above by Orangemen appear to be nothing to worry about. The People, however, are comprised of more than just Orangemen. There are plenty of individuals all over Scotland that agree with the sentiments above but that have never set foot in an Orange lodge.

As we moved into the 21st Century, The People found a new, better place to meet up. It was called the internet. The beauty of online social media was that there were no borders, so The People on both sides of the North Channel could speak with each other instantaneously. There were, of course, Facebook pages dedicated to Orange lodges and bands, but the main meeting places for The People were Rangers sites and forums.

Follow Follow was one such forum, where, although many threads discuss purely football matters, other themes pop up as well. Remember the story about Edward Carson visiting Glasgow with the involvement of John Ure Primrose, the Chairman of Rangers FC? Some of The People expressed pride at their team being part of Unionist history.

> It's good to know that the Chairman of Rangers FC, Sir John Ure-Primrose, shared a platform with the great Carson.[36]

> Great read, thanks. God, we knew what we stood for in those days.[37]

> When glasgow was a conservative, unionist city. shame its now a republican nationalistic hovel now.[38]

Even before the internet came on the scene, The People from Scotland and Northern Ireland were able to meet up and mingle. There were the annual trips by the NI contingent to Glasgow for the July parades and those from Glasgow going to Belfast a day or two later. A more regular event was the ferry-loads of The People coming over to Ibrox for Rangers games. In fact, Rangers had become more of a focus for Unionists from both Scotland and Northern Ireland than the Orange Order. There was, however, a serpent in this Garden of Eden.

When the devolved Scottish Parliament was set up, a strange voting system was to be employed, called the D'Hondt Method. Everyone had two votes; one for a direct, first-past-the-post candidate, the other for a political party under a PR system, which caused MSPs to be chosen from a list. It was a lot more complicated than that[39] and was designed to stop any single party being in control. It worked fine at first, with Labour having to ally with the Liberal Democrats and then the SNP allying with the Greens to form a minority government. In 2011, however, the unthinkable happened.

There are 129 members of the Scottish Parliament, which means that 65 seats are needed for a majority, something that no party had yet achieved. In 2011, though, the SNP were returned with 69 seats; a thing that was not supposed to happen.[40] The SNP were able to form a government on their own, with no need for support from anyone. Of course, everyone knew what was going to happen; there was going to be a referendum on Scottish independence.

Before all that, though, in 1998, the Good Friday Agreement was signed.[41] A good many of The People were unhappy about the Agreement. A referendum was held in Northern Ireland to gauge support for the Agreement. (A similar one was held in the Irish Republic.) 71.1% voted in favour with a high turnout of 81.1%.[42] The fact that this means that only 57.7% of the whole electorate of Northern Ireland voted for the Agreement makes it seem not quite so impressive. Analysis of the results suggests that the vote in favour was far higher among Nationalists than it was among Unionists.[43] It is not too much of a stretch, then, to extrapolate that most of the 42.3% against, or not voting, was comprised of The People.

So, what did The People have against the Agreement? Well, there were two elements that had always been anathema to them, the first of which was equality. The state of Northern Ireland had been set up in the first place to maintain some semblance of the Protestant Ascendancy and The People had enjoyed having the upper hand ever since. Now, not only were they going to have to accept Irish Catholics as equals, but it was going to be enshrined in their very constitution!

The other aspect that put a chill up their spines was power sharing. From now on, they were going to have to accept whoever the Nationalists voted for into Stormont and even into government. Even if Sinn Féin members were elected, one of them was going to be Deputy First Minister or even, God forbid, First Minister.

Neither The People in Northern Ireland nor in Scotland were entirely happy about the whole business. After decades of superiority, it suddenly felt as if they were being debased. After a few years, there was dark talk on Rangers forums about Protestants being marginalised. And then their worst fears were realised when it was announced that a referendum on Scottish independence would take place in September 2014.[44]

Even before the referendum was announced, Unionists in Northern Ireland were extremely wary of what it was going to mean. Perhaps it was the fact that the Good Friday Agreement, and the Anglo-Irish Agreement before it, gave the Irish Republic a say in the affairs of Northern Ireland that made the Unionists think they had a right to be involved in any vote on Scottish independence. As Dr David Hume, of the Grand Orange Lodge of Ireland put it, the Ulster Scots were 'stakeholders' in Scotland and the UK.[45] Nobody in either Scotland or Northern Ireland, however, was brave enough to voice what their real fear was.

In 2020, a YouGov survey found that 54% of the British public could not care less if Northern Ireland left the UK or not.[46] It is unclear where the survey took place, but it is more than probable that it was predominantly English people that were asked. Back in 2018, the new Northern Irish Secretary, Karen Bradley, admitted that she had not the first clue about politics in Northern Ireland before she got the job. Even afterwards she still seemed confused.[47] And, in 2019, Boris Johnson's father, Stanley, expressed the opinion that the Irish should just be left to 'shoot each other.' He said that this would be the opinion of Margaret Thatcher, but he made it patently clear that he agreed with this assessment. He apologised afterwards, but it was still out there.[48]

These surveys and statements showed everyone something that they had suspected for years; that the English wish Northern Ireland would just disappear. The evidence is anecdotal, but it has been clear for a long time that most English people rue the day that their ancestors ever set foot on the Emerald Isle. And James VI (James I in England) is probably roundly cursed by all and sundry for shipping all those Scottish Protestants to Ulster in the first place. So why were they still holding onto it? The answer was rather obvious.

The only reason Westminster was still so interested in Northern Ireland was that it meant so much in Scotland. Scotland, or, more specifically, the tax revenues from Scotland's oil, was of extreme importance to Westminster. The Anglo-centric ministers in London believed that most of Scotland wanted to keep Northern Ireland in the UK since their fellow

Scots lived there. The fear of The People was that a YES victory in the independence referendum would betray that this was no longer the case. Even if there were problems between Scotland and Westminster over how independence should work, it would still mean that the UK Government would have no reason anymore to hold onto Northern Ireland.

As if this was not enough to cope with, in 2012 The People had to go through a traumatic experience. Rangers, the club that had taken the place of the Orange Order as the focus for all The People's hopes and hates, was liquidated. A new club was formed and, still in denial about the death of the old one, The People convinced themselves that liquidation had not happened at all. On this occasion, let us be kind and allow them their delusion and pretend that the new club is 'still Rangers'.

Back to the referendum on Scottish independence, and The People, on their forums, were adamant that they were not going to accept it if Scotland voted for independence. There were dark references to Edward Carson and armed insurrection, which have, of course, all long since disappeared. We can still read, though, Ruth Dudley Edwards's article comparing the SNP with the IRA, blaming Irish Catholic immigrants for sectarian bigotry in Scotland and implying that those Irish Catholics' anti-Englishness was responsible for the calls for Scottish independence.[49] This evil, old witch was, as usual, doing her damnedest to stir up sectarian and racial tensions, possibly ending in violence. At the very least, she was giving The People excuses not to accept a YES victory.

As we know, the YES side lost, but not by as much as unionists would have liked. The People celebrated by attacking independence supporters in Glasgow's George Square and giving Nazi salutes.[50] This was ironic considering the way they had abused the SNP online throughout the campaign by calling them Nazis![51]

For all The People had determined that they were not going to accept a result they did not like, they were not prepared to grant the other side the same courtesy. The abject lies told by the *Better Together* campaign, (see my book, *Fear and Smear*) not least of which was that Scotland would be out of the EU if it became independent, made it difficult to accept the result of the referendum. Calls for another referendum have got The People all riled up again.

One thing that *did* please The People was that they got their political party back. In answer to the original referendum, the Scottish Tories began to call themselves The Scottish Conservative and *Unionist* Party again. Since then, they have gone out of their way to suck up to The People. Murdo Fraser, a Tory list MSP, has a long history of anti-Celtic and often sectarian tweets.[52] In August 2021, he had the following to say:

> I can think of supporters of both Celtic and Rangers among the ranks of Conservative, Labour and Liberal Democrat politicians in Scotland.
> But whilst there are a number of high profile Celtic fans within the SNP ranks, I cannot think of a single SNP MP or MSP who identifies as a Rangers supporter.
> Indeed, too often we seem to see naked hostility towards the club and its fans.[53]

Shades of Ruth Dudley Edwards's pot-stirring there. The only evidence he had to offer in support of his claim was that the Scottish Government had condemned the behaviour of Rangers supporters in George Square but had ignored the behaviour of supporters of the Scottish national team in London. Anyone that witnessed both incidents, even in the media or online, knows that there was no comparison. Fraser's comments were straight from the pages of *Follow Follow*.

Speaking of *Follow Follow*, The People were adamant on this particular forum that no Rangers supporter should be voting SNP. In fact, they went further and claimed that supporting Rangers was incompatible with supporting the SNP.

> You might like Rangers but if you support SNP or Independence then you don't support Rangers and you're not one of us and can fuck off.[54]

> There is a clear agenda within the ranks of the SNP to try and destroy the name of one football club,

while trying to do everything it can to bend over backwards for another football (sic).[55]

Now please explain to me how an snp supporter fits in supporting our club given they are supporting the regime that essentially wants us dead and buried at any opportunity.[56]

Of course, this is all nonsense and nothing more than a rationalisation of The People's hatred of the SNP and fear of Scottish independence. If one reads their forums, they also express the belief that the media in Scotland is against them and are totally under the control of the SNP. This, too, is utter nonsense and even a casual perusal, viewing or listening to Scottish media will quickly let one discover that the opposite is true.

For years now, the Scottish media have been attacking the Scottish Government at every opportunity. Even when it comes to matters that are reserved to the Westminster Government, the media are ready to blame Nicola Sturgeon. The Scottish Government finds itself blamed for things like immigration, unemployment and reductions in benefits, even though those matters are the responsibility of the UK Government.[57]

A prime example of this was the criticism levelled at the Scottish Government over the shortage of ambulances during the ongoing Covid pandemic. When the Scottish Government mentioned asking the army to help, the right-wing press had a field day, claiming that Nicola Sturgeon had been humiliated.[58] What we were not told in Scotland, however, was that the army was also being deployed in England for the same reason.[59]

The Daily Record normally does not allow comments on its online articles, but it makes an exception when it comes to anything critical of the Scottish Government. And, of course, The People are all over every one of them, saying how the SNP are destroying Scotland and throwing in the odd piece of abuse against Nicola Sturgeon. The Daily Record panders to this crowd constantly, even to the extent of decrying Scotland itself.

In September 2021, last-minute plans were being put in place for the COP26 Climate Conference, which was going to be held in Glasgow in November. US President Joe Biden expressed eagerness to get started, saying, 'As we look ahead to the UK hosting Cop26, which I'm really anxious to attend in Glasgow in November.'[60] The Daily Record decided to twist Biden's words with the following headline:

Joe Biden 'anxious' *about* visiting Glasgow for COP26 climate conference.[61] (My italics.)

The implication was that Biden was nervous about coming to Scotland and Glasgow in particular. Why would that be? The answer was obvious: the SNP were in charge both of Scotland and of Glasgow. Usually, the Daily Record falls over itself to promote Scotland, especially Glasgow, where it happens to be based. The paper could not, however, be seen to be positive about anything that involved the SNP. One of The People, an evidently right-wing, Trump-supporting individual, rose to the bait:

Can you imagine this clown walking around Govanhill with Krankie (Nicola Sturgeon). Am I in Detroit he says.[62]

This kind of offensive (and ungrammatical) comment would normally be removed by the Daily Record, but not on this occasion. And in case anyone thinks that the Record would not be that oversensitive, they should have a look at the story about the Glasgow Council leader (SNP, of course) being slammed for calling those responsible for graffiti, 'Wee neds.' According to the leader of Glasgow's Labour group, the Council Leader was stigmatising young people![63] So, why was this considered offensive, but the comment above was okay? That is a rhetorical question, by the way.

Speaking of the Labour Party, it has become almost a political irrelevance in Scotland. In the 2019 UK General Election, Scotland only returned 1 solitary Labour MP, while 6 Tory MPs were elected. Even the Liberal Democrats won 4 seats. Of course, the vagaries of the First-Past-the-Post system played a major part in this. The SNP won 48 seats with 45% of the overall vote, while the Tories got only 6 seats from 25.1%. Labour's 18.6% only merited 1 seat and the Liberal Democrats' 4 seats came from a paltry 9.5% of the vote.[64]

Neither Labour nor the Tories, however, want the system to change, since it would affect the way they have dominated elections in England in modern times. Besides, it is possible that electors would just vote in a different manner, rather than for the same or a different party under a PR system.[65] Paradoxically, both Labour and the Tories rely on the PR system to get seats in the Scottish Parliament.

In the 2021 Scottish Parliament elections, only 5 Tory and 2 Labour MSPs were elected directly. The other 26 and 20 respectively were voted via the List under Scotland's weird and wonderful PR system. How ridiculous this system is shows up when one looks at the percentages. In the Regional List vote, the SNP got 2 seats with 40.34%, the Tories 26 with 23.49%, Labour 20 with 17.91% and the Greens an incredible 8 seats with only 8.12%.[66]

Conversely, in the Constituency elections, the SNP won 62 seats with 47.7% of the vote, while the Tories only got 5 with 21.89%. Labour's vote looks quite respectable at 21.59%, but they only got 2 seats. The Liberal Democrats won out again, getting 4 seats with 6.94% of the vote.[67]

The main thing to take from these figures, however, is how much the Tory vote has improved over the last 10 years, both in the Scottish and UK elections.[68] That ruse of reverting to the old name of the Scottish Conservative and Unionist Party seemed to have paid off. Most observers agree that politics in Scotland has come down to a straight choice between the SNP and the Tories.

As they consider themselves to be über-British, The People, of course, were in favour of Brexit and voted accordingly on both sides of the North Channel. They were in the minority, though, and, in Scotland and Northern Ireland, the Remain vote won convincingly.[69] To their delight, however, neither vote mattered a jot. England had overwhelmingly voted to leave the EU, meaning that the overall UK decision was also Leave.

The Democratic Unionist Party in Northern Ireland were overjoyed and, a year later, they had another reason to celebrate.

After his side had lost the referendum, David Cameron resigned, and Theresa May won the subsequent leadership contest. In order to cement her position, she decided to hold a general election. The outcome of this was that the Tories fell short of a majority and had to make arrangements with the DUP so they could govern. The DUP now held the balance of power in the UK, just like the Irish Nationalists had over a hundred years before.

Many of the Tories might well have been happy to grant the DUP's dearest wishes and send tanks rumbling into the Bogside, but it was not to be. Instead, the Unionist party was handed an outright bribe of £1billion. Of course, this did not mean that Arlene Foster and her crew were jetting off to the Bahamas to live a life of luxury, (Definitely *not* the life of Reilly!) the money was to be used by the NI government. It would, however, provide an electoral boost for the DUP when improvements were made in everybody's life in NI thanks to them.[70]

Theresa May had managed to make a deal with the EU to facilitate Brexit, but she still needed to get it through Parliament. The right-wingers in her party were unhappy about the deal she had made and were determined to throw it out. The major problem they had was with what was called the 'Irish Backstop'.[71] Essentially, this meant that Northern Ireland would remain in the EU for a certain amount of time until a solution could be found to the possibility of a 'hard border' between Northern Ireland and the Irish Republic. To keep trade going between Britain and Northern Ireland, Britain would have to stay in the single market for the same period. The right wing of the party was outraged and went on the attack.

The DUP joined this right-wing faction in turning on Theresa May, not realising that they were cutting their own throats in the process. Boris Johnson, and others of his ilk, would throw their parents under a bus to get their own way, but the DUP naively thought they could trust him.[72] All the attacks resulted in Theresa May resigning and Johnson became leader with a remit to get Brexit, a real Brexit, done and dusted. If that meant abandoning promises to the DUP, then so be it.

As Theresa May had done, Johnson held a general election to seek a mandate for his idea of Brexit; he was returned with a whopping majority of 80 seats.[73] (All the constant propaganda about Jeremy Corbyn's Labour being anti-Semitic obviously worked.) Johnson did not need the DUP to get his agreement with the EU passed through Parliament, but still they supported him.[74] More fool them.

The *Irish Protocol* was the price Johnson paid to get Brexit rushed through. This was worse for the DUP than anything Theresa May had suggested. There would only be a year's grace and then a hard border would be drawn right down the Irish Sea, cutting Northern Ireland off from the British mainland. There would be customs checks whenever anyone travelled from Northern Ireland to Britain and vice-versa. It was the DUP's nightmare come true.

To be honest, Boris Johnson did not have a lot of choice in the matter. The EU was determined to maintain the terms of the Good Friday Agreement, with no hard border between Northern Ireland and the Irish Republic. More importantly, for Johnson at any rate, the Americans would not stand for any change to the Good Friday Agreement. It did not matter who was in the White House, Irish Americans can make a powerful bloc when they have a cause they all believe in. And the only cause that unites them all is the 'Old Country,' even though, for many of them, their view of Ireland comes from the romanticised, Hollywood version in films like *The Quiet Man*.

The People in Northern Ireland care nothing for Boris Johnson's reliance on a trade deal with America; all they care about is staying in the UK. They argue that their statelet is just like any other part of the UK, but only when it suits them. Their banning of same-sex marriage and abortion, which was undone by the Westminster Government during a period when the Stormont Government was not meeting, belies that argument.[75] Nevertheless, they still persist in airing it and the Protocol brings them dangerously closer to a reunification with the rest of Ireland.

When the period of grace came to an end in 2021, there were demonstrations by Unionists in Northern Ireland, annoyed, apparently, that they could no longer get British sausages.[76] The anger, obviously, went much deeper than that and went to the very heart of The People's attitudes to the Good Friday

Agreement. Some observers believe that the DUP thought that signing up for Johnson's Brexit would mean the end of the Agreement.[77] The People had never been that keen on the Agreement since power sharing destroyed any semblance of the Protestant Ascendancy. They obviously underestimated how far the Tories would go to stay on America's good side.

To any reasonable person, it was clear that the Tories were to blame for...er...duping the DUP. The DUP, however, and The People in NI in general, could not afford to antagonise the Tories. Remember, The People in Scotland were relying on the Scottish Tories to keep independence at bay. And Stanley Johnson was not the only one making frightening allusions to abandoning Northern Ireland. Remember those far-right Brexiteers we met in Chapter 3, who made it plain that they did not care about anything but their own, narrow concerns?

> When will remainers get it through their thick skulls that we want brexit at any cost? Even if it means tanking the economy. Even if it means mass unemployment. Even if it means a crashing pound. Even if it means starving. We say loud and proud...YES to brexit, NO to foreigners![78]

Now, those characters sound as if they could not care less if either Scotland or Northern Ireland or both leave the UK. The need for The People to keep Scotland in the Union was more important than ever, and that meant keeping in with the Tories. Luckily, The People in NI had found reasons to blame others for the Protocol; reasons provided by right-wing newspapers in England.

The *Telegraph* had an article in September 2021 that laid out its evidence for the opinion that both the EU and the USA were working to a secret agenda. That agenda was the break-up of the UK. It seemed the EU was looking to punish the UK for leaving, while America was trying to bring about a united Ireland. And, of course, the Irish Republic was in on the conspiracy.[79]

This disgusting rabble rousing played right into the hands of the DUP. Already, before this article appeared, the DUP were threatening to quit Stormont and were already going to boycott north-south ministerial meetings.[80] There were also warnings of violence returning to the streets, as it already had in April, when Unionists rioted in Belfast.[81] The warnings seemed more like a threat and it was clear that The People in Northern Ireland were looking to recreate the days of Edward Carson and the Home Rule Crisis. Now, there was something that The People in Scotland could get their teeth into and the winners, in the sphere of Scottish politics, were going to be the Tories.

Fig.42 The Lady Boys of Bangkok.

Fig.43 David Roberts. An Evangelical against all LGBT people,
who supports the pseudo-feminists that are anti-trans.

Fig.44 Goya processing centre in Brookshire, Texas.

Fig.45 Cookie Monster wearing a poppy.

Fig.46 David Starkey.

Fig.47 David Miller.

Fig.48 Joseph Chamberlain. As Secretary of State for the Colonies 1895-1903, he became the face of the British Empire.

Fig.49 Unionist poster from the General Election 1924. It shows the then Prime Minister, Ramsay MacDonald, being slow in building the houses Labour had promised.

15
Conclusion

Dietrich Bonhoeffer was a Lutheran pastor in Germany, who, unlike others of his church, would not kowtow to Nazi ideology. He was an outspoken critic of the regime and ended up being imprisoned and, eventually, hanged for his stance. While he was a prisoner, he took the opportunity to do a lot of thinking and writing. His ideas have become extremely influential, especially those on how Christians should relate to politics and society.

Not all of Bonhoeffer's writing was concerned with religion. Obviously, considering his own circumstances, he turned his thoughts to why Germany had become what it had. His conclusion was that Germans, or mankind in general for that matter, were not inherently evil; they were *stupid*. And so was born what has become known as *Bonhoeffer's Theory of Stupidity*. And, as the man himself put it,

> Against stupidity we have no defense. Neither protests nor force can touch it. Reasoning is of no use. Facts that contradict personal prejudices can simply be disbelieved — indeed, the fool can counter by criticizing them, and if they are undeniable, they can just be pushed aside as trivial exceptions.[1]

Bonhoeffer saw stupidity as a sociological problem, rather than a psychological one as stupid people tended to be those that followed a herd mentality and were easy prey to anybody with a lunatic theory that seemed to chime with their own prejudices. This, unfortunately, is still the case, as we have seen by the number of people convinced that Covid is nothing but a dangerous hoax intended to curtail our freedoms. Such folk would rather believe someone with an archaeology degree than a scientist that is a qualified and experienced expert in virology.[2] But then, we already know how Britain feels about experts.

And it is not just Covid that showed up the stupidity of a huge part of the British public, as we have seen, it has cropped up again and again. In fact, the whole history of working-class Tory voters is a story of stupidity from start to finish. We could make excuses for those living at the end of the Nineteenth Century if it were not for the fact that others were forming what was to become the Labour Party at the same time.

We can, of course, make allowances for the xenophobia and racism of the working classes in Victorian times. They were poorly educated and only encountered foreigners when they went abroad to fight against them. Meanwhile, they were bombarded with racist images in adverts and all manner of imperialist propaganda. Even into the 20th Century, as we have seen, such propaganda persisted and so did racist and xenophobic attitudes. As time went by, there was less and less excuse for this insular way of thinking and nowadays there is no excuse at all. And yet, there are still plenty of people that think this way.

We have all met British folk on holiday that have brought their own tea bags, tins of baked beans and even bacon with them because they do not trust Johnny Foreigner to be able to provide these things. They will only eat and drink in places owned by fellow Brits for the same reason. Meanwhile, at the extreme end of this vile spectrum, there are folk decrying the RNLI for rescuing asylum seekers braving the English Channel in small boats.[3] There are even stories of fishermen stopping the RNLI from going to save people in trouble.[4]

In Scotland, the stupidity of racists is shown by how many of them try to blame the SNP for taking in asylum seekers. They cannot get it through their skulls that the Scottish Government has no powers concerning immigration; those powers are reserved to Westminster.

They still cling to their delusions, though, like these individuals discussing asylum seekers:

> Virtue signalling only hurts people. That's exactly what the SNP do. That's all they are good at.[5]

> Thats what you get with the SNP they need the vote.[6]

> I thought sturgeon was happy to house migrants without limits.[7]

Equally brainless are the ones blaming Nicola Sturgeon for the COP26 gathering in Glasgow.[8] There are suggestions that the conference, with delegates from all over the world, might have helped spread Coronavirus. The conference was actually organised and hosted by the UK Government; nobody in the Scottish Government even got an invite. As we have seen, though, when it comes to the Coronavirus Pandemic there is no end to the stupidity elicited.

One example among many is the complaint that there should be no need for any further lockdown since most people have now been vaccinated.[9] This, however, ignores the fact that a sizable minority have refused to take the vaccine and many of the same people also refuse to wear a mask. And yet, these are the very one complaining about their freedom being impinged upon when a new variant might mean another lockdown. Maybe if they were not so stupid they might realise that they are the ones causing the need for lockdowns.

Bonhoeffer was not the only academic to write about stupidity. Economic historian Carlo Cipolla even went as far as writing a whole book on the subject, *The Basic Laws of Human Stupidity*.[10] In the book, Cipolla outlines five laws, which apply to both individuals and groups. The most interesting of these is the Third Law, which states,

> A stupid person is one who causes harm to another person or group without at the same time

obtaining a benefit for himself or even damaging himself.[11]

Brexit and all the dire consequences that have ensued, which the Brexiteers were warned about, immediately springs to mind. Even worse on the scale of stupidity are the Unionists in Northern Ireland, who missed out on all the negative effects of Brexit but are determined to suffer empty supermarket shelves like the rest of the UK.

One could go through every chapter of this book and conclude that working-class Tory voters are essentially thick. In fact, they fulfil all the requirements of Cipolla's Third Law of Human Stupidity. Even those folk kicking up a fuss about trans women can easily be described as stupid. After all, they go on about what *could* happen if trans women are allowed into female changing rooms etc. The fact is, however, that trans women have been permitted to use such facilities since 2010[12] and none of the scare stories they disseminate *have* come to pass during the eleven years since.

There is also a fear of a loss of identity among lesbian women, which was notably outlined in an article by the BBC headlined, *We're being pressured into sex by some trans women*.[13] The only instance of *pressure*, though, was provided by lesbian porn star Lily Cade, who backed out of a film scene where she was to have sex with a trans woman.[14] Not all women are in the same position as Cade and it is difficult to understand how lesbian women can possibly feel pressured into having sex with trans women.

Actually, what seems to be the main concern of many lesbians is that they might lose their label. The LGB Alliance is at the forefront of this argument, with women appearing at LGBT+ conferences and demonstrations with signs saying, 'Lesbians don't have penises.'[15] Strangely, this obsession with identity and labels goes against everything that gays and lesbians used to stand for. LGB groups used to argue, against the prevailing zeitgeist, that nobody could help whom they fall in love with. Now, Lesbians seem to be using the same kinds of argument that people once used against them.

Tom Robinson was a leading light in the Gay Liberation movement in the 1970s, while his song, *Glad to Be Gay*, became a kind of anthem for gay people in the UK. The media responded with glee when he later married a woman and became a father. It seemed to make it look as if being gay was a choice after all, as the right-wing press had often claimed. Actually, it proved nothing of the sort. As long-time LGBT+ and human-rights activist said,

> I'm campaigning for queer rights because people should be able to love who they wish, without fear of prejudice or discrimination. That includes the right to be gay, straight or bisexual. I don't have a problem with people switching their affections from one sex to the other. It's their life. Sexual liberation is about people's right to make their own choice about who they love – and not be victimised![16]

That sums up what the whole fight was supposed to be about in the first place. Nowadays, it seems that many are fighting to hold onto labels that were given to them by others. Perhaps it is time that Existentialism made a comeback. Jean-Paul Sartre and Simone de Beauvoir must be turning in their graves!

Sometimes, 'Wokeness' and 'Cancel Culture' appear to go too far. For example, art historian, Andrew Graham-Dixon took part in a debate at Cambridge University about whether good taste existed or not. He argued that it does, in fact, exist and gave examples of *bad* taste to underline his point. He cited Nazi Germany, where various types of art were banned and quoted directly from *Mein Kampf* to show the thinking behind the ban. To lighten things up a bit, Graham-Dixon parodied Hitler by reading out the quotes in a faux German accent. He also explained how vile and ridiculous he considered the Nazi views on art to have been.[17]

Incredibly, there were scores of complaints about what Graham-Dixon had said and the Union President had to apologise for not putting a stop to it at the time. The art historian was subsequently banned by the debating society.[18] Apparently, issue was taken at the racist language he used, even though he had done it in character as parody and explained his own feelings on the matter. Of course, the anti-woke brigade was all over this story, and it was hard to argue against them.

Such occurrences actually undermine the whole idea of 'wokeness' and anyone with a social conscience ends up being lumped in with these idiots. Considering the types that attend Cambridge University, one cannot help but wonder if these students were acting to deliberately make being 'woke' appear ridiculous. This method of *reductio ad absurdum* is a common way of undermining practically anything. The British media are past masters at this sort of thing, as are right-wing politicians. It makes one question whether those Cambridge students were offended at all.

Among this catalogue of stupidity, it is perhaps tempting to exclude those working-class people that live in the countryside and who support blood sports. After all, they do not fulfil Cipolla's Third Law inasmuch as they vote Tory as part of a *quid pro quo* arrangement. Then again, what kind of moron gets pleasure out of the suffering of animals? They might not fit into Cipolla's theories but, by any other measure, they are not exactly overendowed with grey matter.

There is not a lot of point outlining *all* the stupidity behind why working-class people vote Tory; you have probably worked most of it out for yourself. The thing is, though, that those stupid people simply do not realise that they *are* stupid, so there is no reasoning with them. Better education might seem to be a solution but then, they would argue that such education was indoctrination. An additional consideration is that stupid people believe that the rest of us are the ones that are stupid. As one commenter says about Bonhoeffer,

> Bonhoeffer,
> About to come under attack from the woke mob in 3,2,1 as his theory explains their disgusting mindset aptly.[19]

Finally, how thick working-class Tory voters can be is shown in the way they make excuses for their favoured politicians no matter what. The story emerged at the end of November 2021 about how Boris Johnson had drunken parties at 10 Downing Street the year before, while the whole UK was in lockdown and people were fined for having relatives round for Christmas dinner. Incredibly, there were people making excuses for Johnson.

Funny how this is brought up now almost a year later who gives a t o s s[20]

Aye like everyone else was observing Xmas lockdown... most of the offices all had their Xmas di's (sic) and people were still crammed into each other's house for Xmas and new year even within the health and ambulance services, the Xmas parties were in full swing with food being brought in from outside for the events so.. who's kidding who here?[21]

Sometimes all you can do is shake your head!

NOTES

Introduction

[1] https://archive.ph/SLnJr
[2] https://tinyurl.com/sxu36359
[3] Quoted in AB Cooke and John Vincent – <u>The Governing Passion</u> p.3
[4] https://archive.ph/cH2dh

Chapter 1

[1] https://archive.ph/EcODn
[2] https://archive.ph/nsHv5
[3] https://archive.ph/bpJIQ
[4] https://archive.ph/vcxsV
[5] https://archive.ph/jFnRf
[6] https://archive.ph/Gjc19
[7] https://archive.ph/3ZHdK
[8] https://archive.ph/qGHMZ
[9] https://archive.ph/wuMSv Sexuality
[10] ibid
[11] https://archive.ph/mlOtu
[12] https://archive.ph/Ns0Lw
[13] https://archive.ph/HxEb6
[14] https://archive.ph/SxWYE
[15] ibid
[16] https://tinyurl.com/rcmhnxc p258
[17] https://www.youtube.com/watch?v=aS44El_V7SM
[18] https://archive.ph/2PJJ6
[19] https://archive.ph/bjvDh
[20] https://archive.ph/ChSzP
[21] https://archive.ph/ZmUCI
[22] ibid
[23] ibid
[24] ibid
[25] https://archive.ph/HUC2b
[26] https://archive.ph/v6Rm6
[27] https://archive.ph/imxX8
[28] https://archive.ph/zg8w3
[29] https://archive.ph/LyLNG
[30] https://archive.ph/XLYRE
[31] https://archive.ph/LyLNG
[32] https://archive.ph/y04cg
[33] https://archive.ph/cZTi3

[34] ibid
[35] https://archive.ph/HUC2b
[36] https://archive.ph/Z1B7H
[37] https://archive.ph/qaGKG
[38] https://archive.ph/XGkUv
[39] https://archive.ph/nJi3L
[40] https://archive.ph/ZmUCI
[41] https://archive.ph/Vhitg
[42] https://www.youtube.com/watch?v=qpBrkGFd24g
[43] https://www.youtube.com/watch?v=qHwCbIEVmG0
[44] https://archive.ph/YwZbn
[45] https://archive.ph/w5ilT
[46] https://archive.ph/RNf4
[47] https://archive.ph/g1kl1
[48] https://archive.ph/lmtvm
[49] ibid
[50] https://archive.ph/BJQ8Q

Chapter 2

[1] https://archive.ph/DhJtR
[2] https://archive.ph/6VsFg
[3] https://archive.ph/1GdhT
[4] https://archive.ph/weixa
[5] https://archive.ph/sV4em
[6] https://archive.ph/3rdCD
[7] https://archive.ph/hHZeT
[8] https://archive.ph/5h4lo
[9] https://archive.ph/RoYEV
[10] https://archive.ph/dJ4Lt
[11] https://archive.ph/DvSYs
[12] https://archive.ph/KlxIe
[13] https://archive.ph/ALzSa
[14] https://archive.ph/HsKOj
[15] ibid
[16] https://archive.ph/XY5IG
[17] Yahoo Answers, from where I got these quotes, has closed down. I cannot find similar quotes elsewhere, so I chose to leave these as they are.
[18] ibid
[19] https://archive.ph/nWy7D
[20] https://www.youtube.com/watch?v=-eJn3j7Qr9A
[21] https://archive.ph/dU6ij
[22] https://www.youtube.com/watch?v=-eJn3j7Qr9A

[23] https://archive.ph/SVGn5
[24] https://archive.ph/iu1y
[25] https://archive.ph/fSssc
[26] https://archive.ph/KaPaE
[27] https://archive.ph/jNe4B
[28] https://archive.ph/yezHW
[29] https://archive.ph/FabeK
[30] https://archive.ph/zxr92
[31] https://archive.ph/oEBRS

Chapter 3

[1] https://archive.ph/1E6Dq
[2] https://archive.ph/2RqXQ
[3] https://archive.ph/g8BM2
[4] https://archive.ph/wNTdB
[5] https://archive.ph/Q1TPF
[6] https://archive.ph/UA5JJ
[7] https://archive.ph/gcfTW
[8] https://archive.ph/efpGb
[9] https://archive.ph/3rypw
[10] https://archive.ph/Qw91u
[11] https://archive.ph/920aj
[12] https://archive.ph/gKa6s
[13] https://archive.ph/GvZjr
[14] https://tinyurl.com/cp64k82b
[15] https://archive.ph/upePR
[16] https://archive.ph/ichv2
[17] I cannot remember where I read this and cannot find where he said it.
[18] https://archive.ph/gfrih
[19] https://archive.ph/CAxoP
[20] https://www.youtube.com/watch?v=4xoM6-1SWl4
[21] https://archive.ph/ZumZb
[22] https://archive.ph/QhClt
[23] https://archive.ph/Nh661
[24] https://archive.ph/9VWhV
[25] https://archive.ph/jpUCZ
[26] https://archive.ph/oVkSz
[27] Quoted in David Jablonsky - Churchill and Hitler: Essays on the Political-Military Direction of Total War p.26
[28] https://archive.ph/32lbB
[29] David Jablonsky - Churchill and Hitler: Essays on the Political-Military Direction of Total War p.26

30 https://archive.ph/WHWDE
31 https://tinyurl.com/232etm35
32 ibid p63
33 https://archive.ph/hFTb3
34 https://archive.ph/Pugqe
35 https://archive.ph/xPX5S
36 https://archive.ph/2yC6
37 https://archive.ph/MTQ2O
38 https://tinyurl.com/232etm35 p63
39 https://archive.ph/W9Sla
40 https://archive.ph/JSeNp
41 https://archive.ph/12GRb
42 ibid
43 ibid
44 https://archive.ph/4guGc
45 https://archive.ph/yACRK
46 https://tinyurl.com/4natxsy5
47 https://archive.ph/12GRb
48 https://archive.ph/ytyZm
49 https://archive.ph/AHmOn
50 ibid
51 The four volumes are available to read here:
https://archive.ph/NTGYJ
52 https://archive.ph/oVkSz
53 https://archive.ph/FNgrB
54 https://www.youtube.com/watch?v=Xt5ixn8V2C4 position 39.20
55 https://archive.ph/6KdsU
56 https://archive.ph/BJQ8Q
57 https://archive.ph/2Qw1o
58 https://archive.ph/M2mAg
59 https://archive.ph/ZGMwd
60 https://archive.ph/ofGrM
61 https://archive.ph/2CKOt
62 https://www.youtube.com/watch?v=Xt5ixn8V2C4

Chapter 4
1 https://archive.ph/1pQw3
2 https://archive.ph/Apmzy
3 ibid
4 https://archive.ph/lciJh
5 https://archive.ph/fufRD
6 https://archive.ph/0ReeP

271

[7] https://archive.ph/UJJYi
[8] https://archive.ph/QHzI9
[9] https://archive.ph/6MHLx
[10] https://archive.ph/UJJYi
[11] https://archive.ph/lPnx
[12] ibid
[13] ibid
[14] https://tinyurl.com/t58re5kp
[15] https://archive.ph/NnzXf
[16] https://archive.ph/N5Kqu
[17] https://archive.ph/fnOOo
[18] https://archive.ph/VkQy9
[19] https://tinyurl.com/fp42asbz
[20] https://archive.ph/Ck99K
[21] https://archive.ph/Vfx9R
[22] https://archive.ph/NTFK
[23] https://archive.ph/Q28DZ
[24] https://archive.ph/74Qqd
[25] https://archive.ph/6X1pE
[26] https://archive.ph/lPnx
[27] https://archive.ph/Vfx9R
[28] https://archive.ph/M7GJn
[29] https://archive.ph/ubxga
[30] https://archive.ph/3Mvrn
[31] https://archive.ph/MsN3
[32] https://archive.ph/v4QxJ
[33] https://archive.ph/eYtpT
[34] https://archive.ph/v9xIJ
[35] https://archive.ph/vARu1
[36] https://archive.ph/ecL0s
[37] https://archive.ph/lWBXi
[38] https://archive.ph/vqf3A
[39] ibid
[40] https://archive.ph/gA8wm
[41] Ibid

Chapter 5

[1] https://archive.ph/V7gN7
[2] https://archive.ph/My4q9
[3] https://archive.ph/TPHLo
[4] https://archive.ph/25plw
[5] https://archive.ph/hq7Pd

[6] ibid
[7] https://archive.ph/Xsjlj
[8] https://archive.ph/IGNUS
[9] https://archive.ph/sxIWG
[10] https://archive.ph/w1v3q
[11] https://archive.ph/xQoRc
[12] https://archive.ph/fgArq
[13] https://archive.ph/2COh7
[14] https://archive.ph/ubdr8
[15] https://archive.ph/bYZVg
[16] https://archive.ph/aL5DQ
[17] https://archive.ph/1klg1
[18] https://archive.ph/KSXd5
[19] https://archive.ph/DyyF8
[20] https://archive.ph/Aa1X2
[21] ibid
[22] https://archive.ph/PfgsP
[23] ibid
[24] https://archive.ph/AjvLF
[25]https://archive.ph/LVgGV
[26] https://archive.ph/vUYyG
[27] https://archive.ph/xOChh
[28] https://archive.ph/aso9o
[29] https://archive.ph/8WLNC
[30] https://archive.ph/eKMlF
[31] https://archive.ph/KLxNQ
[32] https://archive.ph/2COh7
[33] https://archive.ph/aFPOs
[34] https://archive.ph/adVQL
[35] https://archive.ph/Aa1X2
[36] https://archive.ph/MU7AX
[37] https://archive.ph/PSRmj
[38] https://archive.ph/R6Fbk
[39] ibid
[40] https://archive.ph/fM9mV
[41] https://archive.ph/Czsls
[42] https://archive.ph/FTDNo
[43] ibid
[44] https://archive.ph/QmcY4
[45] https://tinyurl.com/r29mnkem
[46] Ibid

Chapter 6

[1] https://archive.ph/NXOlt
[2] https://archive.ph/tbwY2
[3] https://archive.ph/TI8aO
[4] https://tinyurl.com/ssh5hhc
[5] https://archive.ph/vG5RZ
[6] https://tinyurl.com/3428md5x
[7] https://archive.ph/7kO8O
[8] https://tinyurl.com/4arbkyr4
[9] ibid
[10] ibid
[11] ibid
[12] ibid
[13] https://archive.ph/7kO8O
[14] https://archive.ph/wNyJA Section 5.
[15] https://tinyurl.com/yen5vn7a
[16] https://archive.ph/uBOpK
[17] https://tinyurl.com/depn8xsy
[18] https://archive.ph/aWQTm
[19] https://archive.ph/yHhte
[20] https://archive.ph/ar65b
[21] https://archive.ph/rUpDN
[22] https://archive.ph/3wdv
[23] https://archive.ph/72iwl
[24] ibid
[25] https://archive.ph/n7qyJ
[26] https://archive.ph/4mk8Z
[27] https://archive.ph/IvGrw
[28] https://archive.ph/O0QDQ
[29] https://archive.ph/8dXIj
[30] https://archive.ph/9kgMX
[31] https://tinyurl.com/drstuy
[32] https://archive.ph/bLn9h
[33] https://archive.ph/QM521
[34] https://archive.ph/AgAuf
[35] https://archive.ph/ASKg3
[36] https://archive.ph/yOVWN
[37] https://archive.ph/TImGf
[38] https://www.youtube.com/watch?v=fSBx0pqTSL0
[39] https://www.youtube.com/watch?v=qJ_Nql0p8UA
[40] https://archive.ph/yy623
[41] https://archive.ph/Efuvx
[42] https://archive.ph/DDFEr

[43] https://archive.ph/G68nH
[44] https://archive.ph/TozNP
[45] https://archive.ph/G68nH
[46] https://archive.ph/6TbFZ
[47] https://archive.ph/qiLOW
[48] https://archive.ph/TImGf
[49] https://archive.ph/Kawqs
[50] https://archive.ph/3Suds
[51] https://archive.ph/lQlev
[52] https://archive.ph/ISVYP
[53] https://archive.ph/St22U
[54] https://archive.ph/ewp46
[55] https://archive.ph/3VyHr
[56] https://archive.ph/PpG2S
[57] https://archive.ph/krTBO
[58] https://archive.ph/LaWgs
[59] https://archive.ph/5v8UE
[60] ibid
[61] https://archive.ph/8MBKm
[62] https://archive.ph/r6q9m
[63] ibid
[64] https://archive.ph/D5UVz
[65] https://archive.ph/ovtMc

Chapter 7
[1] https://archive.ph/Q6xWU
[2] https://archive.ph/y2OdF
[3] https://tinyurl.com/2pf9vw3z
[4] https://archive.ph/8mtfL
[5] https://archive.ph/ZMn3y
[6] https://archive.ph/8mtfL
[7] https://archive.ph/sy7qe
[8] https://archive.ph/9itpz
[9] https://archive.ph/9G7Qa
[10] https://tinyurl.com/mhs3emta
[11] https://archive.ph/iM8Ql
[12] https://archive.ph/oICm3
[13] ibid
[14] https://tinyurl.com/mhs3emta
[15] https://archive.ph/Kh04a
[16] https://archive.ph/GokCE
[17] https://archive.ph/INjNp

[18] https://archive.ph/uT0zk
[19] https://archive.ph/rszVu
[20] https://archive.ph/V8X7A
[21] https://archive.ph/DD1wm
[22] https://archive.ph/fxKn1
[23] https://archive.ph/2f6Qg
[24] https://archive.ph/Q3NjT
[25] https://tinyurl.com/4f68wnbj
[26] https://archive.ph/HD4Ky
[27] https://tinyurl.com/yu64794x
[28] https://tinyurl.com/yj9n2wt7
[29] https://tinyurl.com/yu64794x
[30] https://archive.ph/oU4e3
[31] https://archive.ph/adnsa
[32] https://tinyurl.com/2dnv6sps Section headed 'Jewish Mothers'
[33] https://archive.ph/fozC7
[34] https://tinyurl.com/j5mec5n
[35] https://archive.ph/dX0BA
[36] https://archive.ph/H9gfc
[37] https://archive.ph/jGIfT
[38] ibid
[39] https://archive.ph/gzaW9
[40] https://archive.ph/lsSmS
[41] https://archive.ph/gzaW9
[42] https://archive.ph/7Lr3L
[43] https://archive.ph/hJdI2
[44] ibid
[45] https://archive.ph/7IidR
[46] https://archive.ph/88Dal
[47] https://archive.ph/Trkzq
[48] ibid
[49] https://archive.ph/O3SLH
[50] https://archive.ph/DEL5I
[51] https://archive.ph/ddYNP
[52] https://archive.ph/1Aspt
[53] https://archive.ph/LlCSK
[54] ibid
[55] https://archive.ph/Uiq3g
[56] https://archive.ph/XXJzd
[57] https://archive.ph/e8aeb
[58] https://archive.ph/hIPjQ
[59] ibid
[60] https://archive.ph/hIPjQ

61 ibid
62 https://archive.ph/X7uw6
63 https://archive.ph/Trkzq
64 https://archive.ph/dkT7E
65 https://archive.ph/9XfIs
66 https://archive.ph/ysATh
67 https://archive.ph/03E3Z
68 ibid
69 https://archive.ph/CBtsX
70 https://archive.ph/4LkLG
71 ibid
72 https://archive.ph/nNZwf
73 https://archive.ph/hpKHD
74 https://archive.ph/c4Rn8

Chapter 8

1 https://archive.ph/9ARV2
2 https://archive.ph/NadPF
3 https://archive.ph/rP1gI
4 https://archive.ph/NSoiU
5 https://archive.ph/40blZ
6 https://archive.ph/BVHn
7 https://archive.ph/SRU9s
8 https://archive.ph/4Mo84
9 https://archive.ph/HSb4o
10 https://archive.ph/rZUZA
11 https://archive.ph/Rdssc
12 https://archive.ph/yeeyT
13 https://www.youtube.com/watch?v=Co1QGoJWRrg
14 https://archive.ph/Nbic3
15 https://archive.ph/oI6B1
16 https://archive.ph/CIUC1
17 https://archive.ph/MFjK2
18 https://archive.ph/2uIP0
19 Kellow Chesney – The Victorian Underworld (1970) Chapter Ten
20 https://archive.ph/fKAUF
21 https://archive.ph/Y1Qth
22 https://tinyurl.com/j3r6tj28
23 https://archive.ph/6ptEU
24 https://archive.ph/VOChf
25 https://tinyurl.com/2y3x6wnd
26 ibid

[27] https://archive.ph/jkRb7
[28] https://archive.ph/G1lnI
[29] https://archive.ph/qte0f
[30] https://archive.ph/Q442x
[31] https://archive.ph/oBLhz
[32] ibid
[33] Pat Anderson – <u>Up to Our Knees: ANTI-CATHOLIC BIGOTRY IN SCOTLAND</u> (2016)
[34] https://archive.ph/LQXgQ
[35] ibid
[36] https://archive.ph/1pBgv

Chapter 9

[1] https://archive.ph/cX2Jg
[2] https://archive.ph/GG1Qt
[3] https://archive.ph/71Q6o
[4] https://archive.ph/i9hdC
[5] https://archive.ph/CGBOb
[6] https://archive.ph/i9hdC
[7] https://archive.ph/mMOsF
[8] https://archive.ph/DQgaL
[9] ibid
[10] https://archive.ph/stHnF
[11] https://archive.ph/PRsuU
[12] https://archive.ph/TqEoY
[13] https://archive.ph/puUYK
[14] https://archive.ph/GjYXt 'Four Great Women and a Manicure'
[15] https://archive.ph/O6tU0
[16] https://archive.ph/vRBnr
[17] https://archive.ph/X1sGa
[18] https://archive.ph/kmyMI
[19] https://archive.ph/URIaZ
[20] ibid
[21] https://archive.ph/CfHHn
[22] https://archive.ph/4Ioxc
[23] https://archive.ph/zxBX4
[24] https://archive.ph/Vizu7
[25] https://archive.ph/2zq6S
[26] https://archive.ph/CfHHn
[27] https://tinyurl.com/yrvmjm7h
[28] https://archive.ph/noTRE
[29] https://archive.ph/X2w3y

[30] https://archive.ph/ncS7P
[31] ibid
[32] https://archive.ph/xH6yl
[33] https://tinyurl.com/2eytf76f
[34] https://archive.ph/gzKwn
[35] https://archive.ph/W5l6s
[36] https://archive.ph/VFylc
[37] https://tinyurl.com/2eytf76f
[38] https://archive.ph/Pecri
[39] ibid
[40] https://archive.ph/p3dsW
[41] https://www.youtube.com/watch?v=GGgiGtJk7MA
[42] https://archive.ph/hbp57
[43] https://archive.ph/ux0vj
[44] https://archive.ph/QScGm
[45] https://archive.ph/hbp57
[46] https://archive.ph/hbk50
[47] https://archive.ph/FlvYD

Chapter 10

[1] https://archive.ph/tkntZ
[2] https://archive.ph/0gIaf
[3] https://archive.ph/EczEX
[4] https://archive.ph/oopdP
[5] https://archive.ph/2eHd6
[6] https://archive.ph/Brydz
[7] https://archive.ph/g9ME2
[8] https://archive.ph/3N8Bd
[9] https://www.youtube.com/watch?v=EM4cor8PK4I
[10] https://archive.ph/HVFhT
[11] ibid
[12] https://archive.ph/Wecnf
[13] ibid
[14] https://archive.ph/BaXpy
[15] https://archive.ph/KqqIa
[16] https://tinyurl.com/3bkmrudy
[17] https://www.youtube.com/watch?v=lJW_2wLt704
[18] https://www.youtube.com/watch?v=VYHG1rtwIEc
[19] https://archive.ph/UwyhE
[20] https://archive.ph/gHo7t
[21] https://archive.ph/YvbAB
[22] https://archive.ph/gHo7t

[23] ibid
[24] https://archive.ph/YvbAB
[25] https://archive.ph/N2N0z
[26] https://archive.ph/QCwih
[27] https://archive.ph/2QQXX
[28] https://archive.ph/EOyTP
[29] https://archive.ph/N4dVO
[30] https://archive.ph/gicSd
[31] https://archive.ph/VdpMW
[32] https://archive.ph/gicSd
[33] https://archive.ph/C1cf4
[34] https://archive.ph/Shj4L
[35] https://archive.ph/3wWpo
[36] https://archive.ph/eoLoj
[37] https://archive.ph/QGvJC
[38] https://archive.ph/73uUR
[39] https://archive.ph/LGDld
[40] https://archive.ph/ZGrmd
[41] https://archive.ph/gaxVr
[42] https://archive.ph/OfNHR
[43] https://archive.ph/L54J6
[44] https://archive.ph/BS1gn
[45] https://archive.ph/L54J6
[46] https://archive.ph/1g1zq
[47] https://archive.ph/a34wH
[48] https://archive.ph/eYuNK
[49] https://archive.ph/Hw3FP
[50] https://archive.ph/OYayj

Chapter 11

[1] https://archive.ph/g8XV7
[2] ibid
[3] https://archive.ph/gXMAj
[4] https://www.youtube.com/watch?v=6Mq59ykPnAE
[5] https://www.youtube.com/watch?v=xp94BNovs0o
[6] Time and the Politics of Nostalgia (1995) – Stuart Allen, Karen Atkinson and Martin Montgomery p.380. The article is available for download as a PDF here: https://tinyurl.com/48822td9
[7] https://www.youtube.com/watch?v=vcrO8SWZJFc
[8] https://www.youtube.com/watch?v=V0TYvzAHzwo
[9] https://archive.ph/ZvuZM
[10] https://archive.ph/Eygv1

[11] https://archive.ph/QovuN
[12] https://archive.ph/Eygv1
[13] https://archive.ph/fZ4q3
[14] https://archive.ph/wOMRV
[15] https://archive.ph/CKgoD
[16] https://archive.ph/w3YZ5
[17] https://archive.ph/CKgoD
[18] https://archive.ph/dbSQI
[19] William L Shirer – <u>The Rise and Fall of the Third Reich</u> p.227. The book can be read online, or downloaded, at
https://tinyurl.com/axhaw6sf
[20] https://archive.ph/tIdK5
[21] https://archive.ph/GmDG2
[22] ibid
[23] https://archive.ph/qytfU
[24] https://archive.ph/hT6x9
[25] https://archive.ph/IQ3zs
[26] https://archive.ph/ZEaMH
[27] ibid
[28] https://archive.ph/GmDG2
[29] https://archive.ph/9V3g7
[30] ibid
[31] https://archive.ph/qytfU
[32] https://archive.ph/hT6x9
[33] https://archive.ph/Yaucp
[34] https://archive.ph/cBu5o
[35] https://archive.ph/l7VZg
[36]https://archive.ph/VZgvv
[37] Ibid

Chapter 12

[1] https://tinyurl.com/n23xmar2
[2] https://archive.ph/nVDAR
[3] https://archive.ph/woPMm
[4] https://tinyurl.com/9rm6cxmf
[5] https://archive.ph/GEwSQ
[6] https://tinyurl.com/2a7bb438
[7] https://archive.ph/YSi7N
[8] https://www.youtube.com/watch?v=POo-euCSlxk (The 'immoon system' bit starts at 10mins 20secs.)
[9] https://tinyurl.com/322ev7n3
[10] https://archive.ph/ZLyTP

11 https://www.youtube.com/watch?v=8S8Js-tEmlg
12 ibid
13 ibid
14 https://archive.ph/tL7YX
15 ibid
16 https://archive.ph/bwnvT
17 https://tinyurl.com/4k9z4mh3
18 https://archive.ph/uMPru
19 https://tinyurl.com/567mxpek
20 https://archive.ph/Y5oe0
21 https://archive.ph/SXTYt
22 https://archive.ph/jHp4t
23 https://archive.ph/94rss
24 https://archive.ph/jk93W
25 https://tinyurl.com/42d9s6ex
26 https://archive.ph/Jfn6l
27 ibid
28 https://greatreset.com/
29 https://archive.ph/Jfn6l
30 https://archive.ph/vO6Tk
31 https://archive.ph/gK6uB
32 https://www.youtube.com/watch?v=PAJ3YhlUegk
33 ibid
34 https://www.youtube.com/watch?v=obRG-2jurz0
35 https://archive.ph/gQhAC
36 https://archive.ph/iMWqi
37 ibid
38 Revelation 13:16-17 (King James Version)
39 https://archive.ph/cI5vR
40 https://archive.ph/mHzNm
41 https://archive.ph/rvhY8
42 https://archive.ph/mHzNm
43 ibid
44 https://archive.ph/F2aTp
45https://archive.ph/PfSIV
46 https://archive.ph/WZIFL
47 https://archive.ph/CuoUA
48 https://archive.ph/UbSDh
49 https://archive.ph/7pK23
50 https://archive.ph/mudJD
51 https://archive.ph/wwwkB
52https://www.youtube.com/watch?v=HAbI_1ySbCY&feature=emb_logo

[53] https://tinyurl.com/pfd7p4tp Page 5
[54] https://archive.ph/anI0c
[55] https://archive.ph/9as3f
[56] https://archive.ph/pVSjW
[57] https://archive.ph/klmL3
[58] http://archive.vn/imMHm
[59] https://archive.ph/pVSjW
[60] https://archive.ph/ldMv1
[61] https://archive.ph/eRUz4
[62] https://archive.ph/tKofG
[63] https://archive.ph/9as3f
[64] https://archive.ph/tKofG
[65] https://archive.ph/bnVr5
[66] https://archive.ph/rLMyP
[67] https://archive.ph/jgfcy
[68] ibid
[69] https://archive.ph/rbref

Chapter 13

[1] https://archive.ph/LAsJi
[2] https://archive.ph/UKYwm
[3] ibid
[4] https://archive.ph/8Peex#selection-2093.37-2097.192
[5] https://archive.ph/OHl4O
[6] https://archive.ph/Me6ie
[7] https://archive.ph/pLL2r
[8] https://archive.ph/XkgKF
[9] https://archive.ph/woPFF
[10] https://archive.ph/d68yN
[11] https://archive.ph/tXVR2
[12] ibid
[13] https://archive.ph/JXsRC
[14] https://archive.ph/kQWm3
[15] https://archive.ph/hxBXY
[16] https://archive.ph/sh3fx
[17] https://www.youtube.com/watch?v=C9QuSCZUoC8
[18] https://archive.ph/KLenF
[19] https://archive.ph/A3Q7m
[20] https://archive.ph/0eepX
[21] https://archive.ph/5yezD
[22] https://archive.ph/JyatQ
[23] https://archive.ph/nDdiD

[24] https://archive.ph/lg938
[25] https://archive.ph/9xTqo
[26] https://archive.ph/0eepX
[27] https://archive.ph/SYLu7
[28] https://archive.ph/4Awqn
[29] https://archive.ph/0ymbe
[30] https://archive.ph/cTWwf
[31] https://archive.ph/0ymbe
[32] https://archive.ph/4Awqn Comments section.
[33] https://archive.ph/nLR1K
[34] ibid
[35] https://archive.ph/bPCy2
[36] https://archive.ph/UF32R
[37] https://tinyurl.com/2scnbrj5
[38] ibid
[39] https://archive.ph/fBx2s
[40] https://archive.ph/a6pse#selection-14747.4-14747.8
[41] ibid
[42] https://tinyurl.com/3wjv6e3r
[43] ibid
[44] https://archive.ph/Qc4dp
[45] https://tinyurl.com/3wp5m2ff
[46] ibid
[47] https://archive.ph/T2T57
[48] ibid
[49] https://archive.ph/F1Vw6
[50] https://archive.ph/I66ao
[51] ibid
[52] https://archive.ph/h0FRv
[53] https://archive.ph/MfQPH
[54] https://archive.ph/xbCkU
[55] https://archive.ph/xl9f3
[56] https://archive.ph/QEx1M
[57] https://archive.ph/AHmOn
[58] https://archive.ph/9Ssxf
[59] https://archive.ph/5Y0JX
[60] https://archive.ph/S96S3
[61] https://archive.ph/b4uTa
[62] https://archive.ph/qc3lg
[63] https://archive.ph/SLS9S
[64] https://archive.ph/wVIPR
[65] https://archive.ph/KD91H
[66] https://archive.ph/aFzRV

[67] ibid
[68] https://archive.ph/omEOz
[69] https://archive.ph/hpH5a
[70] https://www.youtube.com/watch?v=2tVjZ9hA4SQ
[71] https://archive.ph/vK1Wo
[72] https://archive.ph/ydO2P
[73] https://archive.ph/H9syE
[74] https://archive.ph/ydO2P
[75] https://tinyurl.com/6vpk6r9f
[76] ibid
[77] ibid
[78] ibid
[79] ibid
[80] https://archive.ph/NBXKh
[81] https://archive.ph/dyh9A
[82] https://archive.ph/FzbNz
[83] https://archive.ph/K3LsH
[84] https://archive.ph/A5zZ9
[85] https://archive.ph/hBfQw

Chapter 14

[1] https://archive.ph/BdsL1
[2] https://archive.ph/sHVpK
[3] https://archive.ph/f1J0H
[4] https://archive.ph/t1x1H
[5] ibid
[6] https://archive.ph/18Eke Section VII
[7] https://archive.ph/BnQJR
[8] https://archive.ph/X72Hr
[9] https://archive.ph/gJHDc
[10] https://archive.ph/EqbON
[11] https://archive.ph/aHwOC
[12] https://archive.ph/ZynDV
[13] https://archive.ph/rQIKh
[14] https://archive.ph/qtzb8
[15] https://archive.ph/VxOBe
[16] ibid
[17] https://archive.ph/8pPsT
[18] A copy can be downloaded here: https://archive.ph/3g7I0
[19] https://archive.ph/Ktr3q
[20] https://archive.ph/zg8w3
[21] https://archive.ph/AvsJI

[22] ibid

[23] **https://archive.ph/AvsJI** Chart in section UK Parliament

[24] **https://archive.ph/PuEwr** Merger with the Conservative Party

[25] **https://archive.ph/pIACe**

[26] **https://archive.ph/pQ4pR**

[27] **https://archive.ph/9cwq0**

[28] **https://archive.ph/5gNNf**

[29] **https://archive.ph/jgBOf**

[30] **https://archive.ph/j9qq0**

[31] **https://tinyurl.com/yby28t6h** p.3

[32] **https://archive.ph/AvsJI** 1992

[33] **https://archive.ph/AvsJI** 1997

[34] **https://archive.ph/Q3dzk**

[35] **https://archive.ph/kGWKJ**

[36] **https://archive.ph/ZynDV**

[37] ibid

[38] ibid

[39] **https://tinyurl.com/56r2rd8u**

[40] **https://archive.ph/NuogW**

[41] **https://archive.ph/hFF3b**

[42] **https://archive.ph/pDB6F** Turnout

[43] **https://archive.ph/SB2jr**

[44] **https://archive.ph/vxgq7**

[45] **https://archive.ph/tQ7D3**

[46] **https://archive.ph/glHTn**

[47] **https://archive.ph/h20q7**

[48] **https://archive.ph/Hv5zK**

[49] **https://archive.ph/IEnW7**

[50] **https://archive.ph/IhSLK**

[51] **https://archive.ph/59VLk**

[52] **https://archive.ph/HxAqj** 2 Oct 2017

[53] **https://archive.ph/QQvJN**

[54] **https://archive.ph/XYTxV**

[55] **https://archive.ph/47hl3**

[56] **https://archive.ph/aUg48**

[57] **https://archive.ph/u8hHc**

[58] **https://archive.ph/DRJjq**

[59] **https://archive.ph/5kH07**

[60] **https://archive.ph/GSwp5**

[61] **https://archive.ph/sQWVZ**

[62] ibid

[63] **https://archive.ph/GQKWZ**

[64] **https://archive.ph/2RpUQ** 2019

[65]https://archive.ph/Y1c0L
[66] https://archive.ph/Lqrhq Results: Overall
[67] ibid
[68] https://archive.ph/2RpUQ
[69] https://archive.ph/JSpkZ Results by Constituent Countries
[70] https://archive.ph/x0I3g
[71] https://archive.ph/SzecM
[72] https://archive.ph/24jVe
[73] https://archive.ph/xPZH3
[74] https://archive.ph/24jVe
[75] https://archive.ph/wryLi
[76] https://archive.ph/R2IVv
[77] https://archive.ph/IPrTd
[78] https://archive.ph/1WPLa
[79] https://archive.ph/iY3Ol
[80] https://archive.ph/4aDAb
[81] https://archive.ph/ps4F2

Chapter 15

[1] https://archive.ph/3XHxW
[2] https://archive.ph/QPUfp
[3] https://archive.ph/KGlLA
[4] https://archive.ph/9QHPR
[5] https://tinyurl.com/8f5mzwjd (Comments)
[6] ibid
[7] ibid
[8] https://archive.ph/GIoSm
[9] https://archive.ph/xlv9v
[10] https://archive.ph/cSHCa
[11] https://archive.ph/AzRYg
[12] https://archive.ph/6Zflz
[13] https://archive.ph/Rb4tb
[14] ibid
[15] https://archive.ph/eg075
[16] https://archive.ph/M9J4h
[17] https://archive.ph/yUitO
[18] https://archive.ph/vUCe7
[19] https://archive.ph/maF11
[20] https://tinyurl.com/yckxdmar
[21] ibid

Printed in Great Britain
by Amazon